Acknowledging the Divine Benefactor

Acknowledging the Divine Benefactor

The Second Letter of Peter

Terrance Callan

PICKWICK Publications · Eugene, Oregon

ACKNOWLEDGING THE DIVINE BENEFACTOR
The Second Letter of Peter

Copyright © 2014 Terrance Callan. All rights reserved. Except for brief quotations in critical publications or reviews, no part of this book may be reproduced in any manner without prior written permission from the publisher. Write: Permissions. Wipf and Stock Publishers, 199 W. 8th Ave., Suite 3, Eugene, OR 97401.

Pickwick Publications
An Imprint of Wipf and Stock Publishers
199 W. 8th Ave., Suite 3
Eugene, OR 97401

www.wipfandstock.com

ISBN 13: 978-1-62564-826-6

Cataloguing-in-Publication Data

Callan, Terrance

Acknowledging the divine benefactor : the second letter of Peter / Terrance Callan.

xiv + 220 p. ; 23 cm. Includes bibliographical references and indexes.

ISBN 13: 978-1-62564-826-6

1. Bible. Peter, 2nd—Commentaries. I. Title.

BS2795 C27 2014

Manufactured in the U.S.A.   11/04/2014

In memory of my parents

Contents

Acknowledgments | *ix*
List of Abbreviations | *x*

Introduction | 1
Socio-Rhetorical Interpretation | 1
Discourses in 2 Peter | 4
Rhetography and Rhetology | 11
Text | 32
Author | 32
Addressees | 34
Place and Time of Composition | 35
Outline of 2 Peter | 38

Section 1: 2 Peter 1:1–15
Letter Opening | 39

Unit 1: 2 Peter 1:1–2 Letter Salutation | 40
Unit 2: 2 Peter 1:3–11 Theme of Letter: Peter Proposes Honoring the Divine Benefactor by Living Wisely | 50
Unit 3: 2 Peter 1:12–15 Occasion of Letter: Making it Possible to Remember Peter's Prophetic Teaching after His Death | 76

Section 2: 2 Peter 1:16–2:10a
Letter Body, Part 1
Two Arguments that Jesus Will Come Again | 88

Unit 1: 2 Peter 1:16–18 First Argument: Jesus' Transfiguration Shows that He Will Come Again | 89
Unit 2: 2 Peter 1:19–2:10a Second Argument: The Prophetic Word Shows that Jesus Will Come Again | 99

Section 3: 2 Peter 2:10b–22
Letter Body, Part 2
Prophetic Denunciation of the False Teachers | 129

Unit 1: 2 Peter 2:10b–17 Prophetic Denunciation of the False Teachers' Moral Failings | 130
Unit 2: 2 Peter 2:18–22 Prophetic Analysis of the False Teachers' Destructive Effect on Others | 145

Section 4: 2 Peter 3:1–13
Letter Body, Part 3
Restatement of Letter's Purpose and Resumption of Its Argument | 162

Unit 1: 2 Peter 3:1–4 Peter's Prophetic Reminder of Beneficial Teaching | 163
Unit 2: 2 Peter 3:5–13 Renewed Argument that Jesus Will Come Again | 169

Section 5: 2 Peter 3:14–18
Letter Closing | 188

Bibliography | 201

Author Index | 209

Ancient Documents Index | 213

Acknowledgments

This interpretation of 2 Peter is obviously indebted to the writings and teaching of Vernon K. Robbins. In addition, Professor Robbins read several drafts of this book and made numerous suggestions that have greatly improved the final text.

The translation of 2 Peter is my own. Other biblical quotations are taken from the New Revised Standard Version. Text and translation of other ancient texts are taken from the *Loeb Classical Library* unless otherwise indicated.

Abbreviations

General

acc.	accusative
act.	active
BCE	Before the Common Era
c.	approximately
cf.	compare
ed. eds.	editor, editors
e.g.	for example
etc.	and so forth
fem.	feminine
fut.	future
gen.	genitive
i.e.	that is
impv.	imperative
masc.	masculine
Mt.	Mount
n.	note
no.	number
nom.	nominative
NT	New Testament
pass.	passive
p. pp.	page, pages
pf.	perfect
pl.	plural
pres.	present
ptc.	participle
sg.	singular
St.	Saint
v. vv.	verse, verses

viz.	namely
vol.	volume
vs.	in contrast to

Bible Texts and Versions

א	Codex Sinaiticus
A	Codex Alexandrinus
B	Codex Vaticanus
LXX	Septuagint
P^{72}	Papyrus 72

Ancient Authors and Writings

1–2 Clem.	*1–2 Clement*
1 En.	*1 Enoch (Ethiopic Apocalypse)*
2 Bar.	*2 Baruch (Syriac Apocalypse)*
Pss. Sol.	*Psalms of Solomon*

Diodorus Siculus

| *Hist.* | *Bibliotheca historica* |

Eusebius of Caesarea

| *Praep. ev.* | *Praeparatio evangelica* |

Ignatius of Antioch

| *Eph.* | *To the Ephesians* |
| *Smyrn.* | *To the Smyrnaeans* |

Josephus

| *Ant.* | *Jewish Antiquities* |

Justin Martyr

Dial.	*Dialogue with Trypho*

Philo

Abr.	*De Abrahamo*
Aet.	*De aeternitate mundi*
Conf.	*De confusione linguarum*
Contempl.	*De vita contemplativa*
Jos.	*De Iosepho*
Mos.	*De vita Mosis*
Opif.	*De opificio mundi*
Praem.	*De praemiis et poenis*
QG	*Quaestiones et solutiones in Genesin*
Sacr.	*De sacrificiis Abelis et Caini*
Spec.	*De specialibus legibus*
Virt.	*De virtutibus*

Pliny

Ep.	*Epistulae*

Shepherd of Hermas

Sim.	*Similitude*
Vis.	*Vision*

Suetonius

Domit.	*Life of Domitian*

Modern Works

BDF	Friedrich Blass and Albert Debrunner. *A Greek Grammar of the New Testament* and *Other Early Christian Literature.*

	Translated and revised by Robert W. Funk. Chicago: University of Chicago Press, 1961.
CIG	*Corpus inscriptionum graecarum.* Edited by A. Boeckh et al. 4 vols. Berlin, 1828–77.
TDNT	*Theological Dictionary of the New Testament. 10 vols. Edited by Gerhard Kittel and Gerhard Friedrich. Translated by Geoffrey W. Bromiley. Grand Rapids: Eerdmans, 1964–76.*

Introduction

SOCIO-RHETORICAL INTERPRETATION

In this book I will apply the interpretive analytic known as socio-rhetorical interpretation (SRI) to 2 Peter. The form of SRI that I will use has been developed by Vernon K. Robbins and those associated with him. SRI is a multi-dimensional approach to texts. The first significant stage of this approach was set out by Robbins in two books: *The Tapestry of Early Christian Discourse: Rhetoric, Society and Ideology* and *Exploring the Texture of Texts: A Guide to Socio-Rhetorical Interpretation*. At this stage SRI involved observation and interpretation of five aspects of texts: inner texture, intertexture, social and cultural texture, ideological texture, and sacred texture.

- Inner texture refers to the internal structure of a text, such things as opening-middle-closing, repetitions in the text, progressions, narration, argument, and sensory-aesthetic elements.
- Intertexture is the relationship of the text to things outside itself, the way it incorporates other texts, as well as cultural, social, and historical realities.
- The social and cultural texture of a text consists of its stance toward the culture out of which it arises, its inclusion of cultural values such as honor-shame and purity codes, and its place in its culture.
- Ideological texture "concerns particular alliances and conflicts the language in a text and the language in an interpretation evoke and nurture . . . the way the text itself and interpreters of the text position themselves in relation to other individuals and groups."[1]
- Sacred texture refers to the religious or theological content of a text.

---

1. Robbins, *Exploring the Texture of Texts*, 4.

The great value of SRI in this form is the way it unifies various approaches to the New Testament that are often pursued separately. Each of the items that Robbins calls textures of the text is often pursued on its own. And when any of them is pursued individually, there is at least some tendency to see it as an alternative to other ways of interpreting the text. However, SRI provides a framework within which each of these things has a proper place in developing a complete interpretation of the text.

More recently Robbins has developed SRI in a somewhat different direction that is set forth most completely in the first volume of *The Invention of Christian Discourse*. Beginning with an essay titled "The Dialectical Nature of Early Christian Discourse," Robbins has proposed that there were six basic kinds of early Christian discourse, which he calls "rhetorolects": wisdom, miracle, prophetic, precreation, priestly, and apocalyptic. Each of these is a "distinctive configuration of themes, topics, reasonings, and argumentations"[2] and each blends with the others in early Christian texts.[3]

These six rhetorolects are a Christian counterpart of the classical division of rhetoric into judicial, deliberative, and epideictic. These three kinds of rhetoric are associated respectively with the courtrooms, political assemblies, and civil ceremonies of Greek and Roman city-states. Partly because these were not the most important social situations for early Christians, they developed forms of rhetoric associated with other social situations, namely, the intersubjective bodies, households, villages, synagogues, cities, temples, kingdoms, and empires in which they lived and which they imagined.

In order to understand fully a classical speech in written form, one must take into account the setting in which it was intended to be delivered. For example, one must realize that a judicial speech was delivered by an advocate in a courtroom. In the same way, one must situate the six rhetorolects in the context for which each was composed. Robbins has proposed the following description of these contexts.

- Wisdom discourse is spoken in the context of the universe understood as a household over which God presides as a father. Through the medium of God's wisdom, people who are God's children produce righteous action and speech.

- Miracle discourse arises in a context in which God is understood as the healer, through a bodily agent, of the malfunctioning bodies of

---

2. Robbins, "Dialectical Nature," 356.

3. Definitions of the rhetorolects are given in the glossary of Robbins, *Invention of Christian Discourse*, xxi–xxx. More detailed discussion of rhetorolects in general can be found on 104–20, 489–517 of the same work. Cf. also Robbins, "Conceptual Blending and Early Christian Imagination."

individuals and thus as restoring communities to relationships of well-being.

- Prophetic discourse presumes the context of the universe understood as a kingdom of which God is king. Prophets are individuals to whom God's will has been communicated who call people to act righteously through prophetic action and speech.
- Pre-creation discourse presumes the context of the universe seen as an empire of which God is the emperor with an eternal household consisting of his son and others. People can enter into relationship with the emperor through the members of his household.
- Priestly discourse arises in the context of the universe understood as a temple city. Actions in the temple benefit God in a way that activates divine benefits for humans.
- Apocalyptic discourse presumes the context of the universe understood as an empire of which God is the emperor at the head of an army. The divine army will destroy all the evil in the universe and create a state in which the good experience perfect well-being in the presence of God.

These contexts and their elaborations form what Robbins calls the rhetography of the discourse. The argumentation of the discourse forms its rhetology. As Robbins observes, New Testament interpreters have given relatively little attention to its rhetography. Robbins himself has developed the exploration of rhetography by making use of critical spatiality theory and cognitive theory about conceptual blending.[4] The precise meaning of rhetography is still being clarified.

Some instances of the six rhetorolects are primarily pictorial, i.e., rhetography; this is particularly true of narratives. However, such instances also have an argumentative or persuasive dimension, i.e., rhetology. Other instances of these types of discourse are primarily argumentative. However, such instances also have a pictorial dimension. A still unsettled question is the relationship between the six discourses and the five textures discussed by SRI. In this book I will presume that the five textures mainly contribute either to the rhetography or to the rhetology of the discourses. However, some aspects of these textures may need to be considered separately.

4. This description of the six rhetorolects and of rhetography and rhetology is based on two essays by Robbins: "Socio-Rhetorical Interpretation" and "Rhetography: A New Way of Seeing the Familiar Text;" see also the introduction to Robbins, *Invention of Christian Discourse*. For critical spatiality theory Robbins refers to Gunn and McNutt, *"Imagining" Biblical Worlds* among other works. For conceptual blending theory he refers to Fauconnier and Turner, *The Way We Think*.

DISCOURSES IN 2 PETER

The following outline shows the distribution of discourses in 2 Peter and includes a translation of the text.

I. Introducing Prophetic, Apocalyptic, Precreation, Priestly, and Wisdom (1:1–15)

Step 1: Prophetic blended with >	Apocalyptic	Precreation	Priestly blended with Wisdom
Simeon Peter, slave and apostle of Jesus, writes to those who have received faith like his and wishes them well.	Jesus is Christ and savior	Jesus is God	Peter prays that those he addresses will have abundant grace and peace through knowledge of God and Jesus

1:1 Simeon Peter, slave and apostle of Jesus Christ,
to those who have received faith equal in honor to ours by the justice of our God and savior Jesus Christ.
2 May favor and peace be multiplied for you by full knowledge of God and Jesus our Lord.

Step 2: Prophetic blended with >	Precreation	Priestly	Wisdom	Apocalyptic
Since Jesus' power has given everything needed for life etc., the addressees should supply by their faith, virtue, etc. in order to make a proper return for this gift and continue to receive it until the end	Jesus' power is divine power	The addressees have received what is needed for piety, escape from the corruption in the world, should supply piety etc. and have been cleansed from sin	Jesus' power has provided everything through knowledge; failing to grow in virtue is unfruitfulness; entry into the kingdom will be richly provided	The addressees escape from the world, participate in divine nature, and will enter into the eternal kingdom of the Lord and savior Jesus Christ

3 Since his divine power has given us all things for life and piety through full knowledge of the one who has called us by his glory and virtue, 4 through which [glory and virtue] he has given us the precious and very great promises in order that through these you might become sharers of divine nature, having escaped the corruption in the world by desire,

5 therefore, having brought in all eagerness beside, by your faith supply virtue, and by virtue, knowledge, 6 and by knowledge, self-control, and by self-control, endurance, and by endurance, piety, 7 and by piety, brotherly love, and by brotherly love, love.

8 For possessing and exceeding in these things renders you neither idle nor fruitless for full knowledge of our Lord Jesus Christ.

9 For the one in whom these things are not present is blind, nearsighted, having experienced forgetfulness of the cleansing of his past sins.

10 Therefore, brothers, be more eager to make secure your call and election; for doing these things you will never stumble.

11 For in this way entrance into the eternal kingdom of our Lord and savior Jesus Christ will be richly supplied to you.

Step 3: Prophetic blended with >	Miracle	Apocalyptic
Because of the benefits of following the exhortation in 1:3–11, Peter reminds the addressees of these things and arranges for them to be remembered after his death	Jesus has shown Peter that his death is imminent	Jesus is Christ

12 Therefore, I will always remind you about these things, although you know them and are established in the present truth. 13 But I consider it just, while I am in this tent, to arouse you by remembrance, 14 knowing that putting off my tent is imminent, as also our Lord Jesus Christ revealed to me, 15 and I will be eager for you also to be able always to make remembrance of these things after my departure.

II. Blending Apocalyptic with Miracle, Precreation, Priestly, Prophetic, and Wisdom (1:16—3:13)

Step 1: Apocalyptic blended with >	Miracle blended with Precreation	Priestly
Peter and others have made known to the addressees the power and parousia of the Lord Jesus Christ	They have made it known on the basis of witnessing his majesty and hearing a voice from heaven by which the Majestic Glory declared that Jesus is his beloved son	The mountain is holy

16 For it was not having followed cleverly devised myths that we made known to you the power and coming of our Lord Jesus Christ, but having been eyewitnesses of his majesty. 17 For having received honor and glory from God the father when a voice such as this was borne to him by the magnificent glory: "My son, my beloved, is this one, in whom I am well pleased." 18 And this voice we heard borne from heaven, being with him on the holy mountain.

Step 2: Prophetic blended with >	Apocalyptic blended with Miracle	Priestly
The prophetic word shows that what Peter and others have made known to the addressees is true	The addressees await the dawn of day and rising of the morning star; false teachers will be destroyed, as can be seen from God's past destruction of wicked and salvation of righteous; the past actions include the flood and destruction of Sodom and Gomorrah	Spirit is holy; Jesus is the Master who purchased his followers, probably by means of his death and resurrection; false teachers are impure

19 And we have the more secure prophetic word, which you do well to heed like a lamp shining in a dark place until day dawns and the light-bearer rises, in your hearts 20 first knowing this, that all prophecy of Scripture is not of one's own explanation. 21 For prophecy was never borne by the will of a human being, but being borne by the Holy Spirit human beings spoke from God. 2:1 But there were also false prophets among the people, as among you there will also be false teachers, who will secretly introduce heresies of destruction, even denying the master who purchased them, bringing on themselves imminent destruction. 2 And many will follow their licentiousnesses, because of whom the way of truth will be slandered. 3 And in their greed they will buy you with counterfeit words, whose judgment long ago is not idle and their destruction does not sleep. 4 For if God did not spare the angels who sinned but, having cast them into Tartarus, delivered them to chains of gloom, kept for judgment; 5 and if he did not spare the ancient world but guarded Noah, as an eighth, the herald of justice, having brought a deluge on the world of the impious; 6 and if he condemned the cities of Sodom and Gomorrah, having reduced them to ashes in a catastrophe, having made them an example of the things about to happen to the impious, 7 and he rescued just Lot, worn out by his life amidst the licentiousness of the lawless 8 for by means of seeing and hearing the just man dwelling among them day after day tortured his just soul with respect to their lawless works; 9 then the Lord knows how to rescue the pious from trial and how to keep the unjust confined for the day of judgment, 10 and especially those who go after the flesh in desire for defilement and despise dominion.

Step 3: Prophetic blended with >	Apocalyptic	Priestly	Miracle	Wisdom
Peter criticizes the false teachers; they have followed the way of the prophet Balaam	The false teachers will be destroyed; darkness has been reserved for them; Jesus is savior and Christ	The false teachers are corrupt; the addressees have escaped the defilements in the world	Balaam's donkey spoke	One escapes the defilements of the world through knowledge of Jesus Christ

Stubborn bold ones, they do not tremble, slandering the glories, 11 where angels, being greater in strength and power, do not bear against them a slanderous judgment from (the side of) the Lord. 12 But these, like irrational animals begotten naturally for capture and corruption, slandering things of which they are ignorant, will also be corrupted in their corruption, 13 being wronged as the reward of wrongdoing, considering luxuriousness during the day a pleasure, spots and blemishes luxuriating in their deceits while feasting together with you, 14 having eyes full of an adulteress and not ceasing from sin, enticing unstable souls, having a heart trained in greed, children of a curse. 15 Abandoning the straight way, they have gone astray, having followed in the way of Balaam, son of Bosor, who loved the reward of wrongdoing. 16 And he received a rebuke of his own lawbreaking. A voiceless donkey having spoken with a human's voice prevented the madness of the prophet. 17 These are waterless springs and mists driven by a storm for whom the gloom of darkness has been kept. 18 For speaking boastful words of futility they entice with the desires of the flesh, with licentiousnesses, those who are just escaping from the people who live in error, 19 promising them freedom while being themselves slaves of corruption. For by whatever someone has been overcome, to this he has been enslaved. 20 For if, having escaped the defilements of the world by full knowledge of our Lord and savior Jesus Christ, and again having been implicated in them, people are overcome, for them the last things have become worse than the first. 21 For it was better for them not to have fully known the way of justice than, having fully known it, to turn away from the holy commandment delivered to them. 22 The meaning of the true proverb has applied to them: a dog having turned back to his own vomit, and a sow, having been washed, to wallowing in the mud.

Step 4: Prophetic blended with >	Wisdom	Apocalyptic	Priestly	Miracle
Peter restates the occasion of the letter and resumes replying to opponents after the digression of 2:10b–22	Occasion is reminding addressees of beneficial knowledge	Jesus is savior; scoffers will appear in the last days doubting the promise of Jesus' parousia; day of judgment will lead to a new heaven and earth	The addressees should be sincere etc.; the scoffers indulge their own lusts etc.	The flood is a precedent for the day of judgment

3:1 Beloved, I now write this second letter to you, in which I arouse in your remembrance the pure understanding 2 to remember the words spoken beforehand by the holy prophets and the commandment of your apostles of our Lord and savior, 3 first knowing this, that in the last days scoffers will come with scoffing, going according to their own desires 4 and saying: "Where is the promise of his coming? For since the fathers have fallen asleep all things continue thus from the beginning of creation." 5 For it escapes the notice of those maintaining this that there were heavens long ago and an earth constituted from water and through water by the word of God, 6 through which [water and word] the world of that time was destroyed, having been deluged with water. 7 And the present heavens and the earth are treasured up by the same word, kept for fire on the day of judgment and destruction of impious human beings. 8 And let this one thing not escape your notice, beloved, that one day with the Lord is like a thousand years and a thousand years like one day. 9 For the Lord of the promise does not delay, as some consider delay, but he is patient toward you, not wishing that any be destroyed, but that all come to repentance. 10 And the day of the Lord will come like a thief, on which the heavens will pass away with a rushing noise, and the elements, set on fire, will be dissolved, and the earth and the works on it will be discovered. 11 Since all these things will thus be dissolved, what sort of people is it necessary that you be with holy lives and pieties, 12 awaiting and eagerly seeking the coming of the day of God on account of which the heavens, burning, will be dissolved and the elements, set on fire, are melted. 13 And we await new heavens and a new earth according to his promise, in which justice dwells.

III. Concluding with Prophetic blended with Apocalyptic, Priestly, and Wisdom (3:14–18)

Prophetic blended with >	Apocalyptic	Priestly	Wisdom
The addressees should strive to be found at peace, not be carried away with the error of the lawless, and grow in grace and knowledge of Jesus	They should do so on the basis of the expectations stated in 3:3–13, regard the patience of the Lord as salvation, and await the day of eternity	It should take the form of being without spot or blemish; prayer of praise	This is in accord with the wisdom of Paul; addressees should avoid error and seek knowledge

14 Therefore, beloved, awaiting these things, be eager to be discovered by him spotless and unblemished in peace. 15 And consider the patience of our Lord salvation, as also our beloved brother Paul wrote to you according to the wisdom given to him, 16 so also in all his letters speaking in them about these things, in which [letters] there are some things hard to understand which the ignorant and unstable twist, as they also do the rest of the Scriptures, to their own destruction. 17 Therefore you, beloved, knowing these things beforehand, be on guard in order that you may not fall away from your own firm footing, having been led astray by the error of the lawless. 18 But grow in favor and knowledge of our Lord and savior Jesus Christ. To him be glory both now and into the day of eternity. Amen

As I discuss each section of the text, I will begin with a description of the passage's rhetography, i.e., the way it evokes and elaborates the contexts associated with these discourses. I will then analyze the interweaving of the five textures in the passage—inner texture, intertexture, social and cultural texture, ideological texture, and sacred texture—showing how each contributes to the passage's rhetography and rhetology, i.e., its persuasive impact on those to whom it is addressed. I will conclude by discussing the rhetorical force of the passage.

Some aspects of 2 Peter's rhetography, rhetology, and texture can be seen more clearly and satisfactorily when considering 2 Peter as a whole rather than section by section. An overview of these aspects follows.

RHETOGRAPHY AND RHETOLOGY

Literary Form

The most basic rhetography of 2 Peter is evoked by the literary form of the document. Second Peter is a letter. It begins with a letter salutation (1:1-2) that is very similar to the salutations of other New Testament letters (see discussion of 1:1-2 below). The author of 2 Peter explicitly calls his composition a letter in 3:1.

Second Peter also has the form of a testament. This is a characteristically Jewish literary form in which a notable person, shortly before his death, bids farewell to his associates, giving them ethical advice and/or revelations about the future to guide them after his death. Commentators since Hans Windisch have generally agreed that 2 Peter should be seen as an example of a testament.[5] Richard J. Bauckham develops this understanding of 2 Peter at greatest length.[6] The testamentary character of 2 Peter is clearest in 1:12-15, where Peter refers to his imminent death and says that his purpose in writing is to continue reminding the addressees about his teaching after he dies. It is also clear in 2:1-3 and 3:1-4 where Peter predicts the rise of false teachers.[7] The best-known example of the testament is the *Testaments of the Twelve Patriarchs*. The best example of a testament in letter form is *2 Baruch* 78-86;[8] 2 Timothy is another possible example.[9]

Recognition of 2 Peter as a testamentary letter evokes the mental picture of Peter as writing the letter before his death to provide instruction for those who lived after him. A usual feature of testaments is that they are

---

5. Windisch, *Die Katholischen Briefe*, 87-88; see also Schelkle, *Die Petrusbriefe*, 181; Reicke, *James, Peter and Jude*, 146; Spicq, *Épitres de Saint Pierre*, 193-94; Kelly, *Peter and Jude*, 311; Grundmann, *Brief des Judas und zweite Brief des Petrus*, 55-58; Knoch, *Erste und Zweite Petrusbrief*, 200-202; Paulsen, *Zweite Petrusbrief*, 89-90; Neyrey, *2 Peter, Jude*, 163-64; Vögtle, *Der Judasbrief/Der 2. Petrusbrief*, 122. Harrington, "Jude and 2 Peter," 229. Green (*Second Epistle General of Peter*, 36-38), Davids (*2 Peter and Jude*, 148-49), Green (*Jude & 2 Peter*, 164-67), and Harvey and Towner (*2 Peter & Jude*, 10-11) are not convinced; Charles (*Virtue Amidst Vice*, 49-75) also argues against identification of 2 Peter as a testament.

6. Bauckham, *Jude, 2 Peter*, 131-35; "2 Peter," 3734-35.

7. Bauckham, *Jude, 2 Peter*, 132.

8. Ibid., 133.

9. Luke T. Johnson argues that 2 Timothy is not a testament, but perhaps mainly to evade the implications of this for the authenticity of 2 Timothy (*First and Second Letters to Timothy*, 320-24). On the other hand Raymond F. Collins (*1 & 2 Timothy and Titus*, 182-85) and Benjamin Fiore (*The Pastoral Epistles*, 8-9) regard 2 Timothy as a testament.

pseudonymous.[10] The twelve sons of Jacob were not the actual authors of the *Testaments of the Twelve Patriarchs*, nor was Baruch, Jeremiah's secretary, author of the testamentary letter of Baruch. Thus the mental picture evoked by recognition of 2 Peter as a testamentary letter probably includes awareness that someone other than Peter has presented his message as a testamentary letter from Peter.

In evoking the picture of Peter as writing a testamentary letter, 2 Peter calls to mind the image of Peter as functioning like a prophet as he brings the addressees a challenging message from God. Because this message includes prediction of the eschaton and a call to live in its light, 2 Peter also evokes the image of Peter as an apocalyptic visionary who reveals the divine plan for the world.

This rhetographical frame for 2 Peter as a whole has rhetological implications. Presentation of 2 Peter's message as deriving from Peter, slave and apostle of Jesus Christ and a principal leader of the Christian church, implies that it is authoritative and should be followed. Second Peter carries the authority of prophecy and of apocalyptic revelation.

Within the rhetographical and rhetological frame established by the form of the testamentary letter (found especially in 1:1–2, 12–15; 3:1), 2 Peter displays additional rhetography and rhetology. The main features of this can be summarized as follows:

- 1:3–11 is patterned on a decree honoring a benefactor. Insofar as this section is perceived as resembling a decree, it evokes the mental image of Peter as acting like a civic leader or member of a club who proposes that the addressees honor Jesus for his benefactions by living virtuously. In this highly argumentative section, rhetology is more prominent than rhetography. However, in the latter part of this section (vv. 8–11) the author's arguments make use of vivid pictures.

- 1:16—2:10a constitutes two arguments that Jesus will come again and are thus basically rhetological. However, the arguments are highly rhetographical. They involve telling the story of Jesus' transfiguration in 1:16–18, painting a vivid picture of prophecy as a light that shines in darkness until day dawns in 1:19, describing future false teachers in 2:1–3, and briefly telling three stories of God's past punishment of evildoers and rescue of the upright in 2:4–8.

---

10. Bauckham *Jude, 2 Peter*, 134.

- 2:10b–17 continues the denunciation of the false teachers begun in 2:1–3. As is true in the latter passage, the denunciation in 2:10b–17 presents vivid pictures of the false teachers' multifarious misbehavior.
- 2:18–22 argues that the views of the false teachers are destructive both for those who follow them and for the false teachers themselves. This is another basically rhetological section whose arguments are rhetographical, vividly picturing the false teachers as enticing those who follow them, and describing these followers and the false teachers as slaves of corruption and behaving like dogs and pigs.
- 3:3–4 describes future scoffers who are probably identical to the false teachers described earlier. Their speech is quoted, evoking them clearly.
- 3:5–13 continues the argument that Jesus will come again and is thus basically rhetological. But as often in 2 Peter the argument is very rhetographical, briefly describing the creation of the world, its destruction by the flood, God's relationship to time, God's patience, and the future destruction of the present world by fire and its replacement by new heavens and earth.
- 3:14–18 concludes 2 Peter by repeating briefly the main points made earlier. Like much of 2 Peter it is basically rhetological, but depends on rhetography for the force of its argumentation.

These and other aspects of the rhetography and rhetology of 2 Peter are examined further in the discussion of its sacred texture below.

Inner texture

Much of the inner texture of 2 Peter is best seen in considering each passage. However, one element of its sensory-aesthetic texture, namely its style, benefits from summary overview. This and other aspects of the rhetoric of 2 Peter have been thoroughly explored by Duane F. Watson in *Invention, Arrangement and Style*.

The Style of 2 Peter

The style of a composition can be considered from two perspectives: vocabulary and syntax. Rare words, new coinages, and metaphors and other tropes are ways to ornament vocabulary. Avoiding hiatus of vowels and harsh clash of consonants, using rhythm, and using figures of speech and thought are ways to ornament syntax. Using the period, a sentence the completion of whose sense is suspended until the end, is another way to make syntax ornate. Compositions are said to exhibit grand, middle, or plain style depending mainly on the quantity and quality of ornament.

The style of 2 Peter is striking. Second Peter frequently repeats words. It also uses many words not found elsewhere in the New Testament. According to Bauckham, 2 Peter contains fifty-seven such words. Twenty-five of these words are found in the Septuagint; another seventeen are found in other contemporary Jewish literature; and one more is found in the Apostolic Fathers. Most of the remaining fourteen words are very rare; two of them are not found anywhere else in Greek literature: παραφρονίαν (madness) in 2:16 and ἐμπαιγμονῇ (scoffing) in 3:3.[11]

According to Bauckham, "The incidence of rare words is part of a general impression 2 Peter gives of aiming at ambitious literary effect."[12] Other things that give this impression, according to Bauckham, are the author's characteristic use of pairs of synonyms and the already noted repetition of words. The complex sentences found in 1:3–7 and 2:4–10a, the many figures of speech used in 2 Peter, especially the ladder of virtues in 1:5–7 and the image in 1:19, and the poetic rhythm found in parts of 2 Peter are other indications of 2 Peter's literary ambition.

Second Peter is written in grand style. The poetic rhythm of 2 Peter (and some of the other features mentioned above) probably manifests the author's attempt to write in the Asian style.[13] This was one of the two principal varieties of Greek prose style in the rhetorical schools of the Hellenistic and Roman periods; the other was the Attic style. Unfortunately, few examples of Asianism survive, and we derive our understanding of it largely from those who criticized it.

Just as Asianism was criticized in its own time, many today do not find the style of 2 Peter appealing. However, if 2 Peter is written in this style, its author's literary aspirations are clear. Bo Reicke compares it to European art and literature of the baroque period; this parallel may help us be more appreciative of the style of 2 Peter.[14]

Following Cicero, Eduard Norden described two kinds of Asianism: the delicate and the bombastic. The delicate Asian style was characterized by 1) replacement of the period with short, choppy sentences; 2) each of

11. Ibid., 135–36.
12. Ibid., 137.
13. Reicke, *James, Peter and Jude*, 146–47; Kelly, *Peter and Jude*, 228; Bauckham *Jude, 2 Peter*, 137; Watson, *Invention*, 145–46; Callan, "Style of the Second Letter of Peter."
14. Reicke, *James, Peter and Jude*, 146–47.

which had a marked rhythm; and 3) unusual usage, e.g., nonsensical metaphors and absurd paraphrases. The bombastic style shared the second and third characteristics with the delicate style, but used long instead of short sentences.[15]

Reicke describes the second kind of Asianism as "characterized by a loaded, verbose, high-sounding manner of expression leaning toward the novel and bizarre, and careless about violating classic ideals of simplicity."[16] This is the kind of Asianism that 2 Peter represents. The attempt to write in this style accounts for all the features of 2 Peter mentioned above: unusual vocabulary; figures of speech, including use of synonyms and repetition of words; complex sentences; and rhythm.

The grand style of 2 Peter implies that the author sees himself as expressing powerful and impressive thoughts and that the author is attempting primarily to appeal to the emotions of the addressees, rather than to inform or please them. Writing in the Asian style implies that the author stood outside the mainstream of literary development in the first and second centuries. It would have been possible to write in this style anywhere, even in Rome. The Asian style may imply, however, that 2 Peter was not written in a cultural center, but rather somewhere like Commagene, the location of the Nemrud Dagh inscription that 2 Peter resembles stylistically. The style of 2 Peter makes it likely that its author had received higher education in rhetoric.[17]

The style of 2 Peter serves the general purposes just mentioned, i.e., making his communication impressive and emotionally appealing. Many elements of its style also serve more specific purposes, namely contributing to the mental images the letter evokes or making it more persuasive. I will mention instances of both where they occur.

Intertexture

The oral-scribal intertexture of 2 Peter, i.e., the way it incorporates other texts, is notably complex. Several times 2 Peter quotes from another text, either reproducing its exact words, or reproducing its exact words with one or more differences. We find the following instances of this kind of recitation in 2 Peter:

    1:2a = 1 Pet 1:2a

15. Norden, *Die antike Kunstprosa*, 134–47.
16. Reicke, *James, Peter and Jude*, 147.
17. Callan, "Style of the Second Letter of Peter."

1:17b = Matt 17:5 with differences

2:17b = Jude 13b with one difference

2:20b = Matt 12:45/Luke 11:26 with one difference

2:21 = Job 24:13 with differences

3:2 = Jude 17 with several changes

3:8b = Ps 90:4 (LXX 89:4) with several changes

3:10a = 1 Thess 5:2

3:13a = Isa 65:17; 66:22 with several changes

Second Peter 2:22 is a recitation of a saying using words different from the authoritative source. The verse cites a double proverb. The first part comes from Prov 26:11; the second part seems to come from *The Story of Ahikar* 8:15/18. Bauckham thinks Hellenistic Jews may have combined the two before they were incorporated into 2 Peter.[18]

Second Peter includes several recitations of a text in substantially the author's own words:

1:14 may be such a recitation of John 21:18–19

1:16–18 may be such a recitation of Matt 17:1–8; as noted above 1:17b reproduces the exact words of Matt 17:5 with some differences

2:15–16 is a recitation of Num 22, perhaps as interpreted in targums

3:1–2 is probably such a recitation of 1 Peter

3:15–16 is a recitation of the letters of Paul

Second Peter also includes recitations that summarize a span of text that includes various episodes:

2:4–8 summarizes Gen 6:1—19:29

3:5–6 summarizes Gen 1–7

In all but the first two cases where 2 Peter recites the exact words of a source, 2 Peter also recontextualizes these words. In addition to this, in 2:1—3:3 2 Peter completely recontextualizes Jude 4–18.[19] This is the most significant literary relationship between 2 Peter and another text.

---

18. Bauckham, *Jude, 2 Peter*, 273.

19. On this see Callan, "Use of the Letter of Jude." See also Mayor, *Second Epistle of St. Peter*, xxi–xxv; Chaine, *Les Épitres Catholiques*, 18–24; Windisch, *Katholischen Briefe*, 91–92; Schelkle, *Die Petrusbriefe*, 138–39; Sidebottom, *James, Jude, and 2 Peter*,

Second Peter's use of Jude can be described as a rather free paraphrase.[20] Beginning with the written text of Jude, the author of 2 Peter rewrote Jude, using much of Jude's language, but avoiding direct quotation. The procedure was similar to that used by the author of a work like the one you are now reading who paraphrases the work of others in developing his own presentation. Bauckham says, "This dependence is never slavish. The author takes what he wants from Jude, whether ideas or words, and uses it in a composition that is very much his own."[21] "It is characteristic of our author's use of Jude that he gets an idea from Jude and then gives it a fresh twist or development of his own."[22] Gene L. Green characterizes 2 Peter's use of Jude as *imitatio*.[23]

In addition to these recitations, commentators have proposed that 2 Peter alludes to other texts. These suggested allusions include the following:

1:17 might allude to Ps 2:7 and Isa 42:1

1:19 might allude to Num 24:17

3:9 might allude to Hab 2:3; 3:10, 12; Mal 3:19 + Isa 34:4

Some of these possibilities are discussed at appropriate places below.

To summarize, 2 Peter is related to the following writings of the Old Testament—Genesis, Numbers, Isaiah, Proverbs, and Psalms—and the following writings of what is now the New Testament—Matthew, possibly John, 1 Thessalonians and the letters of Paul in general, 1 Peter, and Jude. At the appropriate points, I will discuss these relationships in more detail. The author knows and uses much of what is now the Christian bible. He does not take over from Jude the quotation of *1 Enoch* in Jude 14–15 or Jude's

---

68–69; Kelly, *Peter and Jude*, 226–27; Grundmann, *Brief des Judas und zweite Brief des Petrus*, 102–7; Knoch, *Erste und Zweite Petrusbrief*, 205–6; Senior, *1 and 2 Peter*, 102; Bauckham *Jude, 2 Peter*, 142–43; Bauckham, "2 Peter," 3714–16; Watson, *Invention*, 160–87; Paulsen, *Zweite Petrusbrief*, 97–100; Neyrey, *2 Peter, Jude*, 122; Vögtle, *Der Judasbrief/Der 2. Petrusbrief*, 122–23; Perkins, *First and Second Peter*, 178; Gilmour, *Significance of Parallels*, 90–91, 120; Harrington, "Jude and 2 Peter," 232–33; Davids, *2 Peter and Jude*, 136–43; Green, *Jude & 2 Peter*, 159–62. Bigg argues that Jude depends on 2 Peter (*St. Peter and St. Jude*, 216–24); so also Wohlenberg (*Der erste und zweite Petrusbrief*, xli–iii) and Moo (*2 Peter and Jude*, 16–18). Lapham argues that in the process of transmission both 2 Peter and Jude have undergone redactive cross-interpolation ("Second Epistle of Peter," 152–54, 157).

20. Sidebottom, *James, Jude, and 2 Peter*, 95, 112.

21. Bauckham, *Jude, 2 Peter*, 236.

22. Ibid., 260.

23. Green, *Jude & 2 Peter*, 161–62; see also his essay "Second Peter's Use of Jude: *Imitatio* and the Sociology of Early Christianity," 1–25.

possible allusion to the *Assumption of Moses* in Jude 9. Perhaps he purposely avoids referring to these texts that are not now authoritative for Christians.

Social and Cultural Texture

The presence of common social and cultural topics in 2 Peter is best seen in the discussion of each section. Jerome H. Neyrey's Anchor Bible commentary on 2 Peter thoroughly explores this aspect of 2 Peter.

Second Peter's basic relationship to the world can be seen as what Robbins, following Bryan Wilson, calls revolutionist, the idea that the world is so thoroughly bad that supernatural powers must destroy it in order to set people free from it.[24] This is the apocalyptic outlook that is fundamental to 2 Peter. One of 2 Peter's main themes is defense of the apocalyptic expectation of Jesus' second coming from those who doubt or deny it. When Jesus comes again, this world will be destroyed and replaced by a new heaven and earth (3:1–13).

Subordinate to this, but very prominent in 2 Peter, is what Robbins calls the introversionist response to the world, i.e., withdrawing from it. Because this world is irredeemably evil and destined to be replaced by a new world, it is necessary to keep oneself separate from this world now, as one awaits the coming of the end of this world and the beginning of the new world. As it is found in 2 Peter, this introversionist response is another aspect of apocalyptic thought. Thus, 2 Pet 1:4 describes the addressees as ones who have escaped from the corruption in the world by desire, and much of the letter is devoted to ethical instruction. 2:20–21 makes it clear that full knowledge (ἐπίγνωσις) of Jesus is the means by which one escapes the pollutions of the world.

The emphasis on full knowledge, which is found throughout 2 Peter, points to a third response to the world in 2 Peter. Robbins calls this gnostic-manipulationist, i.e., the view that one can learn how to overcome the evil in the world. However, in 2 Peter gnostic-manipulationist language is subordinate to introversionist and revolutionist language. In the final analysis, what one needs to know is that it is necessary to live virtuously as one awaits the second coming of Jesus.

The discourse in 2 Peter, principally in its expectation of the return of Jesus and call for virtuous life in preparation for it, seems to be a subculture of apocalyptic Judaism, but countercultural with respect to Greco-Roman culture in general and likewise with respect to those Christians against whom it argues.

24. Robbins, *Exploring the Texture of Texts*, 72–74.

Ideological Texture

I begin by acknowledging some of my own beliefs, assumptions and values as an interpreter of 2 Peter. I am a Roman Catholic who believes that 2 Peter is part of the inspired word of God found in the Bible. I regard this inspired word of God, however, as communicated by means of fully human words. Thus in order to gain access to the word of God, it is necessary to interpret the Bible in the same way one would interpret any human writing. Whatever means we can use to interpret any writing can also be used to interpret the Bible. Reading the Bible and reading other writings are methodologically the same; they differ only in their results. When we have read other writings, we understand only what their human authors have expressed; when we read the Bible, we understand what its human authors have expressed, but also what God has revealed through them.

Because the Bible is the word of God in human words, it is also subject to the limitations of human beings. The limited knowledge of the human authors is reflected in the biblical texts. It is impossible to say beforehand where these limitations are found. When they are discovered, I conclude that this was not the inspired communication of God.

As I have already said above, in this book I approach 2 Peter using socio-rhetorical interpretation. This combines many of the approaches to biblical interpretation currently used by academic biblical scholars. One reason I find this interpretive approach attractive is that it attempts to unify the somewhat fragmented field of academic biblical studies. I agree with the presupposition of socio-rhetorical interpretation that all of these approaches make a contribution to a complete interpretation of a text. Perhaps this partly reflects a Catholic impulse on my part toward inclusion rather than exclusion.

Second Peter probably reflects conflict between Christian groups who claim to embody the authentic faith of Jesus and the apostles. The author of 2 Peter explicitly claims the authenticity of his teaching and rejects the views of others (see 1:16; 3:1-4). His opponents, the "false teachers" (2:1), probably also claim to embody authentic Christianity. From 2 Peter's arguments against them, we can see that they held different views than the author did about eschatology and ethics. The author does not present their rationale for these views, but it seems likely that the "false teachers" regarded them as authentically Christian.

Many interpreters have seen 2 Peter as an expression of an ideology, or theological outlook, they call "early Catholicism." Protestants use this as a pejorative term to designate theological positions rejected by the Protestant Reformation. Ernst Käsemann is the most prominent Protestant interpreter who has criticized 2 Peter as the expression of an early Catholic viewpoint,[25] but many others have followed him in this. Catholics evaluate the same theological outlook differently, understanding it as a legitimate development of Christian theology.[26] Because one's confessional stance determines the meaning of "early Catholicism," it is not a helpful exegetical category.

"Early Catholicism" is also an unsatisfactory category because its content is rather vague. According to Bauckham, following J. D. G. Dunn, early Catholicism has three main characteristics: 1) fading of hope for Jesus' parousia, 2) increasing institutionalization, and 3) crystallization of the faith into set forms.[27] Bauckham argues, correctly I think, that these characteristics are not found in 2 Peter.[28] More specifically Bauckham argues that 2 Peter expresses hope for the imminent arrival of the parousia and does not insist on formal creedal orthodoxy. The only manifestation of institutionalization in 2 Peter is its emphasis on the role of the apostle and particularly that of Peter. This is rather slight evidence of institutionalization. Thus even if "early Catholicism" were a more satisfactory characterization of a particular theological position, it would not be accurate to describe the theology of 2 Peter as early Catholic.

Obviously my own individual location and my use of the socio-rhetorical mode of discourse underlie my whole discussion of 2 Peter. In the course of this discussion, I will call attention to the ways 2 Peter shows its origin in conflict between Christian groups and itself participates in that conflict. The main way I will take account of the ideological texture of 2 Peter is by discussing its sacred texture. The sacred texture of 2 Peter reflects the belief system of its author and thus can be seen as the sphere of ideology within which he writes.[29]

---

25. Käsemann, "Apologia," 169.

26. See Schelkle, *Die Petrusbriefe*, 241–45; Knoch, *Erste und Zweite Petrusbrief*, 226–27.

27. Bauckham, *Jude, 2 Peter*, 8.

28. Ibid., 151–54; Bauckham, "2 Peter," 3728–34. Charles (*Virtue Amidst Vice*, 11–37) also argues against application of the category "early Catholicism" to 2 Peter.

29. Further insight into current discussion of ideological texture in SRI can be found especially in the essays by Kloppenborg, Gowler, Bloomquist, Wanamaker, Sisson, Wachob, and Braun in Gowler, Bloomquist, and Watson, *Fabrics of Discourse*.

Sacred Texture

Theology and Theography

Second Peter uses the word θεός (god) seven times. These seven uses of θεός present the following picture of God:

- there were of old heavens and earth created by the word of God (3:5). Second Peter does not say explicitly that God created the present heavens and earth, but this can probably be assumed.
- God did not spare the angels who sinned, but sent them to Tartarus (2:4)
- God did not spare the ancient world (cf. 3:6), but preserved Noah (2:5)
- God condemned Sodom and Gomorrah, reducing them to ashes and establishing them as a sign of what will happen to the ungodly (2:6), but saved Lot (2:7–8)
- the prophets were men who spoke from God (1:21)
- God the father gave Jesus honor and glory when a voice was conveyed to him by the majestic glory, "My son, my beloved, is this one, in whom I am well pleased" (1:17).
- the present heavens and earth have been treasured up by the word of God for fire on the day of judgment (3:7); this is also the day of God (3:12).
- the justice of God is the source of the addressees' faith (1:1)
- full knowledge of God (and of Jesus) is the source of increasing grace and peace for the addressees (1:2)

The six occurrences of κύριος (lord) that probably refer to God add the following items to the depiction of God in 2 Peter:

- God knows how to save the pious and punish the wicked (2:9), a general conclusion from the specific cases mentioned in 2:4–8
- time is different for God than for humans (3:8)
- God is not slow to keep the promise of Jesus' return and all that will accompany it, but is patient, wanting all to repent (3:9,15)

Although 2 Peter's presentation of God is clearly drawn from the Hebrew Scriptures, the author does not say anything about God's election of, and subsequent dealings with, Israel. Second Peter presents God as God of the whole world and has little to say about the relationship of God to Israel. This probably indicates that the author writes for Gentiles, for whom God's dealing with people in general is more meaningful than is God's involvement with Israel.

It is noteworthy that 2 Peter often avoids making "God" the subject of sentences. The main exception to this is 2:4–8, where the author speaks about God's punishment of sinners and salvation of the righteous. Elsewhere the author is respectfully indirect, making "God" the object of a preposition to indicate that God is the source of something (1:17, 21), or putting "God" in the genitive case (1:1, 2; 3:12). The author also refers to God by speaking of the majestic glory (1:17) and the word of God (3:5).

Even more striking is the emphasis on the word of God in 2 Peter's references to God. This is explicit in the statements, mentioned above, that God created the first heavens and earth by the word, then destroyed them through the word, and has treasured up the present heavens and earth for destruction by the same word.[30] It is implicit in the statement that prophets spoke from God, i.e., they spoke the word of God, and in the story of the transfiguration, when God spoke words concerning Jesus. It may also be implicit in the examples of God's saving the pious and punishing the wicked that are cited in 2:4–8, if they are seen as examples of prophecy that point to the end of the world.

The author of 2 Peter does not attempt to describe God directly, even in the circumspect way this is done in a passage like Rev 4. However, much of the author's discourse about God consists of description of God's activity rather than reasoning about God and is thus theography rather than theology in a strict sense. The author's assertion that the faith of the addressees derives from the justice of God (1:1); his prayer that their grace and peace will increase through full knowledge of God and Jesus (1:2); and most of all his arguments that time is different for God than for humans (3:8) and is patient (3:9) are theological in a strict sense. But everything else the author says about God pictures God's activity and is thus theography. As is evident from the lists at the beginning of this section, the theography of 2 Peter presents a story of God's activity from the beginning to the end of the world.[31]

The most vivid descriptions of God's activity occur in 1:16–18 and 2:4–10a. 1:16–18 describes an occasion when God the father gave honor and glory to Jesus. This is simultaneously theography and Christography, a graphic depiction of Christ. 2:4–10a describes occasions when God punished the wicked and rescued the pious in the past, and argues that God will

---

30. Reicke, *James, Peter and Jude*, 175.

31. On narrative in 2 Peter see Reese, "Narrative Method and the Second Epistle of Peter."

do the same in the future. This is simultaneously theography and eschatography, a graphic depiction of the end times.³²

Christology and Christography

In the first verse of the letter, the author of 2 Peter calls Jesus God. He says that the readers have received faith by the justice τοῦ θεοῦ ἡμῶν καὶ σωτῆρος Ἰησοῦ Χριστοῦ (of our God and savior Jesus Christ). Because there is only one article, the phrase probably refers to Jesus as both God and savior (see the discussion of this verse below).

This is the only place where 2 Peter explicitly calls Jesus God. However, other things 2 Peter says about Jesus more or less clearly imply this same understanding. One of the clearest instances is 1:3 where the author of 2 Peter speaks of τῆς θείας δυνάμεως αὐτοῦ (his divine power), and the antecedent of αὐτοῦ (his) is probably Jesus, the last named substantive (in v. 2). Because the author of 2 Peter sees Jesus as God, he also believes that Jesus possesses divine power.³³ Another clear instance is 1:4 where the author of 2 Peter says that those he addresses are destined to become θείας κοινωνοὶ φύσεως (sharers of divine nature). If divinity is the destiny of those who follow Jesus, Jesus himself is surely divine.

The view that Jesus is divine is probably also implied by 2 Peter's use of κύριος (lord) as a title both for Jesus and for God. In itself "Lord" does not imply divinity. Use of this title indicates a relationship between the one who uses the title, and the one to whom it is applied. Calling someone "Lord" indicates recognition of that person as a superior to whom one gives respect, and even obedience. "Lord" was widely used as a title for God, but also as a title for any other superior (see discussion of 1:2 below). Nevertheless, 2 Peter's use of the title both for Jesus and for God suggests that they are Lord in the same sense of the word, as does the ambiguity of some of 2 Peter's uses of the title; at times it is not clear whether the title refers to Jesus or to God.

Second Peter uses the title "Lord" fourteen times. Seven times Jesus is explicitly said to be the Lord (1:2,8,11,14,16; 2:20; 3:18). In addition, the Lord and savior in 3:2 is very likely to be Jesus; elsewhere in 2 Peter Jesus is explicitly said to be the Lord and savior (1:11; 2:20; 3:18) or God and savior (1:1). The remaining six occurrences of "Lord" probably refer to God and have been discussed above in connection with 2 Peter's theology.

---

32. On the terminology "theography," "Christography" and "eschatography" see Robbins, *Invention of Christian Discourse*, 86–88.

33. Bigg, *St. Peter and St. Jude*, 253.

Other passages also imply the divinity of Jesus. In 1:16 the author of 2 Peter says that he and others were eyewitnesses (ἐπόπται) of Jesus' majesty. Since this term was used to designate the highest level of initiate into the Eleusinian mysteries, it implies that the vision of Jesus transfigured was comparable to that. And if the highest level of initiation involved a vision of the goddess,[34] the word may also suggest that the transfiguration was a vision of Jesus' divinity.

The transfiguration was an occasion on which God, the μεγαλοπρεποῦς δόξης (magnificent glory), gave τιμὴν καὶ δόξαν (honor and glory) to Jesus. This suggests that Jesus' glory is the same as God's and that Jesus is divine. (This may also be implied by 2:10; see discussion of this passage below.) Thus in 3:18 the author of 2 Peter praises Jesus with the kind of doxology usually reserved for God. According to Bauckham, the phrase δόξῃ καὶ ἀρετῇ (glory and virtue) in 1:3 is synonymous with divine power.[35]

The description of Jesus in 2:1 as the master who has purchased his followers might allude to the practice of sacral manumission at Delphi.[36] This involved sale of slaves to a god in order to free them. If this is what the author of 2 Peter has in mind, he thinks of those purchased by Jesus as effectively freed, and only nominally transferred to another owner. This would be another instance of 2 Peter's presentation of Jesus as divine.

Although 2 Peter calls Jesus God and consistently presents him as divine, God and Jesus are clearly distinguished in 2 Peter. They are first distinguished from one another in 1:2, where the author wishes that peace might be multiplied for the readers by the knowledge of both God and Jesus our Lord. Because this phrase closely follows and parallels the phrase in 1:1 that refers to Jesus as God, it is sometimes used to argue that Jesus is not being called God in 1:1.[37] However, we see a similar alternation between identifying Jesus with, and distinguishing him from, God in the first verses of the gospel according to John. In John 1:1-2 the author first says that the Word was with God, then that the Word was God, then (again) that the Word was with God.[38] It seems most likely that both 2 Peter and John consciously intend to identify Jesus with God and to distinguish him from God.

---

34. Fornberg, *Early Church*, 123.

35. Bauckham, *Jude, 2 Peter*, 179.

36. Neyrey, *2 Peter, Jude*, 191–92. According to Dale B. Martin, however, this thesis, first proposed by Deissmann, is now generally rejected because of differences in terminology between the inscriptions that speak of sacral manumission and the New Testament (*Slavery as Salvation*, xvi).

37. Neyrey, *2 Peter, Jude*, 148.

38. Harris, *Jesus as God*, 275. Another parallel to the way 2 Peter both identifies Jesus with, and distinguishes him from, God may be seen in 2 Peter's one reference to

Second Peter sees Jesus as God, yet distinct from God. How can this be? Despite the emphasis on the word of God noted above, the author of 2 Peter does not explain the relationship between Jesus and God by saying that Jesus is the Word of God. The gospel of John first proposed this explanation, and it has been very important in subsequent Christian theology. However, 2 Peter does not seem to identify Jesus and the word of God.

Second Peter offers some explanation of the relationship between Jesus and God by saying that Jesus is the Son of God. This occurs in 1:16–18, 2 Peter's account of the transfiguration. In v. 17 the author says that Jesus received τιμὴν καὶ δόξαν (honor and glory) from God the Father and that a voice was conveyed to him from the μεγαλοπρεποῦς δόξης (magnificent glory) saying, "My son, my beloved, is this one, in whom I am well pleased." In the Hebrew Scriptures "son of God" does not imply a special ontological relationship with God. In the Hellenistic world, however, "son of God" designated divinities who were seen as literal offspring of the gods (see discussion of 1:16–18 below). Since 2 Peter regards Jesus as God, it is very likely that 2 Peter understands the phrase on Hellenistic lines. This would be consistent with the presentation of Jesus as God, yet distinct from God described above. Jesus is God in the sense that he was revealed to be son of God at his transfiguration. He is distinct from God because he is the son, not God himself.

As is clear from the foregoing discussion, the author of 2 Peter has a very exalted understanding of Jesus. This understanding is mainly conveyed by simple assertion, e.g., the references to "our God and savior Jesus Christ" (1:1) and to "his divine power" (1:3), and by implication, e.g., the doxology with which the letter ends (3:18). This understanding is developed further by speaking of things Jesus has done, e.g., giving the addressees faith (1:1) and all things for life and piety (1:3). Presumably the author and addressees have some shared understanding of exactly how and when Jesus did these things, but this understanding is not expressed in 2 Peter. All of this is christological in the strict sense.

1:16–18, however, is a vivid portrayal of Jesus' relationship to God that constitutes Christography rather than Christology, just as it is also theography rather than theology. This passage describes an occasion when God who is glory gave glory to Jesus, when God the father identified Jesus as his son. This has implications for understanding the nature of God and Jesus, i.e., theology and Christology, that I have discussed above. What the

---

the Holy Spirit. In 1:21 the author says that in prophecy, "moved by the Holy Spirit men spoke from God." Prophecy is said to derive both from the Holy Spirit and from God. This suggests an identity between the two, but the use of two different names suggests that they are distinct.

author presents explicitly, however, is a story, a narrative about God and Jesus, rather than reasoning about them. This story evokes in the minds of the addressees a picture of the event narrated and is thus Christography. The author connects the story of this past event to the future coming of Jesus, but does not explicate the connection.

Another vivid portrayal of Jesus in 2 Peter is the reference in 2:1 to Jesus as the master who has purchased his followers. This is simultaneously Christography and soteriography, a graphic depiction of the way Jesus functions as savior.

Soteriology and Soteriography

The author of 2 Peter explicitly calls Jesus savior four times[39] and probably refers to Jesus when he speaks of the savior a fifth time in 3:2. This is the principal role played by Jesus in the letter. It is implicit in the designation of Jesus as Christ, i.e., Messiah,[40] though there is no indication that the author of 2 Peter is aware of this; he seems to use Christ simply as a name for Jesus. The designation of Jesus as Lord is also related to the presentation of Jesus as savior. This is suggested by the linking of the titles "Lord" and "savior" in several passages.[41] It is most explicit in 2:1 where Jesus is described as the master having bought the false teachers opposed by 2 Peter (τὸν ἀγοράσαντα αὐτοὺς δεσπότην—the master who purchased them); "master" is a synonym for "Lord."

Such assertions that Jesus is savior constitute soteriology in the strict sense. However, the description of Jesus as the master who bought the false teachers, and presumably all Christians, is soteriography, a graphic portrayal of the way Jesus saves, i.e., by purchasing his followers from those to whom they are enslaved. The picture might be that of setting free enslaved persons by purchase, something found in both the Old Testament and Greek literature. However, it is more likely that 2 Pet 2:1 pictures transferring ownership of slaves from one master to another. Jesus has purchased his followers from their previous owner, and they have become Jesus' slaves. Thus the author of 2 Peter refers to himself as slave of Jesus Christ in 1:1. Second Peter says nothing about how Jesus made this purchase. Rev 5:9 says that the purchase price was the blood of Jesus, and this may be presumed by 2 Peter. If so, the author of 2 Peter regards Jesus' death as the price he paid to purchase his followers from their previous owner and make them his own slaves.

---

39. 2 Pet 1:1, 11; 2:20; 3:18.
40. 2 Pet 1:1, 8, 11, 14, 16; 2:20; 3:18.
41. 2 Pet 1:11; 2:20; 3:2, 18.

Second Peter 2:1 does not name the previous owner from whom Jesus purchased his followers. However, 2:19-20 strongly suggests they were previously owned by corruption and the defilements of the world. What does it mean to be a slave of corruption (φθορά)? φθορά means destruction; the author of 2 Peter may understand enslavement to corruption to mean "destined for destruction," i.e., mortal. What does it mean to be overcome by the defilements (μιάσματα) of the world? μίασμα means "stain," e.g., a color imparted to a fabric, but it is often used to mean wrongful behavior of various kinds. Enslavement to bad behavior leads to destruction. Second Peter does not explain how this enslavement to corruption and the defilements of the world came to be. However, 2:18 suggests that error, deriving from futile speech, and the desires of the flesh are the cause of this enslavement. See the discussion of this passage below.

I suggested above that the author of 2 Peter understands Jesus as having purchased his followers from enslavement to corruption by his death, even though the author does not say explicitly that Jesus' death was the purchase price. However, the author does speak explicitly about the way followers of Jesus appropriate this salvation. In 1:3 the author says that Jesus' divine power has given them everything pertaining to life and piety through full knowledge of the one who called them by his own glory and excellence (v. 3), i.e., Jesus.[42] Jesus has done this by first calling them and then having them answer the call by recognizing him as savior. The author presupposes that Jesus' death has transferred human beings from enslavement to corruption to his own service. However, this transfer does not take effect until it is known to have occurred. Prior to such knowledge, human beings continue to serve their previous master because they do not know they have a new one. For the author of 2 Peter faith, i.e., full knowledge of Jesus, is absolutely crucial.

The depiction of Jesus as the master who purchased his followers (2:1) and the author's further discussion of freedom and slavery in 2:18-20 reflect a soteriographical story line that underlies these passages.

- At some unspecified point in the past humans were enslaved to corruption and the defilements of the world by error, futility, and the desires of the flesh (2:19-20).
- Jesus purchased humans from this slavery, acquiring them as his own slaves (2:1); the purchase price may have been his death.
- Humans must know about this transfer of ownership in order to take advantage of it. When they know that they have a new master, they

---

42. Bigg, *St. Peter and St. Jude*, 253–54; Kelly, *Peter and Jude*, 300–301; Bauckham, *Jude, 2 Peter*, 178.

can live in freedom from their old master. After having ceased to serve their old master, however, it remains possible to resume doing so (2:20–21). This is the danger the author of 2 Peter seeks to avert.

A full account of 2 Peter's soteriology must include a discussion of ethics and eschatology, which are the main immediate concerns of the letter. In the view of 2 Peter's author, ethics is a matter of remaining in the condition of having been saved by Jesus, and eschatology describes the completion of this salvation.

Ethics

Much of 2 Peter's ethical discourse is rhetology, reasoning about ethics. The central instance of such reasoning is found in 2:20–21, which implies that it is possible to have escaped slavery to the defilements of the world by full knowledge of Jesus and then return to one's former master. Jesus' purchase of human beings from their former master, and their full knowledge of him as their new master, does not eliminate the possibility that they serve their old master. They can undo their salvation by returning to their former way of living. Acknowledging Jesus as their master makes possible a life of freedom from corruption and the defilements of the world, but also requires such a life in order to continue acknowledging Jesus as master. This basis for ethics is similar to that found in the letters of Paul. For 2 Peter virtue is a matter of continuing in the full knowledge of Jesus which is the appropriation of the salvation Jesus accomplished.

Similar ethical reasoning is found in 1:3–11, a series of interlocking enthymemes that argues the necessity of a virtuous life. In vv. 5–8 the author urges the addressees to progress in virtue because having and increasing in these things makes them fruitful for full knowledge of Jesus. Those who have been set free from slavery by recognizing Jesus need to persist in that freedom from slavery by an ongoing full knowledge of Jesus. This is how they make secure their call and election (v. 10), which is the starting point of their salvation (cf. v. 3). Those who do this will receive entrance into the eternal kingdom of Jesus (v. 11). Similarly, in 3:11–13 the author argues that the addressees must be holy and pious because this world is about to be replaced by a new one in which justice dwells.

The main examples of ethical rhetography, are to be found in 2:1–3, 10b–22, which present vivid descriptions of the false teachers' ethical failings and those of their followers. Since the false teachers are destined to appear and be destroyed at the end of the world, the descriptions of them and their vices form part of 2 Peter's eschatography.

ESCHATOLOGY AND ESCHATOGRAPHY

Jesus' salvation of his followers from slavery to corruption is a present reality, but not a final one. At present it is always possible to return to slavery; hence the need for ethics. Salvation only becomes final when this world is destroyed at the end of time. Those enslaved to corruption will be destroyed along with it. Those who have been freed from slavery to corruption will then be definitively free.

The end of the world not only completes salvation in this negative sense, it also completes the life of freedom begun through full knowledge of Jesus. This positive dimension is indicated in 1:3 where the author says that Jesus' divine power has given them everything pertaining to life and piety. By setting them free from impiety, Jesus has given them what they need for piety. And this piety will bring them to life.

In 1:4 the author says that Jesus has given promises in order that through these promises the readers might be θείας κοινωνοὶ φύσεως (sharers of divine nature). Not only do they look forward to life as a result of piety, they are also destined to share divine nature.[43] The most salient characteristic of divine nature is incorruptibility; the immediately following reference to having escaped the corruption in the world makes it very likely that the author equates sharing divine nature with becoming incorruptible.[44] If so, the hope of sharing divine nature is equivalent to that of putting on incorruptibility and immortality in 1 Cor 15:50–55. This will occur when they enter the eternal kingdom of Jesus (2 Pet 1:11).

The promises of definitive freedom from corruption and entry into Jesus' eternal kingdom are part of the prophetic word that points forward to the end of the world (1:19), which is found in Scripture (1:20). What is promised includes the return of Jesus (3:4), destruction of the present heavens and earth (3:10, 12), and the establishment of new heavens and earth (3:13). The author of 2 Peter emphasizes that the future completion of salvation has been promised by Jesus in order to convince those he addresses to maintain this expectation.

---

43. Like the idea that followers of Jesus escape the corruption in the world, the idea that they become sharers of divine nature expresses the meaning of Christianity in terms taken from dualistic Greek philosophical and religious thought. However, these terms are given new meaning (Bigg, *St. Peter and St. Jude*, 255–56; Kelly, *Peter and Jude*, 302–4; Käsemann does not think the terms have been given new meaning ["Apologia," 184]). Just as for 2 Peter the corruption in the world derives from desire, not from the nature of the world; so the followers of Jesus do not share divine nature by essence, but receive a share in divine nature as a gift.

44. Fornberg, *Early Church*, 86–88; Bauckham, *Jude, 2 Peter*, 180–81; Neyrey, *2 Peter, Jude*, 157–58.

Much of 2 Peter's discourse about the end of the world is eschatology in the strict sense, i.e., reasoning about the last times. Thus 1:16–18 and 1:19–2:10a present arguments that Jesus will come again; the second of these passages ends by arguing that the past actions of God show that God will save the pious and punish the wicked in the future (2:4–10a). 2:1–3, 10b–22, and 3:1–4 implicitly argue against the false teachers/scoffers by presenting their appearance as part of what is to be expected at the end of the world. 3:5–7 refutes the argument that the end of the world is unprecedented; 3:8–10a rejects the perception that the end of the world has been delayed.

The author develops these arguments by using vivid pictures of the events that lead to the end of the world and of the end itself, i.e., eschatography. These pictures imply an eschatographical story line extending from the beginning of time to the end of the world. This story line includes the theography, Christography, and soteriography of 2 Peter; all of these ultimately serve 2 Peter's eschatography.

- There were heavens long ago and an earth constituted by the word of God (3:5).
- At some point humans were enslaved to corruption and the defilements of the world by error, futility, and the desires of the flesh (2:19–20).
- God did not spare the angels who sinned, but sent them to Tartarus (2:4).
- God did not spare the ancient world, but preserved Noah (2:5). Through the word of God the world was destroyed in a deluge; this serves as a precedent for another destruction of the world at the end of time (3:6).
- God condemned Sodom and Gomorrah, reducing them to ashes and establishing them as a sign of what will happen to the ungodly (2:6), but saved Lot (2:7–8).
- The three incidents mentioned in 2:4–8 show that God knows how to save the pious and punish the wicked (2:9), and will do so in the future
- borne by the Holy Spirit, human beings spoke from God, serving as prophets (1:21). This prophetic speech included accounts of the incidents mentioned in 2:4–8 and was put in writing (1:20). In this way the prophetic word predicts the end of the world, serving as a light in darkness (1:19).
- God the father gave Jesus honor and glory when a voice was conveyed to him by the majestic glory, "My son, my beloved, is this one,

in whom I am well pleased" (1:17). This shows that Jesus will come again at the end of the world (1:16). This will be the dawn that follows darkness (1:19).

- Jesus purchased humans from slavery to corruption and the defilements of the world, acquiring them as his own slaves (2:1); the purchase price may have been his death.
- Humans must know about this transfer of ownership in order to take advantage of it. When they know that they have a new master, they can live in freedom from their old master. After having ceased to serve their old master, however, it remains possible to resume doing so (2:20–21).
- The prophetic word predicts the appearance of false teachers (2:1–3, 10b–22) or scoffers (3:1–4) before the end of the world.
- The present heavens and earth have been treasured up by the word of God for fire on the day of judgment (3:7); this is also the day of God (3:12).
- One cannot say that God is slow to keep the promise that Jesus will return and this world will come to an end because time is different for God than for humans (3:8); God is patient, giving all an opportunity to repent (3:9); and the time of the end is unknown (3:10).
- On the day of the Lord, the heavens will pass away and the elements will be dissolved (3:10, 12). The false teachers/scoffers and their followers will be destroyed with them (2:1, 3, 12; 3:7).
- After this there will be new heavens and a new earth in which justice dwells (3:13). Holy and pious people will be sharers in divine nature (1:4) and enter the eternal kingdom of Jesus (1:11).

At some points the sequence of events is uncertain. The author does not say when and how humans were enslaved to corruption, but might be thinking of the story told in Gen 3, to which Paul refers in Rom 5:12–21 and elsewhere. The author also does not say when prophets were active. And he does not say when the transfiguration of Jesus occurred or when Jesus purchased humans from slavery to corruption, but may presume the ordering of these events in the synoptic gospels.

TEXT

The text of 2 Peter on which my interpretation is based is that of *The Greek New Testament*, fourth revised edition (UBS). This edition identifies eight passages in which the text is uncertain. In five cases this uncertainty is indicated by enclosing material in the text within brackets; this is the case in 2:6 (twice), 20; 3:11, 18. In two of the remaining three cases, i.e., in 2:4 and 11, this uncertainty is indicated by footnotes rating the reading of the text "C," meaning that the editorial committee had difficulty deciding which variant to place in the text. In the remaining text, i.e., in 3:10, a footnote rates the reading of the text "D," meaning that the committee had great difficulty in arriving at a decision.

The *Novum Testamentum Graecum, Editio Critica Maior IV Catholic Letters* (ECM) text of 2 Peter differs from that of UBS in eight passages. Four of these differences are at points where UBS found the text uncertain, namely in 2:6, 11; 3:10, and 18. In adopting a different reading from that of UBS in 2:6 and 3:18, ECM indicates that the text is uncertain by marking it with bold dots. In adopting a different reading from that of UBS in 2:11 and 3:10, ECM does not indicate that the text is uncertain. ECM also differs from UBS in 2:15; 3:6, and 16 (twice). ECM indicates that all of these but its different reading in 3:6 are uncertain.

ECM also indicates that the text is uncertain in sixteen other passages although its text is the same as that of UBS in these passages. Two of these passages are also ones where UBS indicated textual uncertainty, namely 2:6 and 20. The remaining passages are not marked as uncertain by UBS; the passages are in 1:2, 4 (twice), 9, 12, 21; 2:13, 18 (twice), 19, 22; 3:3 (twice), and 18. Interestingly ECM does not see uncertainty, as UBS does, in 2:4 and 3:11.

The Greek New Testament SBL Edition (SBL) text of 2 Peter differs from that of UBS in six passages. Two of these differences are at points where UBS found the text uncertain, namely in 2:11 and 20. SBL also differs from UBS in 1:9; 2:15, 19; and 3:16.

Most of these textual uncertainties (and some others) are discussed in the notes on each section of 2 Peter. In every case the result is affirmation of the UBS text, with varying degrees of assurance.

AUTHOR

The salutation of 2 Peter names the sender of the letter as Simeon Peter, slave and apostle of Jesus Christ (1:1). This unambiguously identifies its author as Peter, chief of the twelve apostles of Jesus. The rest of the letter is consistent with this in several ways. According to 1:14 Jesus has revealed that the author will soon die; in John 21:18-19 Jesus predicts the death of Peter. According to 1:16-18 the author witnessed the transfiguration of Jesus; Mark 9:2-8 and parallels say that Peter was one of those who witnessed Jesus' transfiguration. In 3:1 the author says that he is writing a second letter; this might be a reference to 1 Peter.

Nevertheless, most commentators do not think Peter actually wrote the letter.[45] Of the twentieth- and twenty-first-century commentaries I have consulted only eight—those of Bigg, Wohlenberg, Mounce, M. Green, Moo, G. Green, Harvey and Towner, and Giese—argue that Peter wrote 2 Peter.[46] Those who do not think Peter wrote 2 Peter take this position for reasons such as the following (listed in order of importance):

- The letter was probably written too late to have been composed by Peter. *Acts of Peter* 36-41 (c. 200) says that Peter was crucified in Rome during the reign of Nero, i.e., during the mid '60s. If so, Peter died too early to have written the letter, as we will see when we discuss the date of the letter below.

- As we have seen, the letter is also a testament, and testaments are usually pseudonymous.

- The language and style of the letter seem unlikely to have been used by Peter; the literary skill and ambition that are manifested in the style of 2 Peter (see discussion above) seem unlikely to derive from a Galilean fisherman whose native language was probably not Greek. An additional problem is that the language and style of 2 Peter differ from the language and style of 1 Peter.

- It seems unlikely that Peter would have made use of Jude in the way 2 Peter does (see the discussion of this above).[47]

---

45. Bauckham, "2 Peter," 3719-24.

46. Bigg, *St. Peter and St. Jude*, 242; Wohlenberg, *Der erste und zweite Petrusbrief*, xxvi; Mounce, *A Living Hope*, 99; Green, *Second Epistle General of Peter*, 13-39; Moo, *2 Peter and Jude*, 23-24; Green, *Jude & 2 Peter*, 150; Harvey and Towner, *2 Peter and Jude*, 9-16; Giese, *2 Peter and Jude*, 6-11. Of course, the authorship of 2 Peter is discussed not only in commentaries but also in New Testament introductions and other writings, and some of these argue that Peter was the author. One example of this is Robinson, *Redating the New Testament*, 173-99. Robinson argues that Jude composed 2 Peter acting as the agent of Peter. Naturally, such arguments also imply an early date for 2 Peter; Robinson suggests 61-62 CE.

47. Bauckham gives a somewhat different list of reasons for doubting the authenticity of 2 Peter ("2 Peter," 3722-24).

For these reasons it seems most likely that an anonymous author composed 2 Peter as a testamentary letter from Peter. Bauckham discusses various explanations that have been offered for the composition of 2 Peter in the name of Peter. He suggests that it is one means by which the church of Rome, represented by Peter, exercised pastoral responsibility for other churches.[48] Neyrey argues that the author of 2 Peter is highly literate, rhetorically sophisticated, and writes from a city in Asia Minor.[49] Such a description is consistent with the implications of the style of 2 Peter; see discussion above.

ADDRESSEES

The addressees of 2 Peter are indicated very generally in 1:1 as those who have received faith equal in honor to ours (i.e., the author of the letter and others). This is a more general specification of addressees than that found in any other New Testament letter except Jude 1. This might mean that the letter is addressed to Christians generally, not a specific group of Christians. For this reason Jude and 2 Peter are often called catholic or general letters. However, both Jude and 2 Peter might have been intended for specific groups even though these groups are not identified in the salutation. This would be especially true for 2 Peter if 3:1 indicates that it has the same addressees as 1 Peter.

The author of 2 Peter says in 3:1 that he is writing a second letter to the addressees. If the first letter was 1 Peter, this implies that 2 Peter is addressed to the same people whom 1 Peter addresses, i.e., residents of Pontus, Galatia, Cappadocia, Asia, and Bithynia (1 Pet 1:1).[50]

In 3:15 the author of 2 Peter says that Paul also wrote to the recipients of 2 Peter. As far as we know, Paul never wrote to people in Pontus, Cappadocia, or Bithynia. Paul did write to the Galatians, however, and he wrote letters to the Ephesians, Colossians, and Laodiceans (see Col 4:16); all of these cities are located in the Roman province of Asia.

If 2 Pet 3:14–15a summarizes what Paul wrote to the recipients of 2 Peter, v. 14 ("be eager to be discovered by him spotless and unblemished in peace") might refer to Eph 4:3 ("being eager to keep the unity of the Spirit in the bond of peace"). Such a reference to Eph 4:3 is consistent with

---

48. Ibid., 3736–40.

49. Neyrey, *2 Peter, Jude*, 128–41.

50. So Chaine, *Les Épitres Catholiques*, 32–33; Grundmann, *Brief des Judas und zweite Brief des Petrus*, 58; Knoch, *Erste und Zweite Petrusbrief*, 199. Mayor (*Second Epistle of St. Peter*, cxxxv) rejects this idea.

understanding 2 Pet 3:1 as implying that 2 Peter is addressed to the addressees of 1 Peter.

If 2 Peter is not addressed to the addressees of 1 Peter, we have no information about the specific identity of those to whom 2 Peter is addressed. However, wherever they lived, it seems likely that they were Gentile Christians whose culture was more strongly influenced by Hellenism than by Judaism, insofar as the two can be distinguished.[51]

PLACE AND TIME OF COMPOSITION

Nothing is known about where 2 Peter was written. If it is not only addressed to the same people as 1 Peter, but also written from the same place, it might have been written in Rome. This might also be indicated by attribution of the letter to Peter, since he was connected with Rome.

The date of 2 Peter is most clearly indicated by the reference to Paul in 3:15-16 (see discussion of this passage below). In 3:15 the author of 2 Peter first mentions what Paul wrote to the recipients of 2 Peter, then states that Paul says the same thing in all his letters. This implies that Paul's letters, originally sent to different places, have been collected.

Exactly when such a collection was made is unknown. Some argue that Paul collected his own letters.[52] Most see the collection as likely to have been made c. 100 because the first references to it date from about that time.[53] The earliest reference to more than one letter of Paul is probably found in the letters of Ignatius of Antioch, written c. 108. In his letter *To the Ephesians*, Ignatius says that Paul makes mention of the Ephesians in every letter (12.2). In his letter *To the Romans*, Ignatius says that he does not command the Romans as Peter and Paul did (4.3), possibly referring to Paul's letter to the Romans. Ignatius seems to know at least Paul's letters to the Ephesians and Romans. He probably knows them by way of a collection of Paul's letters that includes them.

In 3:16 the author of 2 Peter says that the ignorant and unstable twist difficult elements of Paul's letters as they do the other Scriptures. This suggests that the author of 2 Peter regards the letters of Paul as having status comparable to that of the Jewish Scriptures, which were accepted as authoritative by Christians. This presumably happened some time after Paul's

---

51. On this see Fornberg, *Early Church*.

52. Trobisch, *Paul's Letter Collection*; Murphy-O'Connor, *Paul the Letter-Writer*, 114-30.

53. E.g., Kümmel, *Introduction to the NT*, 480-81.

letters were collected. By c. 140 Marcion used a collection of ten letters of Paul that he regarded as authoritative.

Second Peter was probably written sometime between 100 and 140, perhaps about 125.[54] Others argue for different dates; Bauckham gives the most comprehensive survey.[55] Dates proposed by the commentaries I have consulted include the following:

> c. 60 (Bigg)
>
> 63 (Wohlenberg)
>
> early '60s (Giese)
>
> mid '60s (Mounce, M. Green)
>
> 64–110 (Davids)
>
> c. 65 (Moo)
>
> 65–68 (Harvey and Towner)
>
> c. 70 or 80 (Chaine)
>
> 80–90 (Bauckham)
>
> c. 90 (Reicke, Spicq)
>
> late first or early second century (Perkins, Harrington)
>
> c. 100 (Schelkle)
>
> 100–110 (Kelly, Knoch)
>
> 100–125 (James, Paulsen, Vögtle)
>
> 130 (Sidebottom)
>
> 110–50 (Grundmann)[56]

The earliest proposed dates, those of Bigg, Wohlenberg, Giese, Mounce, M. Green, Moo, and Harvey and Towner, are based on the view that Peter is the actual author of 2 Peter; I and most others argue that he is not (see above).

---

54. So also Mayor, *Second Epistle of St. Peter*, cxxcii; and Senior, *1 and 2 Peter*, 99.

55. Bauckham, "2 Peter," 3740–42.

56. Bigg, *St. Peter and St. Jude*, 242–47; Wohlenberg, *Der erste und zweite Petrusbrief*, xxxvii; Giese, *2 Peter and Jude*, 11; Mounce, *A Living Hope*, 99; Green, *Second Epistle General of Peter*, 41; Davids, *2 Peter and Jude*, 130–31; Moo, *2 Peter and Jude*, 24–25; Harvey and Towner, *2 Peter & Jude*, 15; Chaine, *Les Épitres Catholiques*, 34; Bauckham, *Jude, 2 Peter*, 157–58; Reicke, *James, Peter and Jude*, 144–45; Spicq, *Épitres de Saint Pierre*, 195; Perkins, *First and Second Peter*, 160; Harrington, "Jude and 2 Peter," 237; Schelkle, *Die Petrusbriefe*, 178–79; Kelly, *Peter and Jude*, 237; Knoch, *Erste und Zweite Petrusbrief*, 213; James, *Second Epistle General of Peter*, xxx; Paulsen, *Zweite Petrusbrief*, 94; Vögtle, *Der Judasbrief/Der 2. Petrusbrief*, 128–29; Sidebottom, *James, Jude, and 2 Peter*, 99; Grundmann, *Brief des Judas und zweite Brief des Petrus*, 65.

Chaine bases his date on the date at which the views rejected by 2 Peter first appeared. Reicke's date is based partly on the idea that 2 Pet 2:10 is a positive reference to magistrates and society; I interpret the passage differently (see discussion of this passage below). Bauckham, Spicq, Kelly, and Knoch's dates are based on the dates of other early Christian writings whose thought parallels that of 2 Peter. Bauckham and Harrington's dates are based on understanding 2 Pet 3:4 to mean that the generation of the apostles has died; I interpret this passage differently (see discussion of this passage below). Perkins, Schelkle, and Bauckham mention 2 Pet 3:15-16; Perkins and Schelkle see its implications for the date of 2 Peter somewhat the same way I do, although they arrive at a somewhat earlier date than I have suggested. Chaine denies these implications.[57]

Attestation

The earliest writer to mention the second letter of Peter by name is Origen (185–254). He does so in his *Commentarii in evangelium Joannis* on John 5:3, quoted in Eusebius, *Ecclesiastical History* 6.25.8.[58]

> And Peter, on whom the Church of Christ is built, against which "the gates of Hades will not prevail," has left one acknowledged epistle, and let it be granted that there is also a second, for it is doubtful.

Origen also cites or alludes to 2 Peter a number of other times.[59] As can be seen in the passage quoted, Origen refers to the existence of doubts that Peter wrote 2 Peter. Eusebius, writing c. 324, mentions the consequent uncertainty about the canonical status of 2 Peter in *Ecclesiastical History* 3.3.1; 3.25.3. However, Athanasius, writing in 367, included 2 Peter in the New Testament.

The *Apocalypse of Peter* includes the earliest likely allusions to 2 Peter.[60] For example, § 22 of the Greek fragment of the *Apocalypse of Peter* refers to βλασφημοῦντες τὴν ὁδὸν τῆς δικαιοσύνης (slandering the way of justice; cf. also § 28). This entire phrase is not found in 2 Peter, but τὴν ὁδὸν τῆς δικαιοσύνης (the way of justice) is found in 2 Pet 2:21, and elsewhere 2 Peter

---

57. Chaine, *Les Épitres Catholiques*, 28–29.

58. Bigg, *St. Peter and St. Jude*, 201; Spicq, *Épitres de Saint Pierre*, 190; Bauckham *Jude, 2 Peter*, 163. The translation is mine.

59. Bigg, *St. Peter and St. Jude*, 201; Spicq, *Épitres de Saint Pierre*, 190.

60. Bigg, *St. Peter and St. Jude*, 207; Spicq, *Épitres de Saint Pierre*, 189; Bauckham *Jude, 2 Peter*, 162.

makes rather frequent use of βλασφημέω (to slander) and its cognate adjective (2:2, 10, 11, 12); 2 Pet 2:2 says that ἡ ὁδὸς τῆς ἀληθείας βλασφημηθήσεται (the way of truth will be slandered). *Epistle of Barnabas* 15.4 contains an even more likely allusion to 2 Peter. This passage quotes an unidentified "he" as saying, "Behold, the day of the Lord shall be as a thousand years." This is almost certainly a reference to 2 Pet 3:8 because this is 2 Peter's own expansion of the quotation from Ps 90:4 (LXX 89:4) which says only that in God's eyes a thousand years are as one day. Sayings very similar to the one quoted from *Epistle of Barnabas* are also found in Justin, *Dialogue with Trypho* 81; Irenaeus, *Against Heresies* 5.23.2. A possible allusion to 2 Pet 2:1 is found in Justin, *Dialogue with Trypho* 82.1.[61] Such allusions are compatible with a date c. 125 for 2 Peter. Bigg discusses many other possible allusions, both earlier and later.[62]

P[72] (dating from c. 300) provides the earliest copy of 2 Peter, along with copies of Jude and 1 Peter. These texts were part of a codex that included eight other writings, both biblical, i.e., Pss 33 and 34, and non-biblical Christian writings, e.g., Melito's *Homily on Passover*.

OUTLINE OF 2 PETER

I. Letter opening—2 Pet 1:1-15
    A. Salutation—1:1-2
    B. Theme—1:3-11
    C. Occasion of letter—1:12-15

II. Letter body—2 Pet 1:16—3:13
    A. Two arguments that Jesus will come again—1:16—2:10a
        1. First argument—1:16-18
        2. Second argument—1:19—2:10a
    B. Critique of opponents—2:10b-22
    C. Occasion and argument of letter restated—3:1-13

III. Letter closing—2 Pet 3:14-18

---

61. Bauckham *Jude, 2 Peter*, 237.
62. Bigg, *St. Peter and St. Jude*, 202-10; see also Bauckham *Jude, 2 Peter*, 162-63.

Section 1: 2 Peter 1:1–15

Letter Opening

The opening section of 2 Peter is divided into three parts: vv. 1–2 form the salutation of the letter; vv. 3–11 introduce the theme of the letter; and vv. 12–15 state the occasion of the letter.

Second Peter 1:1–15 blends five different kinds of early Christian discourse—prophetic, apocalyptic, precreation, priestly, and wisdom discourse. Prophetic discourse predominates, because it is the discourse of the basic situation(s) implied in the passage. Prophetic discourse presumes the context of the universe understood as a kingdom of which God is king. Prophets are individuals to whom God's will has been communicated who call people to act righteously through prophetic action and speech.[1] Peter, who identifies himself as a slave and apostle, functions as a prophet in calling those to whom he writes to righteous living because he has been called by God to do so. In vv. 1–2 the author identifies himself and those he addresses, and wishes that they might have grace and peace. In vv. 3–11 the author argues that since Jesus' divine power has bestowed all things for life and piety, etc. (vv. 3–4), the addressees should supply virtue abundantly by their faith, knowledge by their virtue, etc. (vv. 5–11). The passage implies that the addressees are in some danger of not adhering to this system of belief and behavior; however, this is not made explicit. In vv. 12–15 the author says that because of the benefits of following the exhortation in 1:3–11, he reminds the addressees of these things and arranges for them to be remembered after his death by putting them in writing.

---

1. For discussion of the basic picture underlying prophetic discourse see chapter 6 of Robbins, *Invention of Christian Discourse*.

UNIT 1: 2 PETER 1:1–2 LETTER SALUTATION

1 Συμεὼν[2] Πέτρος δοῦλος καὶ ἀπόστολος Ἰησοῦ Χριστοῦ
τοῖς ἰσότιμον[3] ἡμῖν[4] λαχοῦσιν[5] πίστιν ἐν δικαιοσύνῃ[6] τοῦ θεοῦ ἡμῶν καὶ σωτῆρος Ἰησοῦ Χριστοῦ,
2 χάρις ὑμῖν καὶ εἰρήνη πληθυνθείη[7] ἐν ἐπιγνώσει τοῦ θεοῦ καὶ Ἰησοῦ τοῦ κυρίου[8] ἡμῶν.

1 Simeon Peter, slave and apostle of Jesus Christ,
to those who have received faith equal in honor to ours by the justice of our God and savior Jesus Christ.
2 May favor and peace be multiplied for you by full knowledge of God and Jesus our Lord.

Rhetography

As a whole the letter salutation evokes a picture of the author writing a letter, probably by making use of a professional scribe who is writing in ink on papyrus. It also evokes a mental picture of the sender and addressees at some distance from one another, but neither his location nor theirs is indicated. They are at least not immediately present to one another; they may be in the same city or town, thousands of miles apart, or anything in between.

The salutation names Simeon Peter as the sender of the letter. "Simeon Peter" may simply evoke the mental image of the man whose name this is. On the other hand, πέτρος (Peter) is an ordinary Greek word meaning "stone" and may not have been used as a name before being applied to

---

2. It is somewhat uncertain whether the original text read Συμεών or Σίμων. The earliest copy of 2 Peter, i.e., P[72], has the latter as does B, while other good texts, e.g., ℵ and A, have the former. The latter is the more common form of Peter's name; apart from this passage Συμεών is found only in Acts 15:14. This makes it seem more likely that Συμεών has been changed to read Σίμων than that the opposite change has occurred. On this see Metzger, *Textual Commentary*, 629.

3. ἰσότιμον (only here in NT) fem. sg. acc. ἰσότιμος = equal in honor, modifies πίστιν.

4. ἡμῖν = τῃ ἡμῶν—Bigg, *St. Peter and St. Jude*, 249.

5. λαχοῦσιν aorist ptc. λαγχάνω = to receive by lot or divine will.

6. ἐν δικαιοσύνῃ = by means of justice.

7. πληθυνθείη aorist pass. optative 3 sg. πληθύνω = to multiply.

8. It is uncertain whether the original text read τοῦ θεοῦ καὶ Ἰησοῦ τοῦ κυρίου or τοῦ θεοῦ καὶ Ἰησοῦ Χριστοῦ τοῦ κυρίου. The former is found in P[72] (which also omits καί) and B, the latter in ℵ and A. It is perhaps easier to understand the addition of Χριστοῦ than its omission.

Simeon.⁹ So "Peter" could evoke the picture of Simeon as a stone, and the further picture of his having received this nickname from Jesus. Especially if one thinks of the account of this naming found in Matt 16:18, the picture of the author as a stone might also be a picture of him as the foundation stone on which the church is built. "And I tell you, you are Peter (πέτρος), and on this rock (πέτρᾳ) I will build my church, and the gates of Hades will not prevail against it."

The salutation further identifies Simeon Peter as both slave and apostle of Jesus Christ. The term "slave" calls up the image of the sender as one of a large group of people in antiquity who were the property of other people. Slaves did many different kinds of work and even had different levels of social status; most were very low status, but some had high status. In saying that he is a slave, the sender does not clearly evoke a picture of how high or low his status may be.

By calling himself an apostle of Jesus Christ, the sender of 2 Peter evokes a picture of himself as having been commissioned by Jesus to act on his behalf in some unspecified way, perhaps including the writing of 2 Peter. In other Christian texts "apostle" particularly designates special envoys of Jesus Christ, including Peter.¹⁰ The term might cause those familiar with these texts, or the traditions embodied in them, to picture many more specific details. These could include stories of Peter's call by Jesus (Mark 1:16-18; Matt 4:18-19; Luke 5:1-11; John 1:41-42); his inclusion in, and leadership of, the twelve apostles who were commissioned to act on Jesus' behalf during his public ministry (Mark 3:13-19; Matt 10:2-4; Luke 6:13-16); Jesus' resurrection appearance to Peter (1 Cor 15:5; Luke 24:34; John 21); and Peter's inclusion in, and leadership of, the apostles after Jesus' resurrection (see Acts 1:15-26; 2:37; 5:1-6, 12-16, etc.). Mark 3:14-15 says that Jesus

> appointed twelve, whom he also named apostles, to be with him, and to be sent out to proclaim the message, and to have authority to cast out demons.

The following verses (3:16-19) give the names of the twelve beginning with "Simon (to whom he gave the name Peter)."

It is not clear what mental image the name "Jesus Christ" might evoke. Since χριστός (Christ) is an ordinary Greek word meaning "anointed," and

---

9. Tal Ilan (*Lexicon of Jewish Names*, 303) mentions one possible earlier use of the name.

10. Paul calls himself an apostle in the salutations of Romans, 1 & 2 Corinthians, Galatians, Ephesians, Colossians, 1 & 2 Timothy, and Titus, as does Peter in the salutation of 1 Peter.

is not otherwise used as a name, this could evoke the picture of Jesus as having had oil poured on him, and a further picture of Jesus as the anointed king who figures in Jewish eschatological expectation.[11] The most extensive portrayal of the Christ of Israel is found in *Psalms of Solomon* 17:21–39. Here are some of the more picturesque sections:

> Behold, O Lord, and raise up unto them their king, the son of David,
> At the time in which you see, O God, that he may reign over Israel, your servant,
> And gird him with strength, that he may shatter unrighteous rulers,
> And that he may purge Jerusalem from nations that trample (her) down to destruction.
> . . .
> And he (shall be) a righteous king, taught of God, over them,
> And there shall be no unrighteousness in his days in their midst,
> For all shall be holy and their king the Christ of the Lord.
> . . .
> He will rebuke rulers, and remove sinners by the might of his word;
> And (relying) upon his God, throughout his days he will not stumble;
> For God will make him mighty by means of (His) holy spirit,
> And wise by means of the spirit of understanding, with strength and righteousness.[12]

Calling Jesus "Christ," therefore, could summon a mental image of him as a righteous king.

The salutation of 2 Peter pictures Simeon Peter addressing a group that has received faith equal in honor to that of the writer and unspecified others. They have received this faith by the justice of "our God and savior Jesus Christ." λαχοῦσιν (received) has the connotation of receiving by lot or divine will; thus the addressees are pictured as having received faith as a gift. Jesus Christ is pictured as acting justly by giving the addressees faith. Since their faith is equal to that of Peter, saying that it derives from Jesus' "justice"

---

11. On first-century expectation of the messiah see, Cullmann, *Christology*, 113–17; Hahn, *Titles of Jesus in Christology*, 136–48; Fuller, *Foundations of NT Christology*, 23–31; Callan, *Origins of Christian Faith*, 7–14; and Fitzmyer, *The One Who Is To Come*.

12. The translation is adapted from that of Charles, *Apocrypha and Pseudepigrapha* 2:649–50. The translation of seventh line in this excerpt (= *Pss. Sol.* 17:32) is based on emendation of the text. All manuscripts agree that the line should read, "For all shall be holy, and their king the Lord Christ" (my translation). On this see Charlesworth, *Old Testament Pseudepigrapha* 2:667–68 note z.

may call up a mental image of Jesus treating people equally. Saying that their faith is equal in honor to that of Simeon Peter and others evokes a picture of people regarding the faith of both groups as equally valuable and estimable.

Describing Jesus as "God and savior" adds new details to the picture of Jesus Christ that has already been evoked by the earlier mention of his name. Referring to Jesus as "God" pictures him as a member of the group of divinities worshiped in the Gentile world, or as the one God worshiped by Israel. Referring to Jesus as savior describes him with a term often used for gods and notable men in both Jewish and Greco-Roman culture, and especially for rulers in the latter.[13] The Greek translation of the Jewish bible frequently calls God savior. For example, Ps 24:5 (LXX 23:5) says, "He will receive a blessing from the Lord and mercy from God his savior." Roman emperors were included among rulers who were called savior. For example, an inscription from Caria in Asia Minor speaks of a statue of the emperor Claudius as a statue of "the savior and benefactor of all people."[14] Calling Jesus savior evokes a picture of him as rescuing people from various problems that beset them. Used in conjunction with Christ, as it is here, calling Jesus savior is probably synonymous with calling him Christ.

Finally, the salutation pictures the writer pronouncing a priestly prayer of blessing on those to whom he is writing. He prays that favor and peace will be multiplied for them by full knowledge of "God and Jesus our Lord." Such a prayer implies a picture of the author as interceding with God on behalf of the addressees. The prayer envisions the future of the addressees as one in which their favor and peace increase. "Favor" does not evoke any very specific picture, simply that of general blessings; "peace" is more specific, evoking the picture of harmony, both internal harmony and harmony in relations with others. Full knowledge of God and Jesus our Lord will produce this increasing favor and peace, and the author's prayer pictures the addressees as attaining this knowledge.

Mentioning God alongside Jesus and saying that Jesus is "our Lord" adds still more details to the pictures of Jesus and God evoked by the previous references to them. Previously the salutation pictured Jesus as God; now it pictures Jesus alongside God. Jesus is further described as "our Lord." Both sender and addressees recognize Jesus as their Lord, i.e., a superior who exercises rightful authority over them. This picture is rather indefinite

---

13. On this see Wendland, "Σωτηρ;" Cullmann, *Christology*, 238–45. Jesus is also described as savior in other early Christian literature, especially the Pastoral epistles; see Luke 2:11; John 4:42; Acts 5:31; 13:23; Eph 5:23; Phil 3:20; 2 Tim 1:10; Titus 1:4; 2:13; 3:6; and 1 John 4:14. Second Peter, using the title "savior" for Jesus five times, does so more frequently than any other New Testament writing.

14. Smallwood, *Documents*, 135.

because "Lord" was used as a title for a rather wide range of people, basically almost anyone who was the superior of someone else.[15] Parables of Jesus often refer to people who are called "Lord." For example, Luke 13:6–9 contains a parable about a man who had a fig tree that did not produce fruit. When the man told the gardener to cut the fig tree down, the gardener suggested giving the tree one more year to produce fruit; in making this suggestion, the gardener addressed the owner as "Lord" (v. 8). Roman emperors were regularly called "Lord." For example, an inscription from Boeotia in Greece speaks of Nero as "Lord of the whole world" and as "the Lord Augustus."[16] "Lord" was used both by Jews and Gentiles to refer to God. Calling Jesus "Lord" recognizes his authority, but does not indicate whether the authority is that of a teacher, a king, or a God. The other titles given to Jesus, however, show that his authority is that of a king and God.

Textural Analysis

Social-cultural texture. 1:1–2 makes use of the formula "X to Y, greeting," by far the most common way to begin a Greek letter in the Roman period.[17] This formula was also used to begin Aramaic letters at this time.[18] This formula can be seen, for example, in the salutation to the letter of James (1:1):

> James, slave of God and of the Lord Jesus Christ,
> To the twelve tribes in the Dispersion:
> Greetings.

Use of this formula informs readers and hearers that what follows is a letter. The prophetic discourse of 2 Pet 1:1–15 is communicated via letter (as is all of the discourse the document comprises).

In Greek letters the name of the addressee often has a noun in apposition with it or is modified by an adjective; likewise the greeting is often expanded slightly.[19] This tendency is taken much further in 2 Peter, as it is in most New Testament letters, including the letter of James quoted above. In the version of the formula found in 2 Peter, there are two nouns in apposition to the name of the sender, with another noun in the genitive case dependent on them. The formula does not name the addressees, but instead

---

15. On this see Cullmann, *Christology*, 195–203; Hahn, *Titles of Jesus in Christology*, 68–73.
16. Smallwood, *Documents*, 64, lines 31 and 55.
17. Exler, *Form of the Ancient Greek Letter*, 62.
18. Fitzmyer, "Aramaic Epistolography," 189.
19. Exler, *Form of the Ancient Greek Letter*, 62–63.

describes them with a complex participial phrase. The greeting is a complex wish for the addressees. Such a salutation does more than simply name sender and recipients, and open the letter with a greeting. It begins to accomplish the purposes of the letter by describing the sender and recipients briefly and praying that one of the letter's main purposes will be fulfilled.

Inner texture. The letter salutation introduces a number of terms that are *repeated* later in the letter (see Appendix A). Also, some terms are repeated within the salutation as well as later in the letter. Ἰησοῦ Χριστοῦ (Jesus Christ) is mentioned twice in v. 1 and six more times later in the letter (1:8, 11, 14, 16; 2:20; 3:18); Ἰησοῦ (Jesus) is mentioned again in v. 2. θεός (God) is mentioned both in v. 1 and v. 2, and five more times later in the letter (1:17, 21; 2:4; 3:5, 12). These repetitions also exhibit *progressive* texture. Verse 1 first refers simply to "Jesus Christ" and then refers to "our God and savior Jesus Christ;" v. 2 refers to "God and Jesus our Lord." The progressive repetition of "Jesus" indicates the central importance of Jesus. Jesus is the source of the sender's identity, the addressees' faith, and the future blessings the sender prays the addressees will receive. The progressive repetition of "Jesus" and "God" also reveals the identity of Jesus, particularly in relationship to God. Jesus is "Christ," "God," "savior," and "Lord," both "God" and distinct from "God."

Another term repeated within the salutation as well as later in the letter is the first person plural pronoun. This is used twice in v. 1, again in v. 2, and 12 more times later in the letter (1:3 [twice], 4, 8, 11, 14, 16, 18; 2:20; 3:15 [twice], 18). This repetition also shows progression. In v. 1 ἡμῖν refers to a group distinct from the addressees; the addressees' faith is equal in honor to that of this group, which includes the sender of the letter and unnamed others.[20] However, ἡμῶν in vv. 1 and 2 seems to designate a group that includes sender and addressees, i.e., those who acknowledge Jesus as Christ, God, savior, and Lord. Use of the first person plural pronoun to refer to a group distinct from the addressees associates the author with unnamed others; he does not send the letter as an isolated individual. Use of the pronoun to refer to a group that includes sender and addressees shows that the two belong to the same group. In some respects the author and others are distinct from the addressees; in other respects they are not.

In v. 1 the author refers to the πίστιν (faith) the addressees have received, and in v. 2 the author expresses the wish that grace and peace may be multiplied for the addressees through ἐπίγνωσις (full knowledge) of God and Jesus our Lord. While these terms are not synonymous, it seems likely

---

20. This group may consist of the apostles (Bigg, *St. Peter and St. Jude*, 249–50; Kelly, *Epistles*, 296–97; Bauckham, *Jude, 2 Peter*, 167).

that faith has a cognitive element, and that the two overlap to some extent. If so, there is a progression from simply having faith to the wish that grace and peace be multiplied by full knowledge. Obviously the effects of full knowledge can be extended; possibly ἐπίγνωσις itself can increase. If ἐπίγνωσις can increase, it is not something one simply attains, but rather something that can and should develop after being attained.

The main *argumentative* force of vv. 1–2 lies in establishing the ethos of the letter's sender. Insofar as the addressees recognize Simeon Peter as an eminent leader of the Christian movement, this recognition gives weight to what he has to say. If they understand the meaning of "Peter" as more than simply a name, this understanding adds to the significance of the sender's identity.

Likewise, the sender's identification of himself as a slave and apostle of Jesus Christ makes explicit some of the significance of his identity. He is servant and emissary of Jesus; this relationship to Jesus is the source of his authority. The exalted character of Jesus makes his slave and apostle an important figure and gives his message great importance.

In saying that the addressees have received faith equal in honor to that of the sender and others, the sender attempts to win their good will and receptivity to the message that follows.

Intertexture. The first part of the sender's greeting in 1:2 (χάρις ὑμῖν καὶ εἰρήνη πληθυνθείη—may favor and peace be multiplied for you) is also found in 1 Pet 1:2.[21] If the addressees are aware of this, the awareness would underline the identity of the sender as Peter. This greeting is also found in *1 Clement*, but with two prepositional phrases inserted between εἰρήνη (peace) and πληθυνθείη (be multiplied). A variation on it is found in the letter of Polycarp with ἔλεος (mercy) in place of χάρις (favor), and a prepositional phrase inserted between εἰρήνη and πληθυνθείη. Another variation is found in Jude 1; ἔλεος replaces χάρις (as in the letter of Polycarp), and καὶ ἀγάπη (and love) is inserted between εἰρήνη and πληθυνθείη.

> *1 Clement* χάρις ὑμῖν καὶ εἰρήνη ἀπὸ παντοκράτορος θεοῦ διὰ Ἰησοῦ χριστοῦ πληθυνθείη
>
> *Polycarp* ἔλεος ὑμῖν καὶ εἰρήνη παρὰ θεοῦ παντοκράτορος καὶ Ἰησοῦ χριστοῦ τοῦ σωτῆρος ἡμῶν πληθυνθείη
>
> *Jude* ἔλεος ὑμῖν καὶ εἰρήνη καὶ ἀγάπη πληθυνθείη

The first four words of 2 Peter's greeting (χάρις ὑμῖν καὶ εἰρήνη) are part of the greeting in every letter of Paul except 1 & 2 Timothy and Titus. Awareness of this might suggest that the sender of 2 Peter is somehow comparable to

---

21. On this see Gilmour, *Significance of Parallels*, 92.

Paul. This might also apply to other letters that begin the same way, namely, 1 Peter and *1 Clement*.

Social-cultural texture. The sender describes himself as a slave and apostle of Jesus Christ. The sender presents himself as occupying two familiar *social roles* in antiquity, those of the slave and the emissary. The slave served his/her master; the emissary went where he was sent to act on behalf of the one who sent him. Description of oneself as a slave of Christ or of God seems to have been fairly common in early Christianity. Paul refers to himself as a slave of Christ in the salutations of Romans and Philippians, as does Jude in the salutation of that letter. Paul refers to himself as a slave of God in the salutation of Titus; James calls himself slave of God and Christ in the salutation of that letter. This usage may have been taken over from the Old Testament.[22] If identification of Simeon Peter as a slave evokes such associations, it may call up the mental image of Simeon Peter as a special agent of Jesus Christ. This is explicitly evoked by the designation "apostle."

The faith of the addressees is described as equal in *honor* to that of Peter and others. In a world where people compete for honor and try to avoid *shame*, the addressees are pictured as having faith that is no less honorable than that of Peter.[23] In referring to the faith the addressees have received from "our God and savior Jesus Christ" and to their need for full knowledge of "God and Jesus our Lord," the author presents the relationship between God/Jesus and the addressees as that between *patron* and *clients*.[24] The patron has given honorable faith to the addressees, the author of 2 Peter, and others. All who have received this faith are equal with respect to faith, but in other ways they are not equal. Writing a letter, and especially a rhetorically ambitious letter like 2 Peter, places the author among the elite of his society with regard to education. Writing in the name of Peter means that the author speaks on behalf of the most eminent leader of the Christian church. In both of these ways the author implies that he represents the *dominant* powers within his context.

Second Peter's discourse about Jesus as God probably reflects the influence of Greco-Roman culture, perhaps as mediated by Hellenistic Judaism.[25] Greco-Roman religion was polytheistic, recognizing the existence of many gods, and rather readily speaking of human beings, especially rulers,

---

22. On use of slavery as a metaphor see Combes, *Metaphor of Slavery*, 43–48.

23. On the value of honor see Neyrey, *2 Peter, Jude*, 3–7.

24. On the patron-client relationship see Neyrey, *2 Peter, Jude*, 7–10; Neyrey discusses the patron-client relationship in 2 Pet 1:1–2 on pages 145–46.

25. On this see Callan, "Christology of 2 Peter."

as gods.[26] An example of this in a Jewish context can be seen in Acts 12:22. After Herod Agrippa delivered an address, those who heard it cried out, "The voice of a god and not of a human!"[27] In the previously mentioned inscription from Boeotia, the emperor Nero is called god. The inscription speaks of Nero as Zeus the Liberator (Νέρων Ζεὺς Ἐλευθέριος) and says that henceforth the citizens of Acraephia in Boeotia will worship Nero at the existing altar dedicated to Zeus the Savior (Διὶ τῷ Σωτῆρι) and will inscribe on the altar, "To Zeus the Liberator, Nero, forever" (Διὶ Ἐλευθερίῳ Νέρωνι εἰς αἰῶνα).[28] As can partly be seen in this inscription, referring to Jesus as savior in this passage describes him with a term often used for gods and notable men in both Jewish and Greco-Roman culture.

Sacred texture. In v. 1 τοῦ θεοῦ ἡμῶν καὶ σωτῆρος Ἰησοῦ Χριστοῦ probably designates Jesus as both God and savior.[29] This same construction (i.e., article-noun-possessive pronoun-καὶ-noun-noun-noun) is found elsewhere in 2 Peter in 1:11 and 3:18, and probably in 2:20. In all of these cases it designates Jesus as Lord and savior. Against this it might be argued that a grammatically parallel phrase in 2 Thess 1:12 is to be interpreted as referring to God and Jesus as distinct from one another.[30] However, in this verse the construction pairs the nouns "God" and "Lord," in that order. These are not as easily understood as applying to one person as either "God" and "savior" or "Lord" and "savior." Note however, the use of the titles "Lord" and "God" (reversing the order of 2 Thess 1:12) for a single person in John 20:28; Suetonius, *Domit.* 13.2. In the former, the apostle Thomas says to the risen Jesus, "My Lord and my God!"

Referring to Jesus as God pictures Jesus as a member of the group of divinities worshiped in the Gentile world, or as the one God worshiped by Israel. Both of these are problematic in different ways. On one hand the early Christians did not recognize the reality of the gods worshiped by Gentiles; on the other hand they did not seem to think that Jesus simply was the God of Israel. Because of this, use of "God" to apply to Jesus is rare in the New

---

26. Harris, *Jesus as God*, 27–28.

27. Josephus tells a similar story in *Ant.* 19.345, 347.

28. Smallwood, *Documents* 64, lines 41 and 46–49.

29. Brown, *Jesus: God and Man*, 22; Brown, *New Testament Christology*, 184; Bigg, *St. Peter and St. Jude*, 250–52; Reicke, *James, Peter and Jude*, 150; Spicq, *Épitres de Saint Pierre*, 208; Kelly, *Peter and Jude*, 297–98; Fornberg, *Early Church*, 142; Bauckham, *Jude, 2 Peter*, 168–69; Knoch, *Erste und zweite Petrusbrief*, 235; Davids, *2 Peter and Jude*, 163; Green, *Jude & 2 Peter*, 175; Harris, *Jesus as God*, 229–38. Harris lists others who hold this view, as well as those who disagree with it, on p. 238. The former is by far the majority position.

30. Brown, *Jesus: God and Man*, 15–16; Brown, *New Testament Christology*, 180; Harris, *Jesus as God*, 265–66.

Testament, though it becomes more common in later Christian literature.[31] Whatever the precise understanding that underlies application of "God" to Jesus, it pictures him as belonging to the divine realm, a supernatural being who exercises some control over the world and human history. It may imply that Jesus is a God who became a human being for a time after which he returned to his original divine condition.

In v. 2 God and Jesus are distinguished from one another, pictured as existing alongside one another. This seems to contradict the identification of Jesus as God in the preceding verse. The contradiction may be intended to prevent too simple an understanding of Jesus as God. In one sense Jesus is God; in another sense Jesus is distinct from God. Something similar to this can be seen in John 1:1–2 where the Word is said both to be with God and to be God. Jesus is further described as "our Lord." "Lord" was used both by Jews and Gentiles to refer to God, so it accords with the identification of Jesus as God in v. 1, but does not require it. One who followed carefully the references to Jesus as both God and distinct from God would probably be puzzled by them. Is this a mistake? If not, how can both be true?

Rhetorical Force

The most striking feature of the salutation of 2 Peter is the way it blends precreation discourse with prophetic discourse by its matter-of-fact identification of Jesus as God. Since this is immediately followed by a phrase that distinguishes the two, we can see that for the author of 2 Peter calling Jesus God is a more complex matter than it later became for Christians. Nonetheless, this aspect of 2 Peter's discourse puts it among the earliest writings to develop a way of speaking about Jesus that later became a defining element of Christian discourse, i.e., the affirmation that Jesus is God. The exalted status the salutation of 2 Peter gives to Jesus, and its emphasis on the centrality of Jesus, prepare for the summary of the letter's main message that follows in 1:3–11.

In the context of the Roman empire, calling Jesus "God," "savior," and "lord" identified him as one of the many divinities people worshiped, which included the Roman emperor himself. Since Jesus was not a widely known divinity, however, he would seem to be a new god, or the god of

---

31. In other New Testament writings Jesus is unambiguously called God only in John 1:1; 20:28; and Heb 1:8, though there are several other passages that are probably to be interpreted as meaning this. Early instances of calling Jesus God outside the New Testament can be found in Ignatius of Antioch, *Smyrn.* 1.1; *Eph.* 1.1; 7.2; 15.3; 19.3. Cf. also Pliny's statement that early Christians chant in honor of Christ as if to God (*Ep.* 10.96.7).

some small and obscure people. The titles "god," "savior," and "lord" claim a place for Jesus alongside, or even pre-eminent to, better known and widely worshiped gods.

For Jews calling Jesus "Christ" was a precise claim regarding his status and role, but one that probably would have been difficult to accept since Jesus had not obviously conquered the powers of evil and established the kingdom of God. Saying that Jesus as Christ was also savior and lord would not have been at all surprising. But calling him "God" would have been an unexpected and problematic way to speak about the Christ.

By the time 2 Peter was written (c. 125), the presentation of Christian prophetic discourse by means of letters was not new. Earlier examples include the letters of Paul, 1 Peter, Jude, James, 2–3 John, *1 Clement*, the letters of Ignatius of Antioch, and the letter of Polycarp. We can be sure that at least the letters of Paul, 1 Peter, and Jude were known to the author of 2 Peter.

Also by the time 2 Peter was written, the composition of such letters in the name of someone other than the actual author was not new. Earlier examples include 1 and 2 Timothy and Titus, written in the name of Paul by someone other than Paul. It is impossible to know whether or not the author of 2 Peter was aware of this, however.

UNIT 2: 2 PETER 1:3–11 THEME OF LETTER

Peter Proposes Honoring the Divine Benefactor by Living Wisely

3 ῾Ως πάντα ἡμῖν τῆς θείας δυνάμεως αὐτοῦ τὰ πρὸς ζωὴν καὶ εὐσέβειαν δεδωρημένης[32] διὰ τῆς ἐπιγνώσεως τοῦ καλέσαντος ἡμᾶς ἰδίᾳ δόξῃ καὶ

---

32. Pf. ptc. δωρέομαι.

ἀρετῇ,³³ 4 δι' ὧν³⁴ τὰ τίμια καὶ μέγιστα ἡμῖν ἐπαγγέλματα³⁵ δεδώρηται,³⁶ ἵνα διὰ τούτων γένησθε θείας κοινωνοὶ φύσεως ἀποφυγόντες τῆς ἐν τῷ κόσμῳ ἐν ἐπιθυμίᾳ φθορᾶς,³⁷
5 καὶ αὐτὸ τοῦτο δὲ³⁸ σπουδὴν πᾶσαν παρεισενέγκαντες³⁹ ἐπιχορηγήσατε⁴⁰
ἐν τῇ πίστει ὑμῶν τὴν ἀρετήν,
ἐν δὲ τῇ ἀρετῇ τὴν γνῶσιν,
6 ἐν δὲ τῇ γνώσει τὴν ἐγκράτειαν,
ἐν δὲ τῇ ἐγκρατείᾳ τὴν ὑπομονήν,
ἐν δὲ τῇ ὑπομονῇ τὴν εὐσέβειαν,
7 ἐν δὲ τῇ εὐσεβείᾳ τὴν φιλαδελφίαν,

33. An instrumental dative; Jesus has called the author and addressees by his own glory and excellence. It is somewhat uncertain whether the original text read ἰδίᾳ δόξῃ καὶ ἀρετῇ or διὰ δόξης καὶ ἀρετῆς. The earliest copy of 2 Peter, i.e., P⁷², has the latter as does B, while other good texts, e.g., ℵ and A, have the former. It may be somewhat easier to understand how ι might have fallen out of the former text and the cases of the nouns corrected to make them objects of the preposition διά, than to understand the reverse of this (Metzger, *A Textual Commentary*, 629). The two formulations have almost the same meaning.

34. The antecedent is δόξῃ καὶ ἀρετῇ (1:3); Bigg, *St. Peter and St. Jude*, 255; Starr, *Sharers in Divine Nature*, 26.

35. The order of the words τίμια καὶ μέγιστα ἡμῖν ἐπαγγέλματα is uncertain because the words occur in five different sequences in different manuscripts. In addition to occurring as the fourth word in the phrase as above (in B), ἡμῖν is also found as the second (in ℵ) and the last word (in P⁷²); in some manuscripts the order of τίμια and μέγιστα is exchanged; and these two variations are combined with each other in different ways. It is difficult to decide which reading was probably original (Metzger, *A Textual Commentary*, 630). Fortunately the order of the words does not greatly affect the meaning.

36. The subject is Jesus; its object is ἐπαγγέλματα.

37. It is somewhat uncertain whether the original text read τῆς ἐν τῷ κόσμῳ ἐν ἐπιθυμίᾳ φθορᾶς, which is the reading found in A B and other texts, or one of a number of variants found in other manuscripts. P⁷² reads τὴν ἐν τῷ κόσμῳ ἐπιθυμίαν φθοράν, and ℵ reads τὴν ἐν τῷ κόσμῳ ἐπιθυμίαν φθορᾶς. Both may have arisen partly from the desire to replace the genitive with the accusative case, since the latter more commonly follows the verb ἀποφεύγω (Metzger, *A Textual Commentary*, 630). ἀποφεύγω is followed by the accusative case in 2 Pet 2:18, 20; occasionally it is followed by the genitive case as it is here, perhaps because ἀπό is followed by the genitive case.

38. καὶ αὐτὸ τοῦτο δέ = and for this very reason also, i.e., therefore. It is somewhat uncertain whether the original text of v. 5 read καὶ αὐτὸ τοῦτο δέ, which is found in P⁷² and B, or one of a number of variants, particularly καὶ αὐτὸ δὲ τοῦτο, which is found in ℵ. The former seems to be unique in Greek literature (Callan, "Syntax of 2 Peter 1:1–7") and so might have seemed to need correction; however, the motive for this correction is obscure.

39. Aorist ptc. nom. pl. of παρεισφέρω to bring in beside; modifies implied subject of ἐπιχορηγήσατε.

40. Aorist pl. impv. of ἐπιχορηγέω = to supply.

ἐν δὲ τῇ φιλαδελφίᾳ τὴν ἀγάπην.
8 ταῦτα⁴¹ γὰρ ὑμῖν ὑπάρχοντα⁴² καὶ πλεονάζοντα οὐκ ἀργοὺς οὐδὲ ἀκάρπους⁴³ καθίστησιν εἰς τὴν τοῦ κυρίου ἡμῶν Ἰησοῦ Χριστοῦ ἐπίγνωσιν·
9 ᾧ γὰρ μὴ πάρεστιν ταῦτα, τυφλός ἐστιν μυωπάζων, λήθην λαβὼν τοῦ καθαρισμοῦ τῶν πάλαι αὐτοῦ ἁμαρτιῶν.⁴⁴
10 διὸ μᾶλλον, ἀδελφοί, σπουδάσατε βεβαίαν ὑμῶν τὴν κλῆσιν καὶ ἐκλογὴν ποιεῖσθαι·⁴⁵ ταῦτα⁴⁶ γὰρ ποιοῦντες οὐ μὴ πταίσητέ ποτε.
11 οὕτως γὰρ πλουσίως ἐπιχορηγηθήσεται ὑμῖν εἴσοδος εἰς τὴν αἰώνιον βασιλείαν τοῦ κυρίου ἡμῶν καὶ σωτῆρος Ἰησοῦ Χριστοῦ.

3 Since his divine power has given us all things for life and piety through full knowledge of the one who has called us by his glory and virtue, 4 through which [glory and virtue] he has given us the precious and very great promises in order that through these you might become sharers of divine nature, having escaped the corruption in the world by desire,
5 therefore, having brought in all eagerness beside,
by your faith supply virtue,
and by virtue, knowledge,
6 and by knowledge, self-control,
and by self-control, endurance,
and by endurance, piety,
7 and by piety, brotherly love,
and by brotherly love, love.
8 For possessing and exceeding in these things renders you neither idle nor fruitless for full knowledge of our Lord Jesus Christ.

---

41. The antecedent is the qualities listed in vv. 5–7; ταῦτα is the subject of the sentence.

42. ὑμῖν ὑπάρχοντα = being yours. ὑμῖν is dative of possession; ὑπάρχοντα = ὄντα as in 2:19; 3:11.

43. The understood object of καθίστησιν is ὑμᾶς; οὐκ ἀργοὺς οὐδὲ ἀκάρπους modifies it.

44. It is uncertain whether the text originally read ἁμαρτιῶν or ἁμαρτημάτων. The former is found in P⁷² and B, the latter in ℵ and A. There is little difference in meaning between the two.

45. There is some uncertainty as to whether σπουδάσατε βεβαίαν ὑμῶν τὴν κλῆσιν καὶ ἐκλογὴν ποιεῖσθαι is the original reading. This is the reading found in P⁷², B, and other texts. However, ℵ, A, and other texts read σπουδάσατε ἵνα διὰ τῶν καλῶν ἔργων βεβαίαν . . . ποιεῖσθαι (A also adds ὑμῶν before ἔργων). Since this appears to be an attempt to replace the complementary infinitive with a ἵνα clause that mistakenly retains the infinitive, the shorter text is likely to be original; Metzger, *A Textual Commentary*, 631.

46. As in v. 8, the antecedent is the qualities listed in vv. 5–7.

9 For the one in whom these things are not present is blind, nearsighted, having experienced forgetfulness of the cleansing of his past sins.
10 Therefore, brothers, be more eager to make secure your call and election; for doing these things you will never stumble.
11 For in this way entrance into the eternal kingdom of our Lord and savior Jesus Christ will be richly supplied to you.

Rhetography[47]

By patterning 1:3–11 on a decree honoring a benefactor, the author evokes a picture of Peter proposing that the addressees, the group of people who have received the gifts and promises mentioned in vv. 3–4, resolve to honor their benefactor by acting as specified in vv. 5–11. When they make such a resolution, they act like the citizens of a city or perhaps the members of an organization such as a club. The intention of the decree is to honor the benefactor for the gifts and promises he has given, both by listing them and by eliciting an appropriate response to them.

The first part of the decree (vv. 3–7) is somewhat abstract and general, evoking only rather vague mental images. The citation of the gifts and promises received (vv. 3–4) evokes a picture of Jesus' divine power as somehow having given both author and addressees all things for life and piety by giving full knowledge of himself; all the things they have received include the promise of sharing divine nature.[48] The response to this benefaction (vv. 5–7) should be a life of abundant virtue.

By contrast, the latter part of the decree (vv. 8–11) presents a series of specific and vivid pictures. By living an abundantly virtuous life the addressees will avoid being idle and fruitless (v. 8). The adjective "idle" pictures those who develop abundant virtue as unlike those who do no work; the adjective "fruitless" pictures them as unlike plants that produce no fruit. In the context of "fruitless," "idle" may picture those who develop abundant virtue as unlike land that has not been cultivated.

Those whose lives are abundantly virtuous will also avoid being blind and forgetful of having been cleansed from sin (v. 9).[49] Anyone without vir-

---

47. For a different account of the rhetography of 1:3–11 along with vv. 12–15, see Sylva, "A Unified Field Picture of Second Peter 1:3–15" in *Reading Second Peter with New Eyes*, 91–118.

48. I have suggested elsewhere that the author of 2 Peter may understand the promise as having been made in John 15:1–17.

49. In the LXX of Job 7:21, Job asks God "why do you not enact τῆς ἀνομίας μου λήθην καὶ καθαρισμὸν τῆς ἁμαρτίας μου (forgetfulness of my lawlessness and cleansing of my sin)? Second Peter 1:9 may be a recontextualization of this verse in which the

tue has impaired vision, either blind or nearsighted. This is a mental image of someone who cannot see, a visualization of someone unable to visualize. Such a person fails to see something important, i.e., the necessity of growth in virtue. The person also has impaired memory, having forgotten the cleansing of past sins. Sin is pictured as something that can be removed by washing, like dirt on the skin. The addressees' sins have been cleaned away, but if they lack virtue, they have forgotten it. It is likely that the cleansing of their past sins is understood to have occurred in their baptismal washing.[50] If so, those who lack virtue are envisioned as having forgotten the significance of their baptism.

Those who live abundantly virtuous lives will make their call and election secure, and they will avoid stumbling (v. 10). The author's reference to call and election may visualize election as a special selection among those who have been called. Perhaps this election is a second stage of selection, like the picture in Matt 22:1–14, where "Many are called, but few are chosen." Cf. also Rev 17:14.

When v. 10 says that by growing in virtue the addressees will make their call and election secure, it may picture their call and election as something that might fall down, like a building. Growth in virtue will make their call and election stand without falling. Perhaps more likely the author envisions their call and election as something they might lose or abandon. Growth in virtue, in contrast, is a response to their call and election that grasps it securely.

In speaking of the possibility that the addressees stumble (v. 10b) the author pictures the life of the addressees as a journey by foot. Interference with that journey is pictured as stumbling on their way. If they trip and lose their footing, they will be in danger of falling. By making their call and election secure, they will avoid stumbling.

Those whose lives are abundantly virtuous will enter the eternal kingdom of Jesus (v. 11). In speaking of "entrance" (εἴσοδος) into the kingdom, the author continues the picture of the addressees as traveling, but now specifies that their goal is the kingdom. "Entrance" refers to a road or way into the kingdom, or perhaps a gate into it. The kingdom is eternal. Since it is the kingdom of Jesus, Jesus is its king.

In order to describe an abundantly virtuous life, the author blends wisdom discourse with prophetic discourse. When the author speaks of "eternal" benefits in the future, apocalyptic discourse blends with prophetic

---

forgetfulness has become that of the sinner and the cleansing from sin an accomplished fact. If so, this is part of the *Intertexture* of 2 Peter.

50. Bigg, *St. Peter and St. Jude*, 260; Kelly, *Epistles of Peter and of Jude*, 308; Bauckham, *Jude, 2 Peter*, 189–90; Green, *Jude & 2 Peter*, 199.

discourse. Apocalyptic discourse, however, is in the background here, with prophetic and wisdom discourse in the foreground.

Textural Analysis

Social-cultural texture. Frederick W. Danker has argued persuasively that 1:3–11 follows the form of a decree honoring a benefactor, with vv. 3–4 forming the preamble and vv. 5–11 the resolution of the "decree."[51] This passage begins the letter by saying that Jesus has bestowed some gifts and promised others (the preamble) and exhorting the addressees to make a proper return for them (the resolution). This effectively introduces the twofold theme of the letter: Jesus' gifts will be completed at his second coming; one makes a proper return for them by a life of virtue, which is also necessary for one to participate in their completion.

Intertexture. Danker gives the following example of a decree honoring a benefactor and says it is typical of hundreds of others:[52]

> In the month of Aphrodision, during the magistracy of Apollophanes, son of Apollo, on the sixth, Xenon, son of Aphthonetos was chairman, and Pantaleon, son of Cleandres, proposed the following:
>
> Whereas (*epeidē*) Theocles, son of Thersites, of Meliboea has proved himself a perfect gentleman (*kalos kai agathos*) in his relations with Iasos and has rendered exceptional service to our citizens who visit Meliboea,
>
> be it resolved (*dedochthai*) that Theocles, son of Thersites, be declared our public friend and representative (*proxenos*); that he be granted exemption from whatever imposts our city has authority to exact and be free to come and go both in war and in peace, without formality of treaty; that he enjoy the privilege of a front seat at the games; and that he be officially recognized with the rest of our city's representatives.

---

51. Danker, "2 Peter 1," 64–82, especially pp. 66, 71. Others who have found his argument convincing include Neyrey (*2 Peter, Jude*, 150–51) and Green (*Jude & 2 Peter*, 179–80); Bauckham (*Jude, 2 Peter*, 173–74) and Davids (*2 Peter and Jude*, 166–67) are not convinced. Bauckham and Davids see this section of 2 Peter as following the pattern of a sermon that includes three parts: 1) a historical section, 2) ethical exhortations, and 3) an eschatological section.

52. Danker, "2 Peter 1," 65, translating the text given in C. Michel, *Recueil D' Inscriptions Grecques* (Brussels: Lamertin, 1900) 463.

A decree in which the inhabitants of Stratonicea honor Zeus Panhemerios and Hekate is much closer to 2 Pet 1:3–11 in both form and content.[53] The decree reads:

> During the magistracy of Ptolemy the clever,
>
> when Sosandros son of Diomedes, secretary of the council, said: "The city has been saved (σεσῶσθαι) again from many great and pressing dangers by the providence of the very great (μεγίστων) gods who protected it, namely, Zeus Panhemerios and Hekate, whose inviolate temples and suppliants and holy assembly were made clearly conspicuous by a decree of Augustus Caesar and the eternal (αἰωνίου) empire of the Roman lords (κυρίων); and it is good to bring all eagerness into (πᾶσαν σπουδὴν ἰσφέρεσθαι) piety (εὐσέβειαν) toward them and to neglect no opportunity to show piety (εὐσεβεῖν) and to supplicate them; and statues of the aforementioned gods are set up in the august council chamber, representing the most illustrious virtues of divine power (τῆς θείας δυνάμεως ἀρετάς), on account of which the whole people together also sacrifices and offers incense and prays and gives thanks always to the so very illustrious gods and is accustomed to show piety (εὐσεβεῖν) toward them by means of procession with hymn-singing and worship";
>
> it seemed good to the council now to choose thirty children of the well-born, whom the superintendent will lead each day into the council chamber, with the public guardians of the children, clad in white and crowned with olive branch, and having olive branches likewise in their hand, who will together with harper and herald sing a hymn which Sosandros son of Diomedes, the secretary would arrange; . . . . [the resolution of the decree continues by addressing various contingencies related to this arrangement].

Like 2 Pet 1:3–11, this decree honors divine benefactors. However, the preamble of the decree is much longer than the corresponding part of 2 Pet 1:3–11, i.e., vv. 3–4. And in content the preamble of the decree resembles not only 2 Pet 1:3–4, but also the remainder of 2 Pet 1:1–11. This is mainly because this preamble not only describes the benefits conferred by the gods, but also describes past responses to this benefaction.

---

53. This is my translation of the text given in *CIG* 2.2715 a, b. The similarity of this inscription to 2 Peter has been discussed by Deissmann, *Bible Studies*, 360–68; and Charles, *Virtue Amidst Vice*, 146–48. In three cases Deissmann restores lacunae in the inscription differently than the editor of *CIG*. In those cases I have followed Deissmann. None of these enters into the similarities with 2 Peter discussed below.

Points of similarity include:

1. The statement that Zeus and Hekate have saved Stratonicea; in 2 Pet 1:1 and 11 Jesus is described as savior, and this is explicated in vv. 3–4;
2. The description of Zeus and Hekate as very great; in 2 Pet 1:4 the promises given by Jesus are said to be very great;
3. The inscription speaks of the eternal domain of the Roman lords; 2 Pet 1:11 speaks of the eternal kingdom of our lord and savior Jesus Christ;
4. The inscription says that the people of Stratonicea should respond to the benefaction of Zeus and Hekate by bringing all eagerness into piety toward them; 2 Pet 1:5–7 says that the addressees should respond to the benefaction of Jesus, having brought in all eagerness beside, by supplying abundantly a number of virtues including piety;
5. Piety is mentioned additional times by both; and
6. The inscription speaks of the statues of Zeus and Hekate as displaying the virtues of divine power; 2 Pet 1:3 speaks of Jesus' divine power and his having called the addressees by means of his glory and virtue.

Neither of these decrees is formally identical to 2 Pet 1:3–11. In the first decree the preamble is a clause introduced by ἐπειδή (since), and the resolution is introduced by an infinitive dependent on the introduction to the decree. In the second decree, the preamble is an accusative-infinitive construction dependent on the introduction to the decree, and the resolution is introduced by the clause "it seemed good to the council."[54] The closest formal parallel to 2 Pet 1:3–4 is provided by decrees included in a letter whose preamble consists of a genitive absolute.[55] The closest formal parallel to 2 Pet 1:5–11 is found in decrees whose resolution is introduced by an expression meaning "therefore."[56]

Danker finds many other similarities between decrees and the first chapter of 2 Peter. Stylistically, though not in form or content, 2 Peter resembles the Nemrud Dagh decree.[57] One difference between these decrees and 2 Pet 1:3–11 is that the former are records of decrees that have been enacted, while the latter effectively proposes the enactment of a decree. The author communicates his prophetic message by proposing that the ad-

---

54. Closer formal parallels to 2 Pet 1:3–4 are found in a decree whose preamble is introduced by ἐπειδή but what follows is a genitive absolute, and a decree whose preamble simply consists of a genitive absolute; cf. Danker, "2 Peter 1," 66.
55. Ibid., 79–80.
56. Ibid., 71.
57. See Callan, "Style of the Second Letter of Peter," 202–24.

dressees honor Jesus for his benefactions by living virtuously. This is true when the letter is considered as a communication from the sender to the addressees occurring within a certain historical setting. However, when the letter is considered apart from that setting, its beginning can be seen as a record of the "decree" proposed by Peter, like the other decrees we have been discussing.

Inner texture. Interpreters disagree about whether 1:3–4 should be understood as the continuation of 1:1–2, or as the beginning of a sentence that continues in vv. 5–7, or as an independent sentence. I regard 1:3–4 as the beginning of a sentence that continues in vv. 5–7.[58] On this understanding, vv. 3–7 are a complex conditional sentence, of which vv. 3–4 form the protasis and vv. 5–7 the apodosis. Verses 3–4 are a genitive absolute introduced by ὡς, on which depend a relative clause and a purpose clause. The main verb of vv. 5–7 is an imperative. If vv. 5–7 are taken as a single clause, the sentence consists of four clauses, which is the maximum length of a period according to Demetrius.[59] The last clause is also the longest, as Demetrius recommends (*On Style* 18). This period is part of the introduction to the message of 2 Peter, a good place to use a period according to Quintilian (*Institutio Oratoria* 9.4.128).

Several terms first mentioned in 1:1–2 are *repeated* in vv. 3–11.[60] Other terms repeated in 1:1–2 are also repeated in vv. 3–11.[61] Other terms are introduced in 1:3–11 and repeated later in the letter (see Appendix B). Still other terms are introduced and repeated in 1:3–11, and in some cases also used later in the letter (see Appendix C). The repetition of ἐπίγνωσις (full knowledge—earlier mentioned in v. 2) in vv. 3 and 8[62] shows *progression*. In v. 2 the author had expressed the wish that grace and peace may be multi-

---

58. Callan, "Syntax of 2 Peter 1:1–7."

59. Demetrius, *On Style*, 16. Quintilian says that an average number of clauses in a period is four, but that it often allows more (*Institutio Oratoria* 9.4.125).

60. ἐπιγνώσεως (full knowledge—1:3, 8) was used earlier in 1:2; note also use of its cognate γνῶσις (knowledge) in 1:5, 6 .
τίμια (precious—1:4) is a cognate of ἰσότιμον (equal in honor) found in 1:1
πίστει (faith—1:5) was used earlier in 1:1.
ὑμῖν (you—1:5, 8, 10, 11) was used earler in 1:1, 2.
κυρίου (lord—1:8, 11) was used earlier in 1:2.
σωτῆρος (savior—1:11) was also used earlier in 1:1.

61. Ἰησοῦ Χριστοῦ (Jesus Christ—1:8, 11) was used twice in v. 1.
The first person plural pronoun (1:3 [twice], 4, 8, 11) was used twice in 1:1 and again in v. 2.

62. Starr discusses the inner texture of 2 Pet 1:1–11 rather extensively on pp. 26–64 of *Sharers in Divine Nature*. On p. 27 he identifies a fourfold repetition of the phrase "in the X of our Lord and Savior Jesus Christ" in vv. 1, 2, 8, and 11. However, these four phrases seem significantly different from one another.

plied for the addressees through ἐπίγνωσις of God and Jesus our Lord. In v. 3 the author says that Jesus' divine power has given him and the addressees everything needed for life and piety through ἐπίγνωσις of the one having called them by his own glory and virtue, i.e., Jesus. This clearly presumes that author and addressees already possess ἐπίγνωσις, and explains why it is the source of grace and peace, i.e., it is the source of everything needed for life and piety.

In v. 8 the author says progressing in virtue as he has recommended in vv. 5–7 makes the addressees neither idle nor fruitless for ἐπίγνωσις of our Lord Jesus Christ. This seems to indicate that ἐπίγνωσις is something the addressees need to preserve or even increase, as well as something they already possess. They preserve or increase it by growing in virtue.[63] The author implies that ἐπίγνωσις is not something static that is simply conveyed to someone once for all time. Rather, it is necessary that one be active and productive in order to attain full knowledge. Specifically, it is necessary to develop the virtues listed in vv. 5–7 in order to arrive at full knowledge of Jesus. This emphasis places wisdom discourse in the foreground at this point in 2 Peter.

The topic of knowledge is obviously of central importance to the letter. It also appears in the letter opening in the references to the virtue of knowledge (γνῶσις) in vv. 5–6, to the danger of forgetting in v. 9, and later in the thrice-repeated statement that reminding the addressees is the purpose of the letter (vv. 12, 13, 15). Stated in terms of this topic of knowledge, the theme of the letter is that one receives the gifts of Christ by ἐπίγνωσις of him, and that one makes a proper return for these gifts and, even more important, continues in ἐπίγνωσις of Christ until their completion, by a life of virtue. The author does not fully explain the significance of knowledge until later in the letter (i.e., in 2:18–22).

---

63. In the phrase εἰς τὴν τοῦ κυρίου ἡμῶν Ἰησοῦ Χριστοῦ ἐπίγνωσιν, εἰς can be taken as indicating the condition to which the qualities in vv. 5–7 bring one, or in a more general sense as indicating the source from which the qualities named in vv. 5–7 proceed. Most commentators argue for the former view, including Windisch (*Katholische Briefe*, 86–87), Schelkle (*Die Petrusbriefe*, 191), Spicq (*Épitres de Saint Pierre*, 214), Grundmann (*Brief des Judas und zweite Brief des Petrus*, 74), Paulsen (*Zweite Petrusbrief*, 111), Knoch (*Erste und zweite Petrusbrief*, 242–43) and Green (*Jude & 2 Peter*, 197). Bigg (*St. Peter and St. Jude*, 258–59), however, opts for the latter because vv. 2 and 3 show that the believer begins with recognition of God; Kelly (*Epistles of Peter and of Jude*, 307–8), Bauckham (*Jude, 2 Peter*, 188–89) and Davids (*2 Peter and Jude*, 185) agree. The author of 2 Peter clearly does think the believer begins with recognition of God and so in some sense thinks the virtues listed in vv. 5–7 should grow out of this. But to me it seems most likely that in v. 8 he presents recognition of God as also growing out of the virtues. One both begins with knowledge of God and then grows in knowledge of God as a result of living virtuously.

Another notable *progression* in vv. 3–11 is the use of the pronouns "we" and "you." The first person plural pronoun occurs three times in vv. 3–4, followed by a second person plural verb. Like the first use of the first person plural in v. 1, the uses in vv. 3–4 might refer to a group distinct from the addressees. On the other hand, since the immediately previous use of the first person plural pronoun (in v. 2) referred to author and addressees, it seems likely that it has the same referent in vv. 3–4. If so, in these verses the author moves somewhat abruptly from speaking about what Christ has done for him and the addressees, to saying that the purpose of this was that the addressees might become sharers of divine nature, i.e., participate in divine nature. This prepares for the exhortation to the addressees in the following verses and the remainder of the letter. In vv. 5–11 we find second person plural verbs and pronouns except for first person plural pronouns in vv. 8 and 11 that refer to Christ as Lord of both author and addressees.[64] This movement from "we" to "you" allows the author to exhort the addressees as one who has much in common with them. Identifying himself with them at the beginning increases the probability that they will be receptive to his message.

Although the author does not say that he himself will become a sharer of divine nature, only that the addressees will do so, it seems highly likely that he expects to share this condition with the addressees. Perhaps he mentions only them in order to emphasize their hope to be in this condition.

The *repetition* of διά (through) in vv. 3–4 is also *progressive*. The author first says that Jesus' divine power has given him and the addressees all things for life and piety through (διά) full knowledge of himself. He further describes Jesus as the one who has called them by his glory and virtue (v. 3). The author then says that through (δι') his glory and virtue Jesus has given them precious and very great promises and says that the purpose of giving these promises was that through (διά) them the addressees might become sharers of divine nature (v. 4).

The threefold *repetition* of διά creates a chain of instrumentality. Full knowledge of Jesus is the means by which one receives all things for life and piety. Jesus' glory and virtue is the means by which one receives precious and very great promises, which are in turn the means by which one becomes a sharer of divine nature. The promises are the means by which one becomes a sharer of divine nature, because that is what they promise. Receiving all things for life and piety is ultimately a matter of sharing divine nature. Jesus' divine power, the source of all things for life and piety, and Jesus' glory and

---

64. Starr, *Sharers in Divine Nature*, 34–35.

virtue, the source of the precious and very great promises, are different expressions of the same thing.

The most notable instance of *repetition* and *progression* in this passage is found in vv. 5–7. The addressees are urged to supply abundantly by means of one virtue another virtue, then by the second virtue a third, by the third a fourth, etc. until they have abundantly supplied seven virtues, eight including the faith with which they began. This involves repetition of each virtue except the first and last; each virtue except the last is seen as a step on the way to the next virtue.

The author has linked the virtues in vv. 5–7 by using the figure of speech known as gradatio or climax. Other examples can be seen in Rom 5:3–5, *Hermas Vis.* 3.8.7 and elsewhere.[65] For instance, Rom 5:3–5 says,

> we also boast in our sufferings, knowing that suffering produces endurance,
> and endurance produces character,
> and character produces hope,
> and hope does not disappoint us, because God's love has been poured into our hearts through the Holy Spirit that has been given to us.

There is no parallel to the precise way the items are linked in 2 Peter, i.e., making the first item the object of the preposition ἐν in an instrumental sense, and the second the object of the verb that governs the entire sequence. The way the author has constructed this sequence also displays other figures of speech. The seven phrases that comprise vv. 5b–7 have approximately the same number of syllables, making them an instance of the figure of speech isocolon. Each of these phrases after the first is connected to the preceding one by δέ; this constitutes the figure of speech polysyndeton, repeated use of conjunctions. Each phrase includes a word in the dative case and one in the accusative; this repetition of case endings constitutes the figure of speech homoeoptoton.[66]

By mentioning a rather large number of virtues and linking them this way the author describes the life he exhorts the addressees to live as abundantly virtuous people. These virtues are patterned on those the author has attributed to Jesus, or the actions of Jesus, in vv. 3–4. Just as Jesus has called the author and addressees by means of his glory and virtue, so they should supply virtue by means of their faith. As Jesus has given them all things for life and piety through full knowledge of him, so they should supply knowledge by means of their virtue. As Jesus has promised that they will become

---

65. In these three examples of climax, all the names of the virtues are feminine.
66. Watson, *Invention*, 98. Watson also sees reduplication here.

sharers of divine nature, having escaped the corruption in the world by desire, so they should supply self-control by means of their knowledge. As Jesus has given them promises, so they should supply endurance by means of their self-control. As Jesus has given them all things for life and piety, they should supply piety by means of their endurance. As all that Jesus has done for them can be seen as a manifestation of love, so they should supply brotherly love by means of their piety, and love by means of their brotherly love.

It is clear that the addressees already have some degree of knowledge and piety. Thus the author must be exhorting them to persist in, and perhaps develop further, these virtues. This may be true of all the virtues the author mentions.

A number of the other repetitions in 1:3–11 also indicate *progression*. After mentioning Jesus three times in 1:1–2, the author does not mention the name of Jesus at all in 1:3–7. However, Jesus is the probable referent of the pronouns αὐτοῦ (his)[67] and ἰδίᾳ (his) in v. 3; in addition Jesus is probably the understood substantive modified by καλέσαντος (call)[68] in v. 3 and the understood subject of δεδώρηται (give) in v. 4. Ἰησοῦ Χριστοῦ (Jesus Christ) is then mentioned explicitly in vv. 8 and 11. Verse 8 speaks of τοῦ κυρίου ἡμῶν Ἰησοῦ Χριστοῦ (our Lord Jesus Christ); v. 11 of τοῦ κυρίου ἡμῶν καὶ σωτῆρος Ἰησοῦ Χριστοῦ (our Lord and savior Jesus Christ). All of this indicates that Jesus continues to be of central importance in 1:3–11, as in 1:1–2. The multiple oblique references to Jesus in vv. 3–4 develop the understanding of Jesus as divine. The explicit reference to "our Lord Jesus Christ" in v. 8 repeats in a different way the identification of Jesus as Lord in v. 2, and adds the identification of him as Christ found twice in v. 1. The explicit reference to "our Lord and savior Jesus Christ" in v. 11 follows the pattern of the reference to Jesus as God and savior in v. 1, but replaces "God" with "Lord." Calling Jesus Lord and savior is less striking than calling him God and savior because "Lord" is a less exalted predicate than "God." But since

---

67. The antecedent is Ἰησοῦ τοῦ κυρίου ἡμῶν (v. 2), the last person mentioned; so Grundmann, *Brief des Judas und zweite Brief des Petrus*, 69; Fornberg, *Early Church*, 144; Bauckham, *Jude, 2 Peter*, 177; Starr, *Sharers in Divine Nature*, 31–34; Davids, *2 Peter and Jude*, 168. Kelly disagrees (*Peter and Jude*, 300); likewise Green understands the antecedent as θεοῦ (*Jude & 2 Peter*, 181). Spicq understands the passage as speaking about Jesus' divine power and his call of the author and addressees, but argues that this should not be seen as asserting anything other than that God was working through Jesus (*Épitres de Saint Pierre*, 210).

68. Grundmann, *Brief des Judas und zweite Brief des Petrus*, 69–70; Bauckham, *Jude, 2 Peter*, 178. Green (*Jude & 2 Peter*, 183) argues that 2 Peter understands God as the one who has called them. In v. 2 the author has referred to full knowledge of God and Jesus our Lord.

the author has already called Jesus "God," he probably calls him "Lord" because he is God.

πάντα (all things) is used in vv. 3 and 5 to indicate that the appropriate response to having received all things for life and piety is to pursue virtue with all eagerness. θείας (divine) is used in vv. 3 and 4 to indicate that the source of the addressees' benefits and the ultimate form of the benefits themselves have the same character, i.e., both are divine. Also in vv. 3 and 4 the repetition δεδωρημένης—δεδώρηται (give) links all things for life and piety with the precious and very great promises, suggesting that the promises given are at least part of what is included in all things for life and piety. The verb "call" is used in v. 3 and the cognate noun "call" in v. 10 to show that the call the addressees have received must be made secure by a life of virtue. Use of the word σπουδή (eagerness) in v. 5 and the cognate verb σπουδάζω in v. 10 emphasizes that it is precisely a life of virtue that is the means of making one's call secure. Use of ἐπιχορηγέω (supply) in vv. 5 and 11 shows that those who supply virtue will have entrance into the kingdom supplied to them. Finally, ποιέω is used twice in v. 10 to indicate that making one's call and election secure is precisely a matter of doing these things, i.e., pursuing virtue.

The *argumentative* character of 1:3-11 is very marked. This is clearly indicated by the use of a conditional sentence in vv. 3-7; use of γάρ (for) in vv. 8, 9, 10, and 11; and use of διό (therefore) in v. 10. 1:3-11 consists of a series of interlocking *enthymemes*.[69] Verses 3-7 form an enthymeme in which the gifts of Christ listed in vv. 3-4 are the basis on which progress in virtue is urged in vv. 5-7. The argument can be restated:

> One who receives everything needed for life and piety should live virtuously.
>
> Jesus' divine power has given the addressees everything needed for life and piety.
>
> Therefore, the addressees should live virtuously.

Verses 3-7 constitute an elaborate and impressive period, increasing the force of the enthymeme.

The author also increases the force of the enthymeme by emphasizing the significance of the gift that has been given to the addressees. He does this in one way by saying that Jesus' divine power is the source of the gift. Speaking of Jesus as having divine power and referring solely to this power in mentioning Jesus makes it clear that the gift proceeds from the most exalted possible source. Likewise, saying that the ultimate purpose of the gift

---

69. On the argumentative character of vv. 3-11 see Watson, *Invention*, 96-97.

is that the addressees become sharers of divine nature makes it clear that the gift has the most exalted possible nature. Such a great gift is deserving of a great response.

The gift is described as all things for life and piety. "Life and piety" might be a hendiadys equivalent to "pious life."[70] Or it might refer to piety as leading to life, i.e., fullness of life, the ultimate goal of human beings.[71] Piety refers to reverence, especially reverence toward God. Showing proper reverence toward God may here be seen as leading to the goal of human life. The author says that he and the addressees have received all things for life and piety, but gives no specific indication of what those things are. We might think they have received freedom from whatever might keep them from piety, or a more positive ability to be pious, or perhaps knowledge of what constitutes piety, or all three.

Having presented the basis for his exhortation in vv. 3–4, the author exhorts the addressees in vv. 5–7, beginning to propose the resolution of the "decree." He urges them to supply a series of virtues, "having brought in all eagerness beside." The author describes the future condition he urges the addressees to enter as one of full eagerness, using a rare verb (παρεισφέρω—to bring in beside) that adds emphasis to the exhortation. In that state of eagerness they are to supply virtues.

Although the author has not explained exactly how one virtue should lead to the next in vv. 5–7, the use of climax strongly emphasizes that these virtues are a series of stages or steps in the development of a virtuous life. Each virtue can and should be the means of progressing to the next virtue. And it seems to be implied that one cannot develop a particular virtue without developing those that form the stages leading to its development. Perhaps it is implied that full development of each virtue will automatically produce the next. The ultimate goal of the virtuous life is love. In order to attain love, one must begin with faith, and move from faith to virtue, from virtue to knowledge, from knowledge to self-control, from self-control to endurance, from endurance to piety, from piety to brotherly love, and finally from brotherly love to love.

Our ability to understand precisely how these virtues are seen as stages in the development of a virtuous life is limited by 2 Peter's lack of any explicit explanation. It is also limited because the terms for these virtues are used rarely, or only here, in 2 Peter. Faith is mentioned only in 1:1, 5; virtue is mentioned only in 1:3, 5; knowledge is mentioned only in 1:5, 6, and

---

70. Reicke, *Epistles of James, Peter and Jude*, 184; Bauckham, *Jude, 2 Peter*, 178; Watson, *Invention*, 97–98.

71. For the latter idea see 1 Tim 4:7–8; Titus 1:1–2.

3:18; piety is mentioned only in 1:3, 6, 7, and 3:11. Self-control, endurance, brotherly love and love are mentioned only in 1:5–7.[72] Some of these terms, however, can be at least tentatively related to others that are used by 2 Peter and explained in light of them. This is particularly true of knowledge and piety. There are many cognates, synonyms and antonyms of these terms in 2 Peter. We can be fairly sure how the author of 2 Peter understood knowledge and piety; understanding the other steps on his staircase of virtues is more speculative.

Although faith is mentioned only twice in 2 Peter, there is reason to think that 2 Peter sees a close relationship between faith and knowledge. To the extent that this is so, what 2 Peter says about knowledge illuminates its understanding of faith. The most direct indication of the close relationship between the two is found in 1:1–7. In v. 1 the letter is addressed to those who have received πίστιν (faith) equal in honor to ours (= Simeon Peter, the sender of the letter, along with unspecified others). In v. 2 the sender wishes that favor and peace may be multiplied for the addressees by ἐπιγνώσει (full knowledge) of God and Jesus. In v. 3 the sender refers to Jesus' having given him and the addressees all things for life and piety through ἐπιγνώσεως (full knowledge) of the one who called them, i.e., Jesus. In vv. 5–7 the sender of the letter says that since Jesus has done this, the addressees should ascend a ladder of virtues whose first rung is πίστει (faith).

This alternation of the terms faith and full knowledge does not explicitly equate the two. But faith at least has a cognitive element; one must know what one believes. And going immediately from speaking about the reception of faith in 1:1 (presupposed in v. 5), to speaking about full knowledge as the means by which favor and peace are multiplied and by which Jesus has given all things for life and piety, suggests that full knowledge is nearly synonymous with faith for 2 Peter. Full knowledge is knowledge of God and especially of Jesus (see also 1:8; 2:20; 3:18). To the extent that faith is synonymous with full knowledge, faith can be understood as faith in God and especially Jesus.

Like faith, virtue is mentioned only twice in 2 Peter. Also like faith, 2 Peter's understanding of virtue can be illuminated by its close relationship to something 2 Peter mentions more frequently, namely justice (δικαιοσύνη). Second Peter uses justice as a general name for the virtue that should characterize Christians. Nevertheless, in 1:3–11, the author's most extensive description of this virtue, he uses different terms. In 1:1 the author

---

72. Terms such as faith and love are common elsewhere in the NT, and terms such as virtue, self-control, and piety that are rare in the NT are more common in other early Christian literature (see Bauckham, *Jude, 2 Peter,* 174–76, 185–87). However, none of this illuminates the way the author of 2 Peter thinks one virtue leads to another.

had said that the addressees received faith by the justice of Jesus. In v. 3 the author says that Jesus has called him and the addressees through his glory and virtue (ἀρετή), using virtue as a synonym for justice. This can be seen as the author's reconfiguration of justice, a term used by Jewish writers to mean right conduct before God,[73] into virtue, a characteristically Hellenistic term for excellence, connoting excellence that is recognized and honored.[74] In Jesus' case it includes both powerful deeds and moral excellence; for the addressees of 2 Peter, it refers mainly to moral excellence.[75]

How can faith be understood as producing this virtue that is so closely related to justice? It seems that faith includes knowledge of how to live virtuously and the necessity of doing so. As we have seen, the author of 2 Peter seems to understand faith as closely related to knowledge of Jesus. And knowledge of Jesus includes knowledge of how to live virtuously. Jesus himself has acted virtuously. Because Jesus is characterized by justice (1:1), knowledge of him is knowledge of justice. Because Jesus has called his followers by means of his virtue (1:3), they know what virtue is.

In 2:20–21 knowledge of "our Lord and savior Jesus Christ" is parallel to knowing the way of justice. 2:20 speaks of escaping the defilements of the world by full knowledge of Jesus and again being implicated in them; 2:21 speaks of fully knowing the way of justice and turning away. Full knowledge of Jesus seems to be equivalent to full knowledge of the way of justice, at least in some measure. And in 2:21 the way of justice is parallel to the holy commandment. The verse speaks first of fully knowing the way of justice and then of turning away from the holy commandment, apparently equating the two. The holy commandment is the commandment to follow the way of justice. This passage not only shows that knowledge of Jesus includes knowledge of virtue, but also indicates why one must live virtuously. Failing to live virtuously negates the freedom from the defilements of the world produced by knowledge of Jesus.

In summary then, faith, which is also full knowledge of God and Jesus, is a dynamic reality. It is not just a thing in itself; it produces other things such as favor and peace (v. 2) and all things for life and piety (v. 3). In 1:5 the author says that faith/full knowledge must produce moral excellence; he implies that it is part of the intrinsic character of faith/full knowledge

---

73. It is also used in this sense in other New Testament literature, especially the gospel of Matthew and the letters of Paul.

74. On the meaning of ἀρετή see Danker, *Benefactor*, 318; Neyrey, *2 Peter, Jude*, 156. In the New Testament apart from 2 Peter ἀρετή is used only in Phil 4:8 and 1 Pet 2:9. This and other such reconfigurations had earlier occurred among Hellenistic Jews such as Philo.

75. Bauckham, *Jude, 2 Peter*, 185; Green, *Jude & 2 Peter*, 192.

to produce virtue. Faith that is truly faith will produce virtue. The connection between faith and virtue that I suggest the author of 2 Peter makes here is similar to the connection between indicative and imperative found throughout the letters of Paul (cf. the reference to faith working through love in Gal 5:6). In terminology 2 Peter is closer to the argument of Jas 2:14–26 that faith must be completed by works. The specific content of the virtue produced by faith is explicated in the remaining steps on the ladder of virtue.

The inclusion of knowledge as the third step on the ladder of virtue shows that faith and knowledge are not completely synonymous. At least in this context there is some distinction between them. If the first step on the ladder of virtue is faith/full knowledge, and this faith/full knowledge produces virtue, the knowledge that virtue in turn produces must be at least somewhat different from the faith/full knowledge with which one began.

Many interpreters see a distinction between knowledge and full knowledge.[76] However, the parallel between 2:20 and 3:18 suggests there is little difference in meaning between the two words. The former speaks of full knowledge, the latter of knowledge, of our Lord and savior Jesus Christ. If the two words are synonymous, 1:8 also explicitly makes the point that living virtuously leads to increased knowledge of the Lord Jesus Christ (as we have seen above). Perhaps the knowledge mentioned as the third step on the ladder of virtue is practical knowledge.[77] The faith/full knowledge that is the first step on the ladder can be understood as theoretical knowledge about Jesus and the need for his followers to live virtuously. This faith leads one to live virtuously and this adds practical knowledge—namely, experience of living as a follower of Jesus—to the theoretical knowledge with which one began. Such an understanding makes it clear how virtue produces an increase of knowledge.

The increased knowledge that results from completing faith by virtue includes knowledge of the danger presented by desire and the consequent need for self-control. In this way the addressees can supply self-control by means of their knowledge. Desire is the source of the corruption in the

---

76. Bigg, *St. Peter and St. Jude*, 253; Bauckham, *Jude, 2 Peter*, 186; Neyrey, *2 Peter, Jude*, 149. Spicq (*Épitres de Saint Pierre*, 213), Grundmann (*Brief des Judas und zweite Brief des Petrus*, 73), and Knoch (*Erste und zweite Petrusbrief*, 242) understand "knowledge" as the ability to distinguish good from evil. Paulsen (*Zweite Petrusbrief*, 111), Davids (*2 Peter and Jude*, 180) and Green (*Jude & 2 Peter*, 193) agree with me in seeing a close relationship between knowledge and full knowledge.

77. This suggests that γνῶσις connotes specifically the knowledge that comes from the experience of trying to live virtuously, which would be one element of the knowledge that is generally synonymous with faith in 2 Peter. Bauckham (*Jude, 2 Peter*, 186) suggests something similar to this.

world (v. 4; cf. 2:10; 3:3), and desire can tempt those who have escaped corruption to embrace it again (2:18). Self-control is necessary to continue completing faith by virtue.

The main kind of desire the author of 2 Peter has in view seems to be inordinate sexual desire, i.e., licentiousness. Licentiousness is equated with desire in 2:18. The false teachers are also said to be licentious in 2:2. In 2:7 licentiousness is said to characterize Sodom and Gomorrah. In 2:14 the false teachers are described as having eyes full of adultery. However, the author may also be thinking of other kinds of desire, namely greed and luxuriousness. According to the author of 2 Peter, the false teachers are characterized by greed (2:3, 14) and they regard luxuriousness during the day a pleasure (2:13).

Self-control is closely related to endurance. Insofar as self-control is successful, it constitutes endurance of the suffering that results from denial of desire. Since the author of 2 Peter regards expectation of Jesus' second coming as the chief support of virtuous living, self-control also requires enduring affirmation of it. Here 2 Peter blends apocalyptic discourse into its Christian wisdom discourse. Self-control requires endurance of both the intrinsic pressure of desire toward its own satisfaction and uncertainty about the second coming of Jesus. This is a feature that someone like Epictetus does not add to his parenesis. But the addressees of 2 Peter are to supply endurance by means of their self-control. Endurance is synonymous with being established in the truth (1:12) and having stability (3:17).

Such endurance is implicitly piety. It is acceptance of the divine order according to which the addressees have been set free from corruption and called to live in freedom from it now while they await the future completion of their salvation when Jesus comes again (cf. 3:11). At the second coming of Jesus the pious will be saved (2:9) and the impious will be destroyed (3:7; cf. 2:5, 6). At this point also apocalyptic discourse blends with wisdom discourse in 2 Peter. Piety is the opposite of the false teachers' slanderous rejection of the second coming of Jesus (3:4) and consequent slavery to corruption (2:19). By means of their endurance of the difficulties involved in living virtuously, the addressees supply piety.

By means of their piety, the addressees must supply brotherly love because love is the culmination of all virtue. Paul argues explicitly in 1 Cor 13 that without love no other virtue means anything. The progression of virtues in 2 Pet 1:5–7 exhibits agreement with this emphasis. In itself the term "brotherly love" refers to love among members of a family.[78] The author of 2 Peter probably uses it to mean love for other followers of Jesus

---

78. Davids, *2 Peter and Jude*, 182–83.

who are seen as equivalent to family members; the author of 2 Peter calls Paul a beloved brother in 3:15, and calls the addressees beloved in 3:1, 8, 14, 17. The virtue of brotherly love is reminiscent of the commandment to love one's neighbor as oneself and even more of the commandment that Jesus' followers love one another as he loved them.[79]

Love begins as love for those close to us, but must ultimately include all. This is closely related to the call to love one's enemies in Matt 5:44 and parallels. In this way the addressees will supply love by means of their brotherly love. Since the author of 2 Peter speaks of Jesus as the beloved son of God the Father (1:17), he may see the love of Christians as imitation of God's love; this is explicit in Matt 5:45-48 and parallels.[80]

The author concludes the resolution of his "decree" with a series of interlocking *enthymemes* that support the argument contained in the preamble and first part of the resolution (vv. 3-7). The first of these is in vv. 3-8, which is a reformulation of the enthymeme in vv. 3-7 indicating why one who receives everything needed for life and piety should live virtuously. Verse 3 says that the addressees have received everything needed for life and piety through ἐπίγνωσις (full knowledge) of the one who called them, namely Jesus. The reformulation argues that this ἐπίγνωσις must issue in a virtuous life in order to be sustained and developed. The argument:

> One should not be idle or fruitless for ἐπίγνωσις of Jesus.
>
> Progress in virtue makes one neither idle nor fruitless for ἐπίγνωσις of Jesus.
>
> Therefore, one should make progress in virtue.

Verses 3-7 and 9 is another enthymeme, a negative reformulation of the enthymeme in vv. 3-8. Verse 9 presumes that receiving everything needed for life and piety is a matter of seeing clearly and being cleansed from one's past sins, and argues that failing to progress in virtue is relinquishing sight and forgetting this cleansing. The argument:

---

79. For the former see Mark 12:31 and parallels; for the latter, John 13:34-35.

80. The foregoing explanation of vv. 5-7 has some similarity to the explanation proposed by the Venerable Bede in his commentary on 2 Peter; it also resembles Grundmann's interpretation of v. 6 (*Brief des Judas und zweite Brief des Petrus*, 73). Windisch (*Katholische Briefe*, 86), Bauckham (*Jude, 2 Peter*, 185), Paulsen (*Zweite Petrusbrief*, 110) and Davids (*2 Peter and Jude*, 178) do not think there is any internal logic to vv. 5-7. This is also asserted by Vögtle (*Tugend- und Lasterkataloge*, 189), but he nevertheless suggests an internal logic with some similarity to the one presented above (ibid., 189-91); so also Schelkle, *Die Petrusbriefe*, 190-91. Charles (*Virtue Amidst Vice*, 145-46, n. 91) rejects the view that the list of virtues is largely random and proposes an understanding of their logical progression (ibid., 140-45, 156-57).

> One should not be blind or forget cleansing of one's past sins.
>
> Lack of virtue is blindness and forgetfulness of the cleansing of one's past sins.
>
> Therefore, one should not lack virtue.

The author presumes that clear vision and remembering the cleansing of one's sins naturally lead to growth in virtue.

Verses 3–10a is yet another enthymeme drawing the conclusion from vv. 3–9 that the addressees should be eager to make secure their call and election. The argument is another indication why one who receives everything needed for life and piety should live virtuously. Verse 3 says that the addressees received everything needed for life and piety through ἐπίγνωσις (full knowledge) of the one who called (καλέσαντος) them, namely Jesus. Verse 10a argues that this call (κλῆσιν) of Jesus must be made secure through a virtuous life. In v. 5 the addressees are urged to be eager (σπουδὴν) to progress in virtue; in v. 10a they are urged to be eager (σπουδάσατε) to make their call secure. The argument:

> It is good to have been called and elected.
>
> This call and election can be lost by failing to live a virtuous life (because such failure is blindness and forgetfulness of the cleansing of one's past sins).
>
> Therefore, the addressees should make their call and election secure (by living virtuously).

Verse 10a then forms two more enthymemes with vv. 10b and 11. First, those who make secure their call and election will never stumble (v. 10b). The argument:

> One should avoid stumbling.
>
> Making one's call and election secure is a way to avoid stumbling.
>
> Therefore, one should make one's call and election secure.

Second, entry into the kingdom of the Lord and Savior Jesus Christ will be supplied abundantly to those who make secure their call and election (v. 11). In v. 5 the addressees are urged to be eager to supply abundantly (ἐπιχορηγήσατε) progress in virtue. Verse 11 says that if they make their call and election secure, entry into the kingdom of the Lord and Savior Jesus Christ will be supplied abundantly (ἐπιχορηγηθήσεται) to them. The abundance of virtue they are urged to supply will be matched or exceeded by the abundance they will receive. The argument:

> One should enter the kingdom of Jesus Christ.
>
> Entry into the kingdom of Jesus Christ will be supplied to those who make secure their call and election.
>
> Therefore, one should make one's call and election secure.

In v. 11 the author uses three titles for Jesus that he has already used, namely Christ (vv. 1 and 8), savior (v. 1), and Lord (vv. 2 and 8). In this context the author presents Jesus as Christ and Lord in that he is king of an eternal kingdom, and savior in that he supplies to the addressees entrance into that kingdom.

References to the kingdom of God are common in the New Testament, particularly in the synoptic gospels, and the New Testament also includes a few other references to the kingdom of Christ. For example, 1 Cor 15:24 speaks of the end as the time when Christ "hands over the kingdom to God the Father." References to Christ's kingdom are also found in Col 1:13 and 2 Tim 4:1 (cf. also Luke 1:33; 22:29–30; John 18:36). Eph 5:5 and Rev 11:15 speak of the kingdom of Christ and God. Though uncommon, such references to the kingdom of Christ are not surprising. As we have seen, identification of Jesus as Christ is identification of him as the eschatological king, implying that he has a kingdom.

Other references to the kingdom of Christ do not speak of entering this kingdom. However, the synoptic gospels often speak of entering the kingdom of God. For example, in Mark 9:47–48 Jesus says,

> And if your eye causes you to stumble, tear it out; it is better for you to enter the kingdom of God with one eye than to have two eyes and to be thrown into hell, where their worm never dies, and the fire is never quenched.

In 2 Pet 1:11 the author uses that same language in connection with the kingdom of Christ. Other references to the kingdom of Christ do not speak of it as an eternal kingdom; in fact 1 Cor 15:24 explicitly excludes this.[81] In speaking of the eternal kingdom of Christ, the author continues to blur the distinction between Jesus and God. As the king of an eternal kingdom, Jesus is presented as divine.

Social-cultural texture. Use of the form of a decree *honoring* a *benefactor* in 1:3–11 obviously continues the presentation of the relationship between Jesus and the addressees as a relationship between *patron* and *clients*. The topic of the patron-client relationship between Jesus and the addressees appears especially in references to the benefactions of Jesus in vv. 3–4 and 9,

---

81. Luke 1:33 says that of Jesus' kingdom there will be no end; Rev 11:15 says that he, either the Lord or his Christ, will reign forever and ever.

in the call for recognition of his patronage in vv. 3 and 8, and in the warning against forgetting it in v. 9.[82]

In v. 1 the author had said the addressees received faith by the δικαιοσύνη (justice) of Jesus. In v. 3 the author says Jesus has called him and the addressees through his glory and ἀρετῇ (virtue), using ἀρετή as a synonym for δικαιοσύνη. As we have discussed above, in the context of his "decree," the author has reconfigured δικαιοσύνη, a term often used by Jewish writers, into ἀρετή, a more characteristically Hellenistic term.

Use of the terms for virtues found in vv. 5–7 can be seen as a development and particularization of the reconfiguration of δικαιοσύνη into Hellenistic terms. This reconfiguration is most prominent in 1:3–11. A number of the terms used for virtues in vv. 5–7 appear only here in 2 Peter. In the remainder of the letter, the author reverts to the language of δικαιοσύνη. However, some of the terms used for virtues in vv. 5–7 are repeated elsewhere, as are various synonyms and antonyms. In this way the reconfiguration of δικαιοσύνη into Hellenistic terms is found throughout 2 Peter.

Some of the terms used for virtues in vv. 5–7, especially ἐγκράτεια and εὐσέβεια, correspond to the terminology of Hellenistic popular philosophy, though they are also found in early Christian literature outside the New Testament.[83] An example of the former can be found in a first century BCE inscription from Asia Minor. The inscription honors Herostratus, son of Dorcalion, describing him as superior in three of the eight virtues mentioned in 2 Pet 1:5–7, namely πίστις, ἀρετή, and εὐσέβεια, as well as in δικαιοσύνη, and as having brought in the most eagerness (τὴν πλείστην ἐισενηγμένον σπουδήν).[84]

The promises given by Jesus (v. 4) are described as precious (τίμια), an adjective that often describes precious stones (e.g., 1 Cor 3:12; Rev 17:4; 18:12). Such stones are precious because they are held in *honor* and desired by many. The author describes the promises given by Jesus as being like such stones.

The goal of escaping the transitory world of mortality and participating in the eternal divine world was widespread in Hellenistic philosophical and religious thought and was taken up by Hellenistic Judaism.[85] For example, Wis 2:23 says, "God created humanity for incorruption (ἀφθαρσίᾳ) and made him the image of his own eternity (ἀιδιότητος)." This language is

---

82. Neyrey, *2 Peter, Jude*, 150–52.

83. Bauckham, *Jude, 2 Peter*, 174–75.

84. The relevant part of the inscription is quoted by Charles (*Virtue Amidst Vice*, 139). The full text is found in Dittenberger, *Orientis Graeci Inscriptones Selectae*, vol. 2 no. 438.

85. Bauckham, *Jude, 2 Peter*, 179–84; Starr, *Sharers in Divine Nature*.

found only here in 2 Peter and can be seen as the author's reconfiguration of apocalyptic discourse into Hellenistic terms in the context of his "decree." Elsewhere he does not reconfigure apocalyptic discourse in this way but simply uses it. For example, in v. 11 he uses the apocalyptic topos of the kingdom of God, though in a distinctive way.

The value of *purity* is invoked as the author exhorts the addressees to piety (vv. 3, 6, 7), self-control (v. 6), and remembering their cleansing from sin (v. 9), and refers to their having escaped corruption that arises from desire (v. 4).[86]

Rhetorical Force

For Christians familiar with other New Testament writings, this section of 2 Peter would probably have constituted a surprising expression of Christian faith in a form and language used by non-Christians. The author was addressing Christians familiar with other New Testament writings and probably wrote as he did in an effort to impress them and so win acceptance of his message. In effect he also offers a Christian alternative to such non-Christian language.

Second Peter 1:3-11 continues and develops the presentation of Jesus as God which first appears in 1:1-2. Since the antecedent of αὐτοῦ (his) in the phrase τῆς θείας δυνάμεως αὐτοῦ (his divine power—v. 3) is probably Jesus, the author describes Jesus as having divine power, which accords well with the identification of Jesus as God in v. 1. Not only does the author say that Jesus has divine power, he uses it by synecdoche in place of mentioning Jesus himself, making divine power such a prominent attribute of Jesus that it can be said to do what Jesus does. Alternatively, this can be understood as picturing Jesus' divine power as a person who gives to others. This picture of Jesus' divine power as giving things to the author and addressees is very general. Something passes from one to the other as a gift, but exactly what and how is not said.

The one who has called the author and addressees (v. 3) is probably Jesus. Later in the letter the author speaks of full knowledge of Jesus in 1:8 and 2:20 (cf. 3:18). This suggests that full knowledge of the one who has called them is full knowledge of Jesus. Thus Jesus is described as having called the author and addressees. The antonomasia of substituting the action of calling for the name of Jesus emphasizes that this action is the most important aspect of Jesus at this point in the author's argument. It presents

---

86. On the value of purity see Neyrey, *2 Peter, Jude*, 10-14; Neyrey discusses purity in 2 Pet 1:3-11 on pp. 153-54.

Jesus as speaking to the author and addressees in order to invite them to be his adherents. None of the circumstances in which this happened are mentioned. Jesus called them through his glory and virtue.[87] This may be another hendiadys = glorious virtue. Virtue is excellence of any kind; glorious virtue is excellence that is well-known and cause for admiration. The author may intend to evoke images of Jesus' miracles and/or resurrection. In view of the reference to Jesus' δικαιοσύνη (justice) in v. 1, the author probably also evokes a picture of the moral excellence of Jesus. Through his manifest excellence, Jesus has called the author and addressees, and by communicating full knowledge of himself has given them all things for life and piety.

Through his glory and virtue Jesus has given the author and addressees "the precious and very great promises" so that through them the addressees "might become sharers of divine nature." Since this is the purpose of the promises, it is also their ultimate content. Divine nature is the nature of God. Since the author has called Jesus God in v. 1 and mentioned his divine power in v. 3, it is apparently also the nature of Jesus. The author uses the same adjective (θείας—divine) to describe both Jesus' power and the nature the addressees are promised to share as divine, suggesting that they will share the nature of Jesus. The word κοινωνοί (sharers) and its cognates are frequently used by Paul to speak of the union of believers with Jesus. For example, in 1 Cor 1:9 Paul speaks of God as the one through whom the Corinthians "were called into the fellowship (κοινωνίαν) of his Son, Jesus Christ our Lord." See also 1 Cor 10:16; Phil 3:10. Perhaps the author of 2 Peter understands the addressees' sharing in divine nature as resulting from union with Jesus.

The most salient characteristic of divine nature is incorruptibility; the immediately following reference to escaping corruption in the world makes it very likely that the author equates sharing divine nature with becoming incorruptible.[88] Thus the author pictures the future condition of the addressees as being one of participation in the incorruptibility of God, perhaps by virtue of their union with Jesus who escaped corruption via resurrection. They will attain this condition after "having escaped the corruption in the world by desire." The author presents the corruption in the world as a result of desire. Perhaps he evokes Gen 3 in which the desire of the first humans

---

87. These terms are often used together in Hellenistic literature; see Bauckham, *Jude, 2 Peter*, 179; Green, *Jude & 2 Peter*, 183.

88. Fornberg, *Early Church*, 86–88; Bauckham, *Jude, 2 Peter*, 180–81; Neyrey, *2 Peter, Jude*, 157–58. Green argues that 2 Peter is speaking about the acquisition of moral character, not about becoming immortal and incorruptible (*Jude & 2 Peter*, 186). Starr concludes that for 2 Peter sharing divine nature means sharing "Christ's nature, viz. his moral excellence in the present, and his eternity and glory in the future" (*Sharers in Divine Nature*, 227).

for the forbidden fruit, when acted upon, makes them mortal. Paul seems to describe such a picture in Rom 7:7–12; this says in part

> If it had not been for the law, I would not have known sin. I would not have known what it is to covet (ἐπιθυμίαν) if the law had not said, "You shall not covet" (οὐκ ἐπιθυμήσεις). But sin, seizing an opportunity in the commandment, produced in me all kinds of covetousness (ἐπιθυμίαν). Apart from the law sin lies dead. I was once alive apart from the law, but when the commandment came, sin revived and I died, and the very commandment that promised life proved to be death to me.

In saying that the addressees escape the corruption in the world, the author presents corruption as a pursuer or captor of the addressees whose power they have eluded.

If non-Christians, Jews like Philo, and Gentiles like Epictetus, were exposed to 2 Peter, its content and manner of speech would probably have seemed more familiar. But the ideas that Jesus is the source of divine blessings and that entry into his eternal kingdom is the goal of a virtuous life would have been surprising. Both Philo and Epictetus would have readily said such things about God, but would have known nothing about Jesus. In addition, someone like Epictetus would have found surprising the idea that people could become sharers of divine nature in the future; Epictetus would have said they were already naturally sharers of divine nature.

In presenting the summary of its prophetic message in the form of a decree, the author of 2 Peter expressed prophetic discourse in strikingly Hellenistic terms. The author used a form and language deriving from the civic life of Hellenistic cities to express a prophetic call to honor God by living virtuously. In doing this the author presented Jesus as God. Such a view was found only among Christians and was highly problematic within the framework of Jewish monotheism. In principle, non-Jewish polytheism could accommodate such a view more readily, though that alone would not make the idea that Jesus was god immediately acceptable.

Second Peter also describes the abundantly virtuous life in Hellenistic terms, expressing wisdom discourse in Greek more than Jewish terms. This is true most of all in the ladder of virtues in vv. 5–7, where the author uses words uncommon in the New Testament, but common among non-Christian writers and also found in early Christian literature outside the New Testament. In this way, too, 2 Peter participates in a trend toward increased Hellenization of early Christianity. In vv. 8–11 the author supports his call for an abundantly virtuous life in terms much more familiar from Jewish wisdom discourse, though also found in other Hellenistic moral teaching.

Finally, 2 Peter describes the future benefits expected from God in Hellenistic terms, expressing apocalyptic discourse in Greek rather than Jewish terms. The author speaks of escaping from the corruption in the world and becoming sharers of divine nature. As we can see from the remainder of the letter, the author of 2 Peter uses this Hellenistic language to express the hope of escaping from the present evil age, which God will destroy, and participating in the new heaven and earth God will create after this destruction. This appears already in 1:3–11 to some extent in the reference to entering the eternal kingdom of Jesus Christ in v. 11.

UNIT 3: 2 PETER 1:12-15 OCCASION OF LETTER

Making It Possible to Remember Peter's Prophetic Teaching After His Death

12 Διὸ μελλήσω[89] ἀεὶ ὑμᾶς ὑπομιμνῄσκειν[90] περὶ τούτων[91] καίπερ εἰδότας καὶ ἐστηριγμένους ἐν τῇ παρούσῃ ἀληθείᾳ. 13 δίκαιον δὲ ἡγοῦμαι, ἐφ' ὅσον εἰμὶ ἐν τούτῳ τῷ σκηνώματι, διεγείρειν ὑμᾶς ἐν ὑπομνήσει,[92] 14 εἰδὼς ὅτι ταχινή ἐστιν ἡ ἀπόθεσις τοῦ σκηνώματός μου καθὼς καὶ ὁ κύριος ἡμῶν Ἰησοῦς Χριστὸς ἐδήλωσέν μοι, 15 σπουδάσω[93] δὲ καὶ ἑκάστοτε ἔχειν[94] ὑμᾶς μετὰ τὴν ἐμὴν ἔξοδον τὴν τούτων[95] μνήμην ποιεῖσθαι.

12 Therefore, I will always remind you about these things, although you know them and are established in the present truth. 13 But I consider it just, while I am in this tent, to arouse you by remembrance, 14 knowing that putting off my tent is imminent, as also our Lord Jesus Christ revealed to me, 15 and I will be eager for you also to be able always to make remembrance of these things after my departure.

---

89. There is some uncertainty whether the original text read Διὸ μελλήσω. This is the reading found in ℵ, A and B, but P[72] reads δι' ου μελησω. An υ has either fallen out of, or been added to, the original text. The latter may be more likely because of the number of witnesses that lack υ.

90. μελλήσω ... ὑπομιμνῄσκειν = ὑπομνήσω (cf. Matt 24:6)—Bigg, *St. Peter and St. Jude*, 263; Bauckham, *Jude, 2 Peter*, 195.

91. τούτων = 1:3–11.

92. Cf. διεγείρω ὑμῶν ἐν ὑπομνήσει (2 Pet 3:1).

93. Fut. of σπουδάζω.

94. ἔχειν with infinitive = to have the means to. The subject is ὑμᾶς.

95. As in 1:12 τούτων = 1:3–11.

Rhetography

The statement of the letter's occasion pictures Peter prophetically reminding the addressees of things they already know. He reminds them by writing this letter, and will always remind them because they will always be able to read or hear again what he has written. In this way Peter is pictured as writing the letter as a testament. He describes the addressees' knowledge as a matter of their being established in the present truth, depicting them as fixed firmly in the truth as though it were a place.

Peter reminds the addressees because he knows his death is imminent. He pictures his life as a matter of dwelling in a tent (v. 13), and his death as putting off the tent (v. 14). It is difficult to be sure of the exact referent of these metaphors. The tent might be an image of the body. In that case the author presents himself as about to end embodied life and begin a purely spiritual life apart from the body after death. On the other hand, the tent might be an image of life itself. In that case the author simply presents himself as about to end life by dying.[96]

Jesus has miraculously revealed the imminence of his death to Peter. This may evoke a picture of the conversation between Jesus and Peter in John 21 (especially vv. 18-19), or a less definite picture of this revelation. Peter speaks of his death as departure (ἔξοδον). This metaphor presents the author's death as a matter of going out of life as if it were a place one could leave. Presenting death as a departure makes opposite use of the imagery involved in speaking about entrance (εἴσοδος) into the eternal kingdom of Jesus (v. 11).

Textural Analysis

Intertexture. Bauckham argues that 1:12-15 has the form of a testament, a kind of writing known especially from Jewish literature.[97] Bauckham thinks 2 Bar. 78-86, Baruch's epistolary testament, and Josephus *Ant.* 4.309-19, Moses' last words, are particularly close parallels. The former text says in part:

> 78 Wherefore I have been the more careful to leave you the words of this epistle before I die, that you may be comforted regarding the evils which have come upon you. . . . Therefore,

---

96. On metaphors in 1:12-15 see Watson, *Invention*, 100. Other tropes and figures of speech in the passage are listed on p. 195.

97. Bauckham, *Jude, 2 Peter*, 194-203. See discussion of literary form under the heading Rhetography and Rhetology in the introduction to this book. Other examples of testaments can be seen in 1 Kgs 2:1-9 and Acts 20:17-38.

if you consider that ye have now suffered those things for your good, that you may not finally be condemned and tormented, then you will receive eternal hope; if above all you destroy from your heart vain error, on account of which you departed hence.

81 And the Mighty One did according to the multitude of His mercies,
And the Most High according to the greatness of His compassion,
And He revealed unto me the word, that I might receive consolation,
And He showed me visions that I should not again endure anguish,
And He made known to me the mystery of the times.
And the advent of the hours he showed me.

82 Therefore, my brethren, I have written to you, that you may comfort yourselves regarding the multitude of your tribulations. For know you that our Maker will assuredly avenge us on all our enemies, according to all that they have done to us, also that the consummation which the Most High will make is very nigh, and His mercy that is coming, and the consummation of His judgment, is by no means far off.

83 Let none therefore of these present things ascend into your hearts, but above all let us be expectant, because that which is promised to us shall come. And let us not now look unto the delights of the Gentiles in the present, but let us remember what has been promised to us in the end. For the ends of the times and of the seasons and whatsoever is with them shall assuredly pass by together. The consummation, moreover, of the age shall then show the great might of its ruler, when all things come to judgment.[98]

Bauckham identifies five conventional elements of the testament form:

1. The hero knows his death is approaching.

2. He wishes his teaching to be remembered after his death.[99]

3. An apocalyptic revelation is sometimes given the hero, forming the basis for predictions made in the testament.[100]

4. A testament could include predictions of the last times and of false teachers to appear then.[101]

---

98. Translation taken from Charles, *Apocrypha and Pseudepigrapha* 2:521–26.
99. Bauckham, *Jude, 2 Peter*, 194.
100. Ibid., 205.
101. Ibid., 237–38, 282.

5. Many testaments include ethical exhortations with eschatological sanctions.[102]

The first two of these elements appear in 1:12–15 as part of the author's presentation of the letter as the testament of Peter, i.e., a statement of Peter's teaching that makes it available after Peter's death. The other three elements appear elsewhere in 2 Peter. All of these conventions also appear in *2 Bar.* 78–86[103] and Josephus *Ant.* 4.309–19, but have a less apocalyptic character in the latter. Insofar as 1:12–15 and other sections of 2 Peter have the form of a testament, they imply that the author is in the situation outlined above. And insofar as the addressees of 2 Peter perceive this section and others as having the character of a testament, these passages evoke this situation in their minds.

Social-cultural texture: 1:12–15 continues to develop the values of *honor vs. shame* and the *patron-client relationship* presented earlier in the letter opening. Authoring a testament honors Peter as chief apostle and patriarch.[104] In his testament Peter functions as mediator of the patron-client relationship between God and the addressees.[105] He solicits recognition of himself as mediator of the patron.

Inner texture: Several terms mentioned earlier in 1:1–11 are *repeated* in 1:12–15 (see Appendix D). Other terms are introduced in 1:12–15 and repeated later in the letter (see Appendix E). Still other terms are introduced and repeated in 1:12–15, and in some cases also used later in the letter.[106]

In 1:12–15 the author resumes speaking about himself as he did when he identified himself as sender of the letter in 1:1. Since that time the author has referred to himself only as part of a group, using first person plural pronouns. In 1:12–15 the author uses first person singular pronouns three times; he also uses four first person singular verbs. He will not use first person singular verbs again until 3:1. He continues to use "you" to refer to the addressees.

---

102. Ibid., 323.

103. Items 1 and 2 are found in sections 78 and 82; item 3 in section 81; item 4 in sections 82–83; and item 5 in sections 78 and 83.

104. Neyrey, *2 Peter, Jude*, 164.

105. Ibid., 164–65.

106. ὑπομιμνῄσκειν (remind) in 1:12 has the cognates ὑπομνήσει (remembrance) in 1:13; 3:1 and μνήμην (remembrance) in 1:15; a verb cognate to the last of these, μνησθῆναι (to remember), is used in 3:2.
σκηνώματι (tent) is used in 1:13, 14.
μου (my) is used twice in 1:14 and again twice in 1:17; the cognate adjective ἐμήν (my) is used in 1:15.

The author *opens* (vv. 12–13) and *closes* the passage (v. 15) by saying that he is reminding the addressees; in the *middle* (v. 14) he speaks about what Jesus has revealed to him. He begins by saying that because of the benefits of doing so, he will always remind the addressees of the things he has just said. This reminder prevents the addressees from falling into forgetfulness, the danger described in v. 9. The author emphasizes that he is reminding them by repeating it three times, using the verb ὑπομιμνήσκω (remind—v. 12), the cognate noun (v. 13), and finally the noun without the prepositional prefix (v. 15). This is the figure of speech paronomasia and at the same time the trope periphrasis, since each uses several words to express an idea that could be expressed by a single word. In the author's final reference to reminding (v. 15), "remembrance" (μνήμην) is the object of a verb that comes last in the sentence, forming the figure of speech adjunction. All of this serves to underline the idea of reminding.

The author reminds them of these things "although you know them and are established in the present truth." In v. 3 the author had said that the addressees have full knowledge of Jesus; here he attributes to them knowledge of the need to grow in virtue for which he has just argued. He underlines this by using the same participle to refer both to their knowledge (εἰδότας—v. 12) and to his (v. 14). This use of the same participle in two different cases is transplacement. Their knowledge is also implicit in the description of what he is doing as reminding them.

Argumentative texture emerges as the author offers reasons for reminding the addressees. He first says that he considers it just (δίκαιον) to do so (v. 13). In this way he presents himself as exhibiting the same virtue he attributed to Jesus in v. 1. And he implies that he exhibits the virtues listed in vv. 5–7 with which he explicates the full meaning of justice. The author considers it just to remind the addressees while he is alive because he knows that his death is imminent.

The author knows that his death is imminent because "our Lord Jesus Christ has revealed it to me." He *repeats* ὁ κύριος ἡμῶν Ἰησοῦς Χριστός (our Lord Jesus Christ) from 1:8 as well as the name "Jesus" from 1:1 (twice), 2, and 11, the title "Christ" from 1:1 (twice) and 11, and the title "Lord" from 1:11.

The author says he will be eager (σπουδάσω) for the addressees to remember the things about which he reminds them, manifesting the eagerness to which he exhorted them in vv. 5 and 10. This letter will make it possible for the addressees to remember these things after the author's departure (ἔξοδον).

1:12–15 begins with an *enthymeme* formed by verses 3–12; verse 12 draws the conclusion from verses 3–11, and especially verses 10–11, that the author will always remind the addressees of what he has just said because of its benefit to them. The presence of this enthymeme is signaled by use of διό in v. 12. The argument can be restated:

> Knowing that one's call and election must be made secure by a virtuous life enables one to make them secure.
>
> Being reminded helps one to retain this knowledge.
>
> Therefore, the author will always remind the addressees.

Despite the author's use of this enthymeme, the *argumentative* force of 1:12–15 lies mainly in the author's further efforts to win the addressees' good will and receptivity to his message and in his further establishment of his own ethos.

The effort to win the addressees' good will can be seen in the author's statement that he reminds the addressees even though they already know the things about which he reminds them (v. 12). The use of the word "remind" in itself implies that the addressees already have this knowledge. The author, however, is not content with the implications of the word "remind," but also says explicitly that the addressees already know what he is telling them. He also says that they are established (ἐστηριγμένους) in the present truth. In all these ways the author minimizes resistance to his message by presenting it as something familiar, and also expresses the letter's theme that the addressees must maintain the status they already have. The addressees already possess full knowledge of God/Christ, but they need to maintain and increase it. Hence his reminder.

The author further establishes his ethos as Peter by presenting himself as writing a testament as his death approaches so that his teaching is available after his death. He also emphasizes this by his statement that Jesus has revealed to him that his death is imminent. In this way the author develops the basis on which the addressees should accept his message. In saying that he will always remind the addressees (v. 12), the author uses the verb μέλλω in the future tense. Because the verb itself has a future meaning, the use of the future tense of the verb is rare and would catch the reader's attention. It seems to have a meaning equivalent to that of the present tense as in Matt 24:6. Bauckham argues that in vv. 12 and 15 the future is used with reference to the present letter in view of its future function.[107] When the author says in v. 15 that he wants the addressees to be able to remember these things always, he uses the rare word ἑκάστοτε to mean always. These aspects of the passage underline the testamentary character of 2 Peter.

---

107. Bauckham, *Jude, 2 Peter*, 195.

Intertexture. In saying that Jesus has revealed the nearness of his death, the author may be evoking the picture described at the end of the gospel of John. John 21 describes Jesus' meeting with his disciples by the Sea of Tiberias after his death and resurrection. After a meal with the disciples, Jesus three times asked Peter if Peter loves Jesus, and Peter three times said that he does. Then in v. 18 Jesus said to Peter,

> Very truly, I tell you, when you were younger, you used to fasten your own belt and to go wherever you wished. But when you grow old, you will stretch out your hands, and someone else will fasten a belt around you and take you where you do not wish to go.

In v. 19 the evangelist comments that Jesus said this to indicate how Peter would die. The saying of Jesus in John 21:18 does not indicate the time of Peter's death very precisely, only that it will occur when he grows old. However, this is probably the basis on which the author of 2 Peter says that Jesus revealed to Peter that his death would be soon after the composition of 2 Peter.[108] If the addressees recognize an allusion to John 21:18, the words of the author would bring this picture to their minds. If they do not, the words would evoke a less specific picture of a revelation by Jesus to the author at some time.

Rhetorical Force

The author presents what he has said in 1:3–11, and what he will say in the remainder of the letter, as a reminder of things the addressees already know. In this way the author attempts to make the addressees receptive to his message. Although the addressees already know these things, the author sets them down in a letter so they can remember them after his death, something the author knows is imminent.

In thus presenting the occasion of the letter as the composition of an epistolary testament, the author presents his prophetic discourse in Jewish terms; the testament form was most developed among Jews. Of course, it has some parallels in Greco-Roman literature. According to William S. Kurz SJ the most elaborate example of a Greco-Roman testament is Plato's *Phaedo* especially its last pages (115–18).[109] This dialogue recounts Socrates' final

---

108. See Bauckham, *Jude, 2 Peter*, 200–201.

109. Kurz, "Luke 22:14–18 and Greco-Roman and Biblical Farewell Addresses," 253–55; cf. also Stauffer, "Abschiedsreden." MacDonald notes similarities between Paul's farewell to the Ephesian elders in Acts 20:17–38 and Hector's farewell to Andromache in *Iliad* 6 (MacDonald, "Paul's Farewell to the Ephesian Elders").

words to his friends and followers before he drank poison as ordered by the Athenian authorities. The other examples Kurz discusses are much briefer and focus on a memorable last saying of the dying person. The testament form is worked out much more fully in Jewish literature. Greco-Roman stories about someone who apparently died, experienced afterlife, and then returned to life to tell others about what he had seen provide another kind of parallel. Examples of this are the myth of Er in Plato's *Republic* (614B–21D) and the story of Thespesius told by Plutarch in *De sera numinis vindicta* 563B–68.[110] Such stories are not very similar to the testament found in Jewish literature except that both contain revelations about the future. Second Peter resembles Jewish literary testaments much more closely than it does any Greco-Roman parallels.

Use of the testament form in 2 Pet 1:12–15 alongside the author's presentation of the letter's message in the form of a decree in 1:3–11 shows the author's intention to combine Jewish with more broadly Hellenistic discourse. Tord Fornberg in *An Early Church in a Pluralistic Society* and Neyrey in *2 Peter, Jude* have called attention to this aspect of 2 Peter throughout the letter. Fornberg sums up the cultural situation represented by 2 Peter as one in which

> the Church is in the process of being grafted into the pluralistic and syncretistic society constituted by the Mediterranean world of late antiquity. The dependence on Judasim gradually declined. Instead a large proportion of the religious terminology of the Church was derived from her heathen environment, at the same time as the Christians were profoundly aware of being a "third race," set apart from Jews and heathen. The Church faced, and had to answer, new questions, but preserved her uniqueness without being absorbed by syncretism.[111]

Its composition as an epistolary testament accounts for 2 Peter's being written in Peter's name by someone other than Peter; testaments are always written in the name of some notable past figure by someone other than that person.

Appendix A: Terms Used in 1:1–2 and Repeated Later in 2 Peter

δοῦλος (slave—1:1) is also found in 2:19, as is the cognate verb δεδούλωται (to enslave) and the antonym ἐλευθερίαν (freedom).

---

110. On this see Kolenkow, "The Genre Testament."
111. Fornberg, *Early Church*, 124.

ἀπόστολος (apostle—1:1) is also found in 3:2.

ἰσότιμον (equal in honor—1:1) has the cognates τίμια (precious) in 1:4 and τιμήν (honor) in 1:17.

πίστιν (faith—1:1) is also found in 1:5.

δικαιοσύνη (justice—1:1) is also found in 2:5, 21; 3:13; the cognate δίκαιος (just) is found in 1:13; 2:7, 8; the antonym ἀδίκους (unjust) is found in 2:9; ἀδικούμενοι (being wronged) is found in 2:13; and ἀδικία (wrong-doing) is found in 2:13, 15.

σωτῆρος (savior—1:1) is also found in 1:11; 2:20; 3:2, 18; σωτηρίαν (salvation) is found in 3:15.

χάρις (favor—1:2) is also found in 3:18.

ὑμῖν (you—1:2) is also found in 1:5, 8, 10, 11, 12, 13, 15, 16, 19; 2:1, 3, 13; 3:1 (twice), 2, 8, 9, 11, 15, 17.

εἰρήνη (peace—1:2) is also found in 3:14.

ἐπιγνώσει (full knowledge—1:2) is also found in 1:3, 8; 2:20; ἐπιγινώσκω (to know fully) is found in 2:21 (twice); γνῶσις (knowledge) is found in 1:5, 6; 3:18; ἐγνωρίσαμεν (to make known) in 1:16; γινώσκω (to know) in 1:20; 3:3; the synonym οἶδα (to know) is found in 1:12, 14; 2:9; the antonym ἀγνοοῦσιν (being ignorant) is found in 2:12; the antonym ἀμαθεῖς (ignorant) is found in 3:16 .

κυρίου (lord—1:2) is also found in 1:8, 11, 14, 16; 2:9, 11, 20; 3:2, 8, 9, 10, 15, 18; κυριότητος (dominion) is also found in 2:10; the synonym δεσπότην (master) is found in 2:1.

Appendix B: Terms Introduced in 1:3-11 and Repeated Later in 2 Peter

δυνάμεως (power) is used in 1:3 and twice later in the letter (1:16; 2:11).

ἰδίᾳ (his) is used in 1:3 and six times later in the letter (1:20; 2:16, 22; 3:3, 16, 17).

δόξα (glory) is used in 1:3 and four times later in the letter (1:17 [twice]; 2:10; 3:18).

ἐπαγγέλματα (promises) is used in 1:4 and again in 3:13; the cognate ἐπαγγελία (promise) is use in 3:4, 8; the cognate verb ἐπαγγελλόμενοι (promising) is used in 2:19.

ἀποφυγόντες (having escaped) is used in 1:4 and twice later in the letter (2:18, 20).

κόσμῳ (world) is used in 1:4 and three times later in the letter (2:5, 20; 3:6).

ἐπιθυμία (desire) is used in 1:4 and three times later in the letter (2:10, 18; 3:3).

φθορᾶς (corruption) is used in 1:4 and three times later in the letter (2:12 [twice], 19); the cognate φθαρήσονται (to be corrupted) is also used in 2:12; the synonym ἀπώλεια (destruction) is used in 2:1 (twice), 3; 3:7; the cognate verb ἀπόλλυμι (to destroy) is used in 3:6, 9.

ἀγάπη (love) is used in 1:7 and the cognate ἀγαπητός (beloved) is used six times later in the letter (1:17; 3:1, 8, 14, 15, 17); the cognate verb ἠγάπησεν (to love) is used in 2:15.

ὑπάρχοντα (being) is used in 1:8 and twice later in the letter (2:19; 3:11).

ἀργούς (idle) is used in 1:8 and the cognate ἀργεῖ (to be idle) is used in 2:3.

λαβών (having received) is used in 1:9 and again in 1:17.

πάλαι (past) is used in 1:9 and the cognate ἔκπαλαι (long ago) is used in 2:3; 3:5.

ἁμαρτιῶν (sins) is used in 1:9 and 2:14; the cognate ἁμαρτησάντων (having sinned) is used in 2:4.

πάρεστιν (to be present) is used in 1:9 and again in 1:12.

διό (therefore) is used in 1:10 and twice later in the letter (1:12; 3:14).

βεβαίαν (secure) is used in 1:10 and again in 1:19.

ποτέ (ever) is used in 1:10 and again in 1:21.

οὕτως (thus) is used in 1:11 and twice later in the letter (3:4, 11).

εἴσοδος (entrance) is used in 1:11; the antonym ἔξοδος (departure) is used in 1:15; the cognate ὁδός (way) is used 2:2, 15 (twice), 21

αἰώνιον (eternal) is used in 1:11 and the cognate αἰῶνος (eternity) is used in 3:18.

Appendix C: Terms Introduced and Repeated in 1:3–11 and in Some Cases Repeated Later in 2 Peter

πάντα (all) is used in 1:3, 5 and five times later in the letter (1:20; 3:4, 9, 11, 16).

διά with genitive (through) is used in 1:3, 4 (twice) and twice later in the letter (3:5, 6)—διά with accusative (on account of) is also used in 2:2; 3:12.

θείας (divine) is used in 1:3, 4.

αὐτοῦ (his) is used in 1:3, 5, 9 and 26 times later in the letter (1:17, 18; 2:1, 2, 3, 8, 11, 12, 13, 19 [twice], 20, 21 [twice], 22; 3:3, 4, 5, 7, 10, 13, 14, 15, 16 [twice], 18).

εὐσέβειαν (piety) is used in 1:3, 6, 7 and again in 3:11; the cognate εὐσεβεῖς (pious) is found in 2:9; the antonym ἀσεβής (impious) is found in 2:5, 6; 3:7.

δεδωρημένης (has given) is used in 1:3, 4.

καλέσαντος (has called—1:3) has the cognate κλῆσιν (call) in 1:10.

ἀρετή (virtue) is used in 1:3, 5.

τούτων (these) is used in 1:4, 5, 8, 9, 10, and seventeen times later in the letter (1:12, 13, 15, 17, 18, 20; 2:12, 17, 19, 20; 3:1, 3, 5, 8, 11, 14, 16).

σπουδήν (eagerness) used in 1:5 has the cognate σπουδάσατε (to be eager) in 1:10; the latter is also found in 1:15; 3:14.

ἐπιχορηγήσατε (to supply) is used in 1:5, 11.

ἐγκράτεια (self-control) is used twice in 1:6.

ὑπομονή (endurance) is used twice in 1:6.

φιλαδελφίαν (brotherly love) is used twice in 1:7; the cognate ἀδελφοί (brothers) is used in 1:10 and again in 3:14.

γάρ (for) is used in 1:8, 9, 10, 11 and eleven times later in the letter (1:16, 17, 21; 2:4, 8, 18, 19, 20, 21; 3:4, 5).

ποεῖσθαι (to make) is used twice in 1:10 and twice later in the letter (1:15, 19).

Appendix D: Terms mentioned in 1:1–11 and repeated in 1:12–15

διό (therefore—1:12) was used earlier in 1:10.

ὑμᾶς (you—1:12, 13, 15) was used earlier in 1:5, 8, 10, 11.

τούτων (these—1:12, 13, 15) was used earlier in 1:4, 5, 8, 9, 10.

εἰδότας (know—1:12, 14) is synonymous with ἐπίγνωσις (full knowledge) mentioned earlier in 1:3, 8; and γνῶσις (knowledge) mentioned earlier in 1:5, 6.

παρούσῃ (present—1:12) was used earlier in 1:9.

δίκαιον (just—1:13) is a cognate of δικαιοσύνη (justice) used earlier in 1:1.

ὁ κύριος ἡμῶν Ἰησοῦς Χριστὸς (our Lord Jesus Christ—1:14) was used earlier in 1:8, and all of the elements of the phrase were used earlier additional times.

σπουδάσω (be eager—1:15) was used earlier in 1:10 and the cognate σπουδήν was used earlier in 1:5.

ἔξοδος (departure—1:15) is an antonym of εἴσοδος (entrance) used in 1:11.

ποιεῖσθαι (make—1:15) was used earlier in 1:10 twice.

Appendix E: Terms Introduced in 1:12–15 and Repeated Later in 2 Peter

μελλήσω (will) is used in 1:12 and again in 2:6.

ἐστηριγμένους (established) is used in 1:12; the cognate ἀστήρικτος (unstable) is used in 2:14; 3:16; the cognate στηριγμοῦ (firm footing) is used in 3:17.

ἀληθείᾳ (truth) is used in 1:12 and again in 2:2; the cognate adjective ἀληθοῦς (true) is used in 2:22.

ἡγοῦμαι (consider) is used in 1:13 and three times later in the letter (2:13; 3:9, 15).

διεγείρειν ὑμᾶς ἐν ὑπομνήσει (to arouse you by remembrance) in 1:13 is very similar to διεγείρω ὑμῶν ἐν ὑπομνήσει (I arouse in your remembrance) in 3:1.

ταχινή (imminent) is used in 1:14 and again in 2:1.

καθώς (as) is used in 1:14 and later in 3:15.

ἔχειν (have) is used in 1:15 and four times later in the letter (1:19; 2:14 [twice], 16).

Section 2: 2 Peter 1:16—2:10a

Letter Body, Part 1
Two Arguments that Jesus Will Come Again

The body of 2 Peter (i.e., 1:16—3:13) is divided into three parts: 1:16—2:10a presents two arguments that Jesus will come again; 2:10b-22 is a critique of those who deny this; and 3:1-13 restates the letter's occasion and argument. The first of these three parts is further divided into two unequal sections, i.e., 1:16-18 and 1:19—2:10a, each presenting an argument that Jesus will come again.

Within the basic prophetic framework established by 1:1-15, 2 Pet 1:16—2:10a is mainly apocalyptic discourse. However, just as other discourses are blended into the prophetic discourse of the former passage, in 2 Pet 1:16—2:10a apocalyptic discourse sometimes functions as a further framework within which other kinds of discourse are used in support of the apocalyptic discourse. In apocalyptic discourse the universe is seen as analogous to an empire ruled by God, from which God will soon eradicate evil and establish righteousness. The evil of the universe and God's control over it are not obvious, but are made known by means of a revelation that exposes the character of the universe and the divine plan for it. According to this plan, the history of the universe is divided into temporal segments leading inevitably to the culmination of that history. Apocalyptic revelation focuses on the place of those who receive the revelation in the unfolding history of the universe. In Christian apocalyptic discourse the final segment of time begins with the second coming of Christ.[1]

---

1. This description of the basic picture underlying apocalyptic discourse is drawn

UNIT 1: 2 PETER 1:16-18 FIRST ARGUMENT

Jesus' Transfiguration Shows that He Will Come Again

16 Οὐ γὰρ σεσοφισμένοις μύθοις ἐξακολουθήσαντες[2] ἐγνωρίσαμεν ὑμῖν τὴν τοῦ κυρίου ἡμῶν Ἰησοῦ Χριστοῦ δύναμιν καὶ παρουσίαν ἀλλ' ἐπόπται γενηθέντες[3] τῆς ἐκείνου μεγαλειότητος. 17 λαβὼν γὰρ παρὰ θεοῦ πατρὸς τιμὴν καὶ δόξαν φωνῆς ἐνεχθείσης αὐτῷ τοιᾶσδε[4] ὑπὸ τῆς μεγαλοπρεποῦς δόξης, ὁ υἱός μου ὁ ἀγαπητός μου οὗτός ἐστιν[5] εἰς ὃν ἐγὼ εὐδόκησα,[6] 18 καὶ ταύτην τὴν φωνὴν ἡμεῖς ἠκούσαμεν ἐξ οὐρανοῦ ἐνεχθεῖσαν σὺν αὐτῷ ὄντες ἐν τῷ ἁγίῳ ὄρει.

16 For it was not having followed cleverly devised myths that we made known to you the power and coming of our Lord Jesus Christ, but having been eyewitnesses of his majesty. 17 For having received honor and glory from God the father when a voice such as this was borne to him by the magnificent glory: "My son, my beloved, is this one, in whom I am well pleased." 18 And this voice we heard borne from heaven, being with him on the holy mountain.

Rhetography

The author begins 1:16-18 by rejecting the idea that his message derives from cleverly devised myths. This evokes, in order to reject, the picture of someone deliberately concocting the story that Jesus would come again. The author of 2 Peter might be envisioned as the creator of the myth, or he might be envisioned as having adopted the myth from its creator, either knowing that it was a concoction, or not. This rejected picture may derive from the false teachers whom the author opposes.

The author's message concerns the δύναμιν καὶ παρουσίαν[7] (power and coming) of Jesus. Reference to the παρουσία of Jesus evokes a picture of Jesus

---

from chapter 8 of Robbins, *Invention of Christian Discourse*.

2. ἐξακολουθήσαντες aorist ptc. ἐξακολουθέω, modifies implied subject of ἐγνωρίσαμεν.

3. γενηθέντες aorist ptc. γίγνομαι, modifies implied subject of ἐγνωρίσαμεν.

4. φωνῆς ἐνεχθείσης αὐτῷ τοιᾶσδε. Genitive absolute. ἐνεχθείσης aorist pass. ptc. φέρω. τοιᾶσδε (= such) fem. sg. gen., modifies φωνῆς.

5. ὁ υἱός μου ὁ ἀγαπητός μου οὗτός ἐστιν is the reading of v. 17 found in P[72] and B. Other texts such as ℵ and A read οὗτός ἐστιν ὁ υἱός μου ὁ ἀγαπητός, probably assimilating the text of 2 Peter to Matt 17:5.

6. Verse 17 is an anacolouthon, lacking a main clause. After a participial phrase and a genitive absolute, the author breaks off and begins a new sentence in 1:18.

7. The word means "presence" (cf. 1 Cor 16:17; 2 Cor 10:10; Phil 2:12) or "coming"

as the emissary of God who will return at some future time to establish God's reign.[8] The picture, however, is only mentioned, not described. Use of this term for the second coming of Jesus was already well-established among Christians when the author of 2 Peter used it.[9] Perhaps the author expects the word itself to evoke a detailed picture of the second coming of Jesus such as we find in passages like 1 Thess 4:15–17, which says that the Lord

> with a cry of command, with the archangel's call and with the sound of God's trumpet, will descend from heaven, and the dead in Christ will rise first. Then we who are alive, who are left, will be caught up in the clouds together with them to meet the Lord in the air.

In 2 Pet 1:16 the author refers to himself and others as ἐπόπται (eyewitnesses) of Jesus' majesty. This word was used for higher-level initiates into mystery cults, meaning that they had seen sacred things.[10] One example of this usage is found in Plutarch, *Alcibiades* 22.3. Plutarch says that Alcibiades was impeached for mimicking the Eleusinian mysteries in his own house and thus committing a crime against the goddesses Demeter and Kore whose mysteries they were. Alcibiades dressed up as hierophant and saluted his companions as μύστας . . . καὶ ἐπόπτας (initiates . . . and higher-level initiates). Insofar as the addressees of 2 Peter perceive this connotation of ἐπόπται, the word might cause them to visualize Peter and others as initiates into a mystery.

To support the truth of his message about the power and coming of Jesus, the author does not explicitly discuss this coming further. Instead he recounts the story told in Mark 9:2–8 and parallels, perhaps especially the version in Matt 17:1–8.[11] Jesus took Peter, James, and John with him up a

---

as the beginning of presence (cf. Jdt 10:18; 2 Macc 8:12; 15:21; 3 Macc 3:17; 2 Cor 7:6, 7; Phil 1:26).

8. Spicq (*Épitres de Saint Pierre*, 220) and Paulsen (*Zweite Petrusbrief*, 118) think that παρουσία here refers to Jesus' first coming rather than the second. Since the word clearly refers to Jesus' second coming in 2 Pet 3:4, it probably has the same meaning here.

9. Cf. Matt 24:3, 27, 37, 39; 1 Cor 15:23; 1 Thess 2:19; 3:13; 4:15; 5:23; 2 Thess 2:1, 8; Jas 5:7, 9; 1 John 2:28.

10. Kelly, *Peter and Jude*, 318; Fornberg, *Early Church*, 123; Bauckham, *Jude, 2 Peter*, 215; Green, *Jude & 2 Peter*, 220.

11. There is another extensive but rather different account of the transfiguration in the *Apocalypse of Peter*, as well as briefer accounts in *Acts of Peter*, 20; *Acts of Thomas*, 143; *Acts of John*, 90; and *Gospel of Philip* 58, 5–10; on these see Bauckham, *Jude, 2 Peter*, 212. As in 2 Peter, the accounts of the transfiguration in the *Apocalypse of Peter*

high mountain. There Jesus was transfigured, his face and clothing becoming white as light. Moses and Elijah appeared and talked to Jesus. A bright cloud overshadowed them, and a voice from the cloud said, "This is my beloved Son, with whom I am well pleased; listen to him."

The author of 2 Peter does not recount this story in detail. What he does say would call the story to the minds of those who knew it. Those unfamiliar with the story of Jesus' transfiguration would only be aware of what the author mentions explicitly. And even those who are familiar with the story would be most aware of the details that are specifically mentioned. The author emphasizes Peter and others' hearing of the words of a heavenly voice, evoking the mental image of the voice speaking and Peter and others hearing it.

The author of 2 Peter does not specify all who accompanied Jesus, only that he himself was present along with some others. Like the accounts in the synoptic gospels, the author mentions that he and the other witnesses of Jesus' transfiguration were on a mountain. However, he calls it the holy mountain, a detail not found in the synoptic transfiguration accounts. Bauckham argues persuasively that the reference to the "holy mountain" in v. 18 indicates that the author sees the words of v. 17 as an allusion to Ps 2:7.[12] If the addressees perceive the reference to Ps 2, it evokes another picture to be laid over the picture of Jesus' transfiguration. This is a picture of God's enthronement of the king of Israel on Mt. Zion.

The author of 2 Peter also explicitly mentions God's participation in the transfiguration, another detail absent from the synoptic accounts. The author says nothing about the witnesses' reaction to what happened or about the presence of Moses and Elijah. More significantly he mentions the transfiguration of Jesus only rather obliquely by saying that he, the author, and others were eyewitnesses of Jesus' majesty and that Jesus received honor and glory from God. This probably refers to the transformation of Jesus, i.e., something that was seen, but it is expressed in such general terms that it could simply be a reference to the words spoken by the voice. The visual dimension is indicated most directly by the author's references to glory. This glory could be visualized as a kind of radiance that passes from God, the magnificent glory, to Jesus. In Matthew's account of the transfiguration, Jesus' clothing became white as φῶς (light) and a φωτεινός (bright) cloud overshadowed Jesus. The author of 2 Peter might envision something like this and intend that the addressees do so.

---

and the *Acts of Peter* are given by Peter himself. These accounts are probably dependent on that of 2 Peter.

12. Bauckham, *Jude, 2 Peter*, 219–21.

In comparison with the synoptic gospels' account of Jesus' transfiguration, however, the author of 2 Peter lets the transformation of Jesus recede into the background of the story.[13] The visual element is apparently less important than the auditory element. The author explicitly reports the words of the voice, "My son, my beloved, is this one, in whom I am well pleased," and emphasizes that he and others heard it. This mental image of the voice speaking, and Peter and others hearing, is the most important aspect of the story for the author. To underline this he adds other details not found in the synoptic accounts. He twice mentions that the voice was borne to Jesus, the first time saying that it was borne by the magnificent glory (v. 17) and the second time that it was borne from heaven (v. 18). He also calls God "the father," which is appropriate because the words of the voice say that Jesus is the speaker's son. This presents Jesus and God as members of a family.

In calling to mind the story of Jesus' transfiguration this passage depicts God's miraculous transformation of the body of Jesus. In focusing on the words of the voice directed to Jesus, it is a precreation portrayal of Jesus' identification as the eternal son of the heavenly emperor. By serving as a revelation of the second coming of Jesus, it somehow pictures this apocalyptic event. This is the aspect of the story that is most important for the author.

Textural Analysis

Inner texture. Several terms mentioned earler in 1:1–15 are *repeated* in 1:16–18 (see Appendix A). Other terms are introduced in 1:16–18 and repeated later in the letter.[14] Still other terms are introduced and repeated in 1:16–18, and in some cases also used later in the letter.[15]

---

13. This is also true of the transfiguration account in the *Apocalypse of Peter*. In this account Moses and Elijah appear in a glorified form, but not Jesus. After the words of the heavenly voice about Jesus, Jesus, Moses, and Elijah are all taken into heaven. This account also refers to the mountain of transfiguration as the holy mountain and speaks of a voice from heaven, details mentioned by 2 Peter but not found in the synoptic transfiguration accounts. The opposite trend can be seen in the accounts of the transfiguration found in *Acts of Peter*, 20; *Acts of Thomas*, 143; *Acts of John*, 90; and *Gospel of Philip*, 58, 5–10; these do not report the words of the heavenly voice, but focus on the transformation of Jesus' appearance.

14. ἐξακολουθήσαντες (having followed) is used in 1:16 and repeated in 2:2, 15.
παρουσίαν (coming) is used in 1:16 and repeated in 3:4, 12.
πατρός (father) is used in 1:17 and repeated in 3:4.
οὐρανοῦ (heaven) is used in 1:18 and five times later in the letter (3:5, 7, 10, 12, 13).
ἁγίῳ (holy) is used in 1:18 and four times later in the letter (1:21; 2:21; 3:2, 11).

15. φωνῆς (voice) is used in 1:17 and 18 and again in 2:16.
ἐνεχθείσης (borne) is used in 1:17 and 18 and three times later in the letter (1:21 [twice]; 2:11).

Repetition of γάρ (for) in 1:16 and 17 signals the *argumentative* character of the passage. Use of γάρ in 1:16 indicates that 1:16–18, and particularly v. 16, explains why the author is eager for the addressees to make remembrance of these things, as he said in 1:15. 1:15–16 thus forms an enthymeme that can be restated:

> Reliable knowledge of the power and coming of Jesus should be kept in mind.
>
> The author did not follow cleverly devised myths in making known to the addressees the power and coming of Jesus.
>
> Therefore he is eager for the addressees always to be able to make remembrance of it.

This argument also makes it clear that an important element of 1:3–7, to which the author refers as "these things" in 1:8, 9, 10, 12, and 15, is the power and coming of Jesus, even though these words have not previously been used. The power and coming of Jesus is at least part of the content of the promises mentioned in 1:4. The author continues to emphasize the importance of knowledge and of Jesus, as he had in 1:1–15.

Other significant repetitions in this passage include the two references to glory in v. 17 and to the voice having been borne to Jesus in vv. 17 and 18. Verse 17 says that Jesus received honor and glory from God the Father and then refers to God as the majestic glory. The glory Jesus received from God was a participation in God's own glory. In 1:3 the author had said that Jesus called him and the addressees by means of his glory; now he informs them about the origin and character of that glory. Verses 17–18 first speak of the voice borne to Jesus by the majestic glory and then call it the voice borne from heaven. This repetition emphasizes the divine origin of the voice.

In 1:16–18 the author resumes the use of first person plural verbs and pronouns found in 1:1–11. In 1:12–15 the author used first person singular verbs and pronouns for himself except in v. 14, where the first person plural refers to author and addressees. In 1:16–18 the author uses first person plural to speak of himself and others, a group distinct from the addressees, as he had in 1:1. The author says he and others were eyewitnesses of Jesus' majesty and heard the voice from heaven. This suggests that the first person plural refers to Peter, James, and John, who witnessed Jesus' transfiguration according to the synoptic gospels (Mark 9:2–8 and parallels). However, when Jesus is called "our" Lord in v. 16, this first person plural includes author and addressees, as it did in 1:1, 2, 8, 11 and probably in 1:3, 4.

The central argument of this passage is that the author's teaching about the power and coming of Jesus is reliable because it rests on the eyewitness testimony of Peter and others. In making this argument the author also enhances his own ethos in presenting himself as an eyewitness of Jesus' transfiguration. Insofar as the addressees perceive this passage as the recitation of an authoritative text, namely the account of Jesus' transfiguration found in the synoptic gospels, it would also gain weight from the authority of the gospels.

Use of γάρ in 1:17 indicates that 1:17–18 supports the assertion that the author and others were eyewitnesses of Jesus' majesty (v. 16) by describing what they saw and heard.

The author implies that what Peter and others experienced when Jesus was transfigured was an experience of Jesus' power and coming.[16] The author's description of the transfiguration does not explicitly mention power; but seeing Jesus' majesty and his reception of honor and glory from God, and hearing the words of the voice, might reasonably be understood as an experience of his divine power. However, in order to be an experience of Jesus' coming, the transfiguration must have anticipated this future event.[17] Bauckham argues that the author of 2 Peter understands the transfiguration as Jesus' appointment by God to the role he will exercise at his second coming, in fulfilllment of Ps 2.[18] Knoch argues that the author understands the transfiguration, and especially the words of the voice, as God's testimony to the power of Jesus and thus the reliability of Jesus' promise to come again.[19]

Perhaps people have denied that Jesus will come again in glory on the basis that Jesus' earthly life was incompatible with such an expectation. If so, the story of Jesus' transfiguration might be an effective response.[20] Jesus' temporary transformation and the words of the voice reveal a dimension of Jesus ordinarily hidden. But even if the author is not responding to this specific objection, the revelation that Jesus is the eternal son of the Father supports the idea that he will come again because this reality has not yet been fully manifested in Jesus' words and deeds. If this is the truth about Jesus, it is reasonable to suppose that at some time he will be clearly and enduringly known by all to be God's son. Attending to the rhetography of this passage shows that the story focuses on God's declaration that the beloved

---

16. Paulsen (*Zweite Petrusbrief*, 120) simply sees the transfiguration of Jesus as a general legitimation of the author's message.

17. Neyrey, "Apologetic Use of the Transfiguration," 510–14; Davids, *2 Peter and Jude*, 202; Green, *Jude & 2 Peter*, 221.

18. Bauckham, *Jude, 2 Peter*, 219–20; so also Watson, *Invention*, 102; Davids, *2 Peter and Jude*, 203–6; cf. Vögtle, *Der Judasbrief/Der 2. Petrusbrief*, 164–65.

19. Knoch, *Erste und Zweite Petrusbrief*, 255.

20. This may also be the reason for including the story of Jesus' transfiguration in the synoptic gospels.

son of God, with whom God is well pleased, is Jesus. The argumentative power of the passage lies in this.

Intertexture. Watson, following Bauckham,[21] argues that 2 Pet 1:16–18 is independent of the synoptic accounts of the transfiguration. He regards the words of the voice in v. 17b as a reconfiguration of Ps 2:7 and Isa 42:1.[22] However, 2 Pet 1:17b is much closer to the words of the voice in the synoptic transfiguration accounts than to Ps 2:7 and Isa 42:1. This makes it seem more likely that 2 Pet 1:17b depends directly on the synoptic tradition and only indirectly on the Old Testament passages underlying it. If so, 2 Pet 1:16–18 is a *recitation* of Mark 9:2–8 and parallels in the author's own words. One part of this recitation, i.e., the words spoken by the voice in v. 17b, can be seen as replication of the exact words of the saying found in Matt 17:5 with one or more differences.[23] There are four differences: 1) οὗτός ἐστιν (this is) follows rather than precedes ὁ υἱός μου ὁ ἀγαπητός (my beloved son), 2) μου (my) is repeated after ἀγαπητός (beloved), 3) ἐν ᾧ has been replaced by εἰς ὃν (in whom), and 4) ἐγώ (I) has been added after εἰς ὃν (in whom).

2 Pet 1:17 ὁ υἱός μου ὁ ἀγαπητός μου οὗτός ἐστιν εἰς ὃν ἐγὼ εὐδόκησα

Matt 17:5 οὗτός ἐστιν ὁ υἱός μου ὁ ἀγαπητός, ἐν ᾧ εὐδόκησα

It is quite likely that 2 Pet 1:16–18 exhibits dependence on at least Matt 17:1–8.[24]

Social-cultural texture. When the author denies that the power and coming of Jesus derive from μύθοις (myths—v. 16), he uses a term common in first-century Greek literature. Sometimes it was used positively to mean stories that expressed truth in non-literal form. At other times it was used negatively, as here, to refer to stories that were false.[25] For example, in *Opif.* 2 Philo says that Moses did not begin his laws μύθους πλασάμενος (by fabricating myths) or adopting ones constructed by others. Similarly, in *Ant.* 1.22 Josephus contrasts Moses with other legislators who followed myths (μύθοις ἐξακολουθήσαντες). μῦθος is also used negatively in the Pastoral Epistles (1 Tim 1:4; 4:7; 2 Tim 4:4; Titus 1:14).

---

21. Bauckham, *Jude, 2 Peter*, 205–10; see also Paulsen, *Zweite Petrusbrief*, 118–19; Davids, *2 Peter and Jude*, 198–99.

22. Watson, "Apocalyptic Discourse," 199–200.

23. So also Gilmour, *Significance of Parallels*, 96–97.

24. Miller, "Independent Attestation?"

25. Windisch, *Katholischen Briefe*, 89; Spicq, *Les Épitres de Saint Pierre*, 218–19; Bauckham, *Jude, 2 Peter*, 213–14; Green, *Jude & 2 Peter*, 217–18.

96   Acknowledging the Divine Benefactor

Since the testament often includes a revelation given to the testator that forms the basis for the testator's teaching,[26] this section continues the presentation of 2 Peter as a testament of Peter. Insofar as the addressees perceive this, the section would cause them once again to visualize Peter as writing this letter shortly before his death to make his teaching available to people after he dies.

παρουσία (coming) is a term often used for the arrival of a divinity or a person of high rank, particularly kings and emperors.[27] For example, when in *Ant.* 9.51-59 Josephus tells the story found in 2 Kgs 6:8-23, he says that Elisha asked God to manifest τὴν αὐτοῦ δύναμιν καὶ παρουσίαν (his power and coming) to Elisha's servant in order to give the servant hope and courage since the Syrian army was lying in wait for Elisha. God then did what the prophet requested, causing the servant to see a multitude of chariots and horses surrounding Elisha (55). Another example: the city of Corinth issued coins to commemorate Nero's visit to Corinth in the year 67. One such coin had the head of Nero on one side encircled by the Latin inscription *Nero Cae[sar] Aug[ustus] Imp[erator]*. This coin had a Roman galley on the other side encircled by the inscription *P M Cleandro [IIVir] Qui[nquennali] Cor[inthi]* (P. M. Cleander being [duumvir] quinquennalis of Corinth) and with *Adve[ntus] Aug[usti]* (coming of Augustus) above the galley; *adventus* is the Latin translation of παρουσία.[28] Use of the word παρουσία pictures the return of Jesus as something similar to these events

In describing God as father the passage makes use of a conception of God widespread in both Jewish and Greco-Roman culture.[29] For example, Deut 32:6 asks the people of Israel concerning God, "Is he not your father, who created you, who made you and established you?" Another example: in Homer Zeus is called πατὴρ ἀνδρῶν τε θεῶν τε (father of both men and gods) (e.g., *Iliad* 1.544; 4.68) or simply πατήρ (father) (e.g., *Iliad* 4.235; 5.33).

Likewise, in having the voice imply that Jesus is the son of God, the passage makes use of the closely related idea that human beings can be called children of God.[30] Such presentation of Jesus as the son of God is very

---

26. Bauckham, *Jude, 2 Peter*, 205; Watson, *Invention*, 102; "Apocalyptic Discourse," 199; Vögtle, *Der Judasbrief/Der 2. Petrusbrief*, 164.

27. Schelkle, *Die Petrusbriefe*, 196 n. 2; Spicq, *Épitres de Saint Pierre*, 220; Green, *Jude & 2 Peter*, 220.

28. Head, *Catalogue of Greek Coins. Corinth*, 70 no. 567; 227 plate XVIII, no. 4; Smallwood, *Documents* 62.

29. See discussions of this in Moore, *Judaism*, 2:201-11; Schrenk and Quell, "πατηρ κτλ.," 951-59, 965-74, 978-82; Hengel, *The Son of God*, 21-56.

30. On this see Cullmann, *Christology*, 270-305; Hahn, *Titles of Jesus in Christology*, 279-346; Fuller, *Foundations of NT Christology*, 31-33; Hengel, *The Son of God*; Young,

common in other early Christian literature. In the Hebrew Scriptures "son of God" does not imply a special ontological relationship with God. "Son of" is an idiom in Semitic languages that expresses a range of relationships in addition to that of biological descent. "Son of God" indicates a relationship with God shared by many people, including the people of Israel as a whole, the king of Israel and the Messiah. An example of the first is found in Deut 14:1 where Moses says to the people of Israel, "You are sons of the Lord your God." An example of the second is found in 2 Sam 7:14. The prophet Nathan, speaking for God, says to David concerning his descendent, "I will be a father to him, and he will be a son to me." Thus, calling someone son of God in this context is not incompatible with Jewish monotheism.

However, in the Hellenistic world, "son of God" designated those who were seen as literal offspring of the gods. Because the Hellenistic world was polytheistic, those who were regarded as sons of gods were ordinarily said to be the son of some particular god. For example, in *Iliad* 1.9 Apollo is called Λητοῦς καὶ Διὸς υἱός (son of Leto and Dis = Zeus). In the first century, however, Roman emperors were simply called "son of god" meaning that they were the sons of their divinized predecessors. For example, an inscription found in Tarsus refers to Augustus as θεοῦ υἱόν (son of god).[31] And Roman emperors were frequently called sons of god on coins. On one side of a coin minted in Ephesus c. 28–20 BCE the head of Augustus is encircled by the Latin text *Imp[erator] Caesar Divi F[ilius] Cos VI Libertatis P[opuli] R[omani] Vindex* (Imperator Caesar, son of god, consul for the 6th time, defender of the liberty of the Roman people); *Divi filius* is a Latin equivalent of θεοῦ υἱός (son of god). On the other side of the coin is a figure of the goddess *Pax* (Peace) encircled by a laurel wreath. Second Peter may understand Jesus' being son of God along Hellenistic lines such as these.

The passage introduces the theme of *challenge and response*. The passage is a response to someone's challenging the honor of Jesus and Peter.[32] In this and other ways the passage continues to embody the value of *honor vs. shame*, as it does the *patron-client relationship* and *purity*. It imputes honor to Jesus, especially in referring to his power and coming, his majesty ,and his receiving honor and glory from God. It also imputes honor to God by referring to God as the majestic glory. And it imputes honor to Peter in defending what he made known to the addressees. It develops the patron-client relationship in defending Peter's mediation of the addressees' patron-

---

"Two Roots or a Tangled Mass;" Dunn, *Christology in the Making*, 13–22, especially 18–19; Callan, *Origins of Christian Faith*, 49–51.

31. Deissmann, *Bible Studies*, 167 n. 1.

32. Neyrey, *2 Peter, Jude*, 171–72 and elsewhere.

client relationship with God. And it develops the topic of purity in referring to the mountain on which the transfiguration occurred as holy.

Sacred texture. The way the author has told this story emphasizes the very close relationship between Jesus and God. The reference to the power of Jesus in 1:16 again evokes the picture of Jesus as possessing divine power from 1:3 and in turn the picture of Jesus as God from 1:1. The divinity of Jesus may be implied by use of the word παρουσία (coming—v. 16) since it was a term used for the epiphany of a god both in Hellenistic religion generally and in Hellenistic Judaism.[33] It may also be implied by use of the word ἐπόπται (eyewitnesses—v. 16) since it was a term used for initiates into mystery cults. Use of this word for the witnesses of Jesus' transfiguration may imply that they saw the divine Jesus.

The similarity between Jesus and God and the distinction between them is indicated somewhat obliquely in the paronomasia involved in speaking of Jesus' μεγαλειότητος (majesty—v. 16) and of God as the μεγαλοπρεποῦς (magnificent—v. 17) glory. The metonymy (and periphrasis) of referring to God as the magnificent glory suggests that this is the most prominent aspect of God at this point in the author's discourse. The statement that Jesus received glory from God who is the magnificent glory suggests that Jesus participates in God's own glory.

The close relationship between Jesus and God appears most of all in the presentation of God as the father who identifies his beloved son, in whom he is well pleased, as Jesus. Because the author has earlier called Jesus God (1:1) and spoken of him as having divine power (1:3), he probably understands Jesus as son of God in that he is ontologically related to God. As the son, however, he is distinct from the father; therefore the author distinguishes Jesus from God in 1:2. The author offers no further explanation of this.[34]

Rhetorical Force

What is most distinctive about this passage is use of the precreation portrayal of Jesus as the son of God, embedded in the miracle story of the transfiguration, as an argument for the apocalyptic expectation of the second coming of Jesus. As I suggested above, the author seems to suppose that if Jesus is the son of God, he must at some time clearly manifest himself as such. In this way, the christological status of Jesus is the foundation for eschatological expectation.

---

33. Kelly, *Peter and Jude*, 318.
34. On this see Callan, "Christology of the Second Letter of Peter," 253–63.

The author does not explicitly expound his understanding of Jesus or explain how it is the foundation for his eschatological expectations. The author clearly perceives the eschatological skepticism he opposes as based partly on the skeptics' view of Jesus, a view he also does not expound. He corrects their view, not by arguing against it explicitly, but by telling a story that presents his alternative view. It is the story of an occasion when he and others witnessed Jesus' majesty: God the father gave Jesus honor and glory by declaring that his beloved son, with whom God is well pleased, is Jesus. This is simultaneously theography, a vivid portrayal of God, and Christography, a vivid portrayal of Jesus. This story about Jesus displaces the skeptics' alternative story according to which the message about Jesus' power and coming is a myth. The vivid quality of the story and the need to reflect on its implications may make it more persuasive than a direct argument would be.

In addition to providing an alternative to the skeptics' view of Jesus, this story also provided an alternative to the many stories about sons of gods told in the Greco-Roman world. These include stories telling how gods such as Apollo and heroes such as Heracles were begotten by Zeus, and stories of Roman emperors such as Augustus as sons of their divine predecessors. Especially Jesus' followers would understand the story of his transfiguration as revealing him to be uniquely son of God and supplanting stories about others as sons of gods.

UNIT 2: 2 PETER 1:19—2:10A SECOND ARGUMENT

The Prophetic Word Shows that Jesus Will Come Again

A. Opening: 2 Peter 1:19–21

Thesis: The Prophetic Word Predicts the Second Coming of Jesus

19 καὶ ἔχομεν βεβαιότερον τὸν προφητικὸν λόγον, ᾧ καλῶς ποιεῖτε προσέχοντες ὡς λύχνῳ φαίνοντι ἐν αὐχμηρῷ τόπῳ, ἕως οὗ ἡμέρα διαυγάσῃ καὶ φωσφόρος ἀνατείλῃ, ἐν ταῖς καρδίαις ὑμῶν 20 τοῦτο πρῶτον γινώσκοντες ὅτι πᾶσα προφητεία γραφῆς[35] ἰδίας ἐπιλύσεως οὐ γίνεται· 21 οὐ γὰρ θελήματι

---

35. There is uncertainty whether the original text read προφητεία γραφῆς or προφητεία καὶ γραφή. The latter is found in P[72]; the former is found in all the other best manuscripts, i.e., ℵ, A, and B, making it the preferred reading.

ἀνθρώπου ἠνέχθη προφητεία ποτέ, ἀλλὰ ὑπὸ πνεύματος ἁγίου φερόμενοι ἐλάλησαν ἀπὸ θεοῦ[36] ἄνθρωποι.

19 And we have the more secure prophetic word, which you do well to heed like a lamp shining in a dark place until day dawns and the light-bearer rises, in your hearts 20 first knowing this, that all prophecy of Scripture is not of one's own explanation. 21 For prophecy was never borne by the will of a human being, but being borne by the Holy Spirit human beings spoke from God.

Rhetography

In 1:19–21 the author begins his appeal to the prophetic word as support for his apocalyptic message about the power and coming of Jesus. The author's appeal to the prophetic word evokes a picture of prophecy as it functioned in Israel. The reference to prophecy of Scripture (v. 20) makes it clear that the prophetic word is written, including the stories about prophets and records of their utterances written in the Jewish Scriptures. The addressees of 2 Peter know the prophetic word through these writings, not by means of direct contact with prophets. This evokes the picture of people studying and pondering the written records of the prophets.

The primary picture evoked by this appeal to the prophetic word is that of prophecy in Israel especially as it is included in the Jewish Scriptures. However, prophecy was also an element of the religion of Greece and Rome.[37] These words could also evoke a picture of prophecy as it functioned in this context.

The author of 2 Peter does not define or describe the prophetic word at all, except to mention that it is found in written form and derives from the Holy Spirit. He obviously presumes that the prophetic word is well known to those he addresses so that the picture his argument requires is summoned by the term alone.

In v. 19 he elicits acknowledgment of the prophetic word's value by picturing it as "like a lamp shining in a dark place until day dawns and the light-bearer rises." These words describe a lamp alight in a dark place, such as a house. It is dark because it is night. During the night the lamp is necessary to see, but it will no longer be necessary when day dawns. The author

---

36. There is uncertainty whether the original text of v. 21 read ἀπὸ θεοῦ or ἅγιοι θεοῦ. The former is found in P[72] and B; the latter in ℵ and A (with an article before θεοῦ). Perhaps the latter reading derived from the former when Π was mistaken for ΓΙ and another Ι inserted at the end of the word; see Metzger, *A Textual Commentary*, 632.

37. Neyrey, *2 Peter, Jude*, 180–81.

makes this simile more vivid by setting up an antithetical contrast between the shining lamp and the dark place and by using a rare word meaning "dark" (αὐχμηρός).

This sequence of events in an ordinary day corresponds to the sequence of events in the history of the world. The present is dark, like night. During this night, the prophetic word supplies light by predicting the power and coming of Jesus. This imagery reconfigures the history of prophecy in Israel into the apocalyptic view of history as composed of the present evil age and the age to come. During the darkness of the present age, the prophetic word predicts the dawn of the age to come.

The second coming of Jesus is pictured as the dawn of day and the rise of the light-bearer, a hendiadys using two terms to express a single reality. "Dawn" refers to the first lightening of the sky at the end of night. The rising of the light-bearer may refer to the appearance of the planet Venus in the sky, the morning star that heralds dawn. In that case, dawn and the rising of the light-bearer are mentioned in reverse of chronological order. Alternatively the rising of the light-bearer may refer to the appearance of the sun over the horizon just after dawn. In either case the light-bearer is a metaphor for Jesus.

In v. 20 the author evokes, in order to reject, a picture of scriptural prophecy as deriving from the prophets themselves, from their own explanation of the world.[38] This picture may be that of the author's opponents who use it as the basis for rejecting prophecy. In v. 21 the author develops in some detail an alternative picture of prophecy as deriving from the Holy Spirit. He says that prophecy does not derive from the will of human beings but occurs when human beings are carried by the Holy Spirit and thereby speak from God.

---

38. ἰδίας in v. 20 refers either to the prophet or to people in general, neither of which is explicitly mentioned in the sentence. Bigg and others argue that it refers to people in general and see the sentence as denying that one can give one's own interpretation to scriptural prophecy (Bigg, *St. Peter and St. Jude*, 269-70; so also Schelkle, *Die Petrusbriefe*, 201; Spicq, *Épitres de Saint Pierre*, 225; Kelly, *Peter and Jude*, 323-24). According to Bauckham (*Jude, 2 Peter*, 229) this is the view of most commentators; more recently Paulsen (*Zweite Petrusbrief*, 122-23) and Harrington ("Jude and 2 Peter," 257) have adopted this view. Bauckham argues that ἰδίας refers to the prophet; he sees the sentence as denying that scriptural prophecy derives from the prophet's own interpretation (Bauckham, *Jude, 2 Peter*, 229-33; so also Davids, *2 Peter and Jude*, 210-13; and Green, *Jude & 2 Peter*, 231-32). In light of the argument of the whole letter (see especially 3:16) reference to the prophet is more likely. The author sees his opponents as dismissing prophecy on the grounds that it is simply the words of the prophets themselves. If this did deny that one can give one's own interpretation to prophecy, it could be seen as the expression of a preference for group orientation over individualism (Neyrey, *2 Peter, Jude*, 181-82), and thus be an element of *social-cultural texture*.

Textural Analysis

Inner texture. 1:19–20 forms a somewhat *elaborate* sentence. The main clause is v. 19a. On this depends a relative clause (v. 19b). A temporal clause (v. 19c) depends on the relative clause, as does a participial phrase (v. 19d–20a). A noun clause (v. 20b) depends on the participial phrase. Like 1:3–7, 1:19–20 consists of four clauses, of which the last is the longest. Use of the ellipsis ἕως οὗ (until) in place of ἕως τοῦ χρόνου ᾧ (until the time when) makes the temporal clause (v. 19c) more compact. The paronomasia προφητικὸν (prophetic—v. 19a)—προφητεία (prophecy—v. 20) brings the conclusion of the period back to its starting point.

Most interpreters see ἐν ταῖς καρδίαις ὑμῶν (in your hearts) in v. 19 as modifying the preceding verb, i.e., they understand it as describing the rising of the light-bearer. On this interpretation the rising is pictured as something that happens in people's hearts. Mainly because this implies that the second coming of Jesus is at least partly an individual, subjective event, unlike the way it is regarded elsewhere in 2 Peter and other early Christian literature, I consider it more likely that the phrase modifies the following participle γινώσκοντες (knowing). The author visualizes the addressees' knowing the true character of prophecy as occurring in their hearts.[39]

Several terms mentioned earlier in 1:1–18 are *repeated* in 1:19–21 (see Appendix B). Other terms are introduced in 1:19–11 and repeated later in the letter (see Appendix C). Other terms are introduced and repeated in 1:19–21, and also used later in the letter.[40]

The author continues to speak of "we" and "you," using a first person plural verb in 1:19 along with a second person plural verb and a second person plural pronoun. This movement from "we" to "you" again allows the author to exhort the addressees as one who has something in common with them.

The thrice-*repeated* references to prophecy indicate that prophecy is the central topic of this short passage. In 1:19 the author supports his appeal to the prophetic word with an explicitly pictorial simile. The author implies that the prophetic word makes visible the future power and coming of Jesus by predicting it; thus expectation of Jesus' return is well founded. It is an even more secure *argument* than the transfiguration because it predicts the power and coming of Jesus more directly. The power and coming of Jesus

---

39. On this see Callan, "Note on 2 Peter 1:19–20," 143–50.

40. προφητικόν (prophetic) is used in 1:19; its cognate προφητεια (prophecy) is used in 1:20, 21; the cognate ψευδοπροφῆται (false prophets) is used in 2:1; the cognate προφήτης (prophet) is used in 2:16; 3:2.
ἀνθρώπου (human being) is used twice in 1:21 and again in 2:16; 3:7.

is not presently visible because it still lies in the future, but probably also because the character of the present world is contrary to the future that will begin with the power and coming of Jesus. The present is like night; the future will be like day. The power and coming of Jesus constitute the dawn of that day.

If the addressees regard the author's comparison of the prophetic word to a light shining in darkness as valid, their spontaneous recognition of the goodness and usefulness of light in the darkness is transferred to the prophetic word and the future it predicts. Likewise, if they regard the comparison of the second coming of Jesus to the coming of dawn and rise of the light-bearer as valid, the goodness and usefulness of dawn is transferred to the second coming of Jesus.

In 1:20–21 the author argues for the value of the prophetic word by presenting it as divine in origin. These verses constitute an *enthymeme* in which v. 21 supports the contention that prophecy is not of one's own interpretation (v. 20). The presence of the enthymeme is signaled by the use of γάρ in 1:21. The argument can be restated:

> Prophecy that derives from human will is of a prophet's own interpretation.
>
> Prophecy of Scripture was never borne by human will, but being borne by the Holy Spirit, prophets spoke from God.
>
> Therefore, prophecy of Scripture is not of a prophet's own interpretation.

In v. 21 the author repeats two key terms, "human being(s)" and "borne," in the two halves of the verse and in a chiastic pattern, i.e., first in the just-stated order and then in reverse order. The verse says that prophecy is not a matter of being borne by human will, but rather of being borne by the Holy Spirit; the repetition of "borne" emphasizes the rejection of one source of prophecy and the affirmation of another. "Borne" is used first in the aorist tense, then in the present tense. The former denies that prophecy ever arose from human will; the latter implies that while they were speaking from God, prophets were being borne by the Holy Spirit. In 1:17–18 the author says that the heavenly voice was "borne" to Jesus; use of the same word to speak of the origin of prophecy pictures prophecy as comparable to the voice borne to Jesus. Just as the voice was borne to Jesus, so prophets, when they speak from God, are borne by the Holy Spirit. By mentioning "human being" at the beginning and the end of v. 21 the author rounds off the sentence by ending where he began. This repetition makes clear the precise participation of human beings in prophecy. Although prophecy does not derive from the will of a human being, it does involve human beings who spoke from God.

The author's portrayal of prophecy as deriving from the Holy Spirit, picturing prophets as speaking under the impetus of the Holy Spirit, is implicitly an argument for its reliability. Explicitly it is an attempt to show that prophecy is not of one's own explanation. This is probably intended to reject the idea that the words of prophets can be dismissed as deriving from themselves. The author uses the nature of prophecy as an argument against a view of prophecy that minimizes its support for the author's apocalyptic expectations.

Intertexture. Watson argues that 1:19 is a *recitation* with modification of Num 24:17.[41] 1:19 probably at least alludes to this passage. Neyrey argues that 1:19 refers instead to Greco-Roman astrological thinking; Venus precedes, and in a certain sense brings, the sun, and so is properly called light-bearer.[42]

In 1:19–21 the author does not cite any prophecies of Jesus' return; he will be more specific about this in 2:4–10a. He presumes that these prophecies exist and invokes the reliability of the institution of prophecy to support belief in the second coming of Jesus. Insofar as one recognizes that God truly has sent prophets to the people of Israel to guide them, one accepts the reliability of what they said, now written down in the Bible.

It seems probable from 2 Pet 2:4–10a that the prophetic word is partly found in Genesis. Thus, the author seems to view the entire Bible as prophetic, not just those parts that concern people explicitly called prophets.[43] This is confirmed by 2 Pet 3:1–13. Here the author again implies that Genesis is prophetic, but also implies that prophecy is found in Psalms, the letters of Paul, Isaiah, and quite possibly other parts of the Bible. The author seems to view the entire Bible as having been produced by prophetic activity.

Social-cultural texture. 1:19–21 begins the author's second *riposte* to his opponents' *challenge* to his *honor* and that of Jesus. The challenge is the assertion that the message about the power and coming of Jesus was a cleverly devised myth.

The author responds by appealing to the prophetic word which he also calls prophecy of Scripture (v. 20) and describes as coming from God through humans borne by the Holy Spirit (v. 21). Stories about prophets and records of their utterances make up a large percentage of the Jewish

---

41. Watson, "Apocalyptic Discourse," 200.

42. Neyrey, *2 Peter, Jude*, 183–84.

43. Kelly, *Peter and Jude*, 321; Bauckham, *Jude, 2 Peter*, 224; Davids, *2 Peter and Jude*, 207–8; Green, *Jude & 2 Peter*, 227.

Scriptures. This material shows how prophecy functioned among the Jews. From time to time God called certain individuals to be prophets, that is people who speak for God, and sent them to call the rest of the people back to fidelity to God (see, e.g., Isa 6; Jer 1). The prophet Amos describes his call to be a prophet thus (Amos 7:14-15):

> I am no prophet, nor a prophet's son; but I am a herdsman, and a dresser of sycamore trees, and the Lord took me from following the flock, and the Lord said to me, "Go, prophesy to my people Israel."

These prophets did not act on their own, but were moved by the Holy Spirit. The Holy Spirit fell on the prophets and impelled them to actions they would and could not take by themselves (e.g., 1 Sam 10:5-6, 10-13). Prophets were most numerous during the time of the monarchy in Israel (c. 1000-500 BCE). By the time 2 Peter was written the prophetic word was available mainly in the Jewish Scriptures.

Prophecy was also part of Greco-Roman culture. For example, one might think of the priestess of Apollo at Delphi, who was known as a prophet, or of the prophets who proclaimed her words. In *De Pythiae Oraculis* 397 B–C Plutarch says about the priestesses that Apollo

> supplies the origin of the incitement, and then τῶν προφητίδων (the prophetesses) are moved each in accordance with her natural faculties. . . . the voice is not that of a god, nor the utterance of it, nor the diction, nor the meter, but all these are the woman's; he provides only the visions and puts a light in her soul in regard to the future.

Utterances of the Delphic oracle were written down in various places. In general, however, it would have been much more difficult to find written records of Greco-Roman prophecy than of Jewish prophecy. Those for whom 2 Peter's words evoked the picture of Greco-Roman prophecy would understand the author's main point, i.e., the divine origin of prophecy. However, 2 Peter's references to prophecy of Scripture and, even more, to the Holy Spirit as the source of prophecy, mean that prophecy at Delphi does not match the circumstances presumed in 2 Peter as closely as does prophecy in Israel, and that the latter is probably the picture intended by the author.

Sacred texture. Second Peter 1:21 contains the one reference to the Holy Spirit in 2 Peter. Its statement that guided by the Holy Spirit humans spoke from God suggests a near identity between the Holy Spirit and God, but also distinguishes them from one another. This is parallel to the way the relationship between Jesus and God is presented in 2 Peter.

Rhetorical Force

1:19-21 begins the author's argument that the prophetic discourse of the Jewish Scriptures promises the apocalyptic second coming of Jesus. The view that apocalyptic expectations were the fulfillment of prophecy is basic to all apocalyptic discourse. The specific expectation of a second coming of Jesus is found only in Christian apocalyptic discourse. The author's opponents apparently reject the validity of this discourse.

The presentation of the prophetic word as a light shining in darkness emphasizes the clarity of the prophetic word. Apocalyptic discourse often acknowledges the obscurity of prophecy even as it claims to know the true meaning of prophecy. For example, in Dan 9, Daniel perceives in the book of Jeremiah that seventy years must be fulfilled for the devastation of Jerusalem (v. 2, referring to Jer 25:11-12; 29:10). Daniel prays for an answer (v. 3), presumably to the meaning of this prophecy, and later receives one (vv. 21-27). Greek and Roman prophecy were also frequently obscure. By contrast with both, the author here emphasizes the clear meaning of prophecy and does not advert to any ambiguity in it. The picture of the prophetic word as a light shining in darkness until day dawns vividly conveys the clarity of prophecy.

B. Middle 2 Peter 2:1-3

The Prophetic Word Predicts the Rise of False Teachers

1 Ἐγένοντο δὲ καὶ ψευδοπροφῆται ἐν τῷ λαῷ, ὡς καὶ ἐν ὑμῖν ἔσονται ψευδοδιδάσκαλοι, οἵτινες παρεισάξουσιν αἱρέσεις[44] ἀπωλείας[45] καὶ τὸν ἀγοράσαντα αὐτοὺς δεσπότην ἀρνούμενοι, ἐπάγοντες ἑαυτοῖς ταχινὴν ἀπώλειαν. 2 καὶ πολλοὶ ἐξακολουθήσουσιν αὐτῶν ταῖς ἀσελγείαις δι' οὓς[46] ἡ ὁδὸς τῆς ἀληθείας βλασφημηθήσεται. 3 καὶ ἐν πλεονεξίᾳ πλαστοῖς λόγοις ὑμᾶς ἐμπορεύσονται, οἷς τὸ κρίμα ἔκπαλαι οὐκ ἀργεῖ καὶ ἡ ἀπώλεια αὐτῶν οὐ νυστάζει.

---

44. This word means "school" or "sect;" here it seems to mean the opinion of a school or sect (Bigg, *St. Peter and St. Jude*, 271-72; Bauckham, *Jude, 2 Peter*, 239-40). The plural is problematic because the word ordinarily refers collectively to all the views of a given group, not, as here, to the various views of a single group. The plural may indicate that the author alludes to traditional apocalyptic warnings, e.g., Justin, *Dial.* 35.3 (Bauckham, *Jude, 2 Peter*, 240).

45. αἱρέσεις ἀπωλείας is a Semitism, i.e., use of a noun in the genitive case in place of an adjective (Bigg, *St. Peter and St. Jude*, 272; Spicq, *Épitres de Saint Pierre*, 229).

46. The antecedent is πολλοί (Bigg, *St. Peter and St. Jude*, 273).

1 But there were also false prophets among the people, as among you there will also be false teachers, who will secretly introduce heresies of destruction, even denying the master who purchased them, bringing on themselves imminent destruction. 2 And many will follow their licentiousnesses, because of whom the way of truth will be slandered. 3 And in their greed they will buy you with counterfeit words, whose judgment long ago is not idle and their destruction does not sleep.

Rhetography

In 2:1–3 the author speaks of the existence of false prophets among the people in order to predict the future arrival of false teachers among the addressees. The author elaborates the picture of prophecy in Israel that he evoked in 1:19–21 by saying that there were false prophets among the people as well as true prophets. It was not always clear which of the people who claimed to be prophets, or were thought to be prophets, were in fact prophets.

This picture of the false prophets corresponds to that of the false teachers. Teaching does not evoke as specific a concrete situation as does prophecy. In speaking of prophecy, the author refers mainly to a past activity that is described in some detail in the Jewish Scriptures. But in speaking of false teaching, the author refers to a present, or even future, activity that is nowhere described in detail. We do not know exactly when, where, and how these other teachers taught; thus the picture evoked by the reference to false teachers is somewhat ill defined as far as we can see. Peter's main point is that they and their teaching are false and that they will be destroyed in the eschatological judgment that is coming soon. The images evoked by these descriptions are clear.

Peter's description of the false teachers, their doctrine, and their destiny evokes a kaleidoscope of pictures, each flashing briefly before the minds of the addressees before being replaced by another. These pictures portray the faults of the false teachers and promise that the false teachers will be destroyed. Implicitly the appearance of the false teachers is part of apocalyptic expectation. This becomes explicit in 2 Pet 3:1–4.

The false teachers are described as secretly introducing their teaching; they hide its true character so that it will be accepted. Its true character is that it leads to destruction, but they conceal this. Implicitly their teaching is a denial of the master who bought them. This pictures Jesus as someone who has bought the false teachers as slaves from their former owner and is now himself their owner. Jesus is a like a householder, or perhaps the owner of an enterprise such as a farm or a mine, who owns slaves who work for him. This picture is emphasized by the antonomasia of using the epithet δεσπότης (master) in place of the name of Jesus. Lying behind this picture of Jesus as the purchaser of the false teachers is probably another picture of Jesus as having paid the purchase price by his own death.

The false teachers are pictured as licentious, referring especially to sexual misconduct. Many are pictured as imitating their licentiousness, and because of this others are described as slandering the followers of Jesus. Following Jesus is described as the way of truth, picturing it as a road that leads human beings to their proper destination. When those who claim to walk on the way of truth follow the licentiousnesses of the false teachers, those who observe this will slander the way of truth, presumably by saying that it leads to licentiousness. The image of the road was invoked earlier in 1:11 and 15.

The false teachers are also described as greedy, i.e., loving money excessively. In this instance it is probably used in a transferred sense, referring to the false teachers' zeal to gain control over the addressees. Because of their greed, the false teachers will use counterfeit words to buy[47] the addressees. Speaking of the false teachers as buying the addresses pictures them as shoppers who use their false teaching to acquire the addressees as possessions.

The judgment of the false teachers that was handed down long ago and their destruction are personified. Judgment and destruction are pictured as sentient beings who might be idle or asleep, but are not. As with other pictures rejected by the author of 2 Peter, this one may derive from the false teachers.

Textural Analysis

Intertexture. Beginning in 2:1 and extending through 3:3, 2 Peter *recontextualizes* Jude 4–18 (see Introduction). Jude is largely a critique of its opponents' immoral behavior.[48] The author of 2 Peter adapted Jude to serve as an *argument* against the teaching of his opponents as well as their behavior. When he adapted Jude, the author of 2 Peter also converted Jude's critique of a group presently confronting its addressees into criticism of a group predicted to confront the addressees of 2 Peter in the future. This may have

---

47. ἐμπορεύομαι is used with this meaning in Philo *Sacr.* 28. Most interpreters understand it as meaning something like "exploit" and see it as referring to literal greed; so Bauckham, *Jude, 2 Peter*, 243; Davids, *2 Peter and Jude*, 224; Green, *Jude & 2 Peter*, 245.

48. For descriptions of the purpose of Jude see Bauckham, *Jude, 2 Peter*, 11–13; Watson, *Invention*, 29–30; Neyrey, *2 Peter, Jude*, 31–32; Thurén, "Hey Jude!."

been required by the testamentary character of 2 Peter. Converting Jude's material into a prediction was mainly a matter of changing the aorist of Jude 4 into future tense in 2 Pet 2:1–3.

Second Peter 2:1–3 recontextualizes Jude 4(–5). In addition to changing its tense, the author of 2 Peter made other changes in Jude 4 (and 5) when adapting it in 2:1–3. His first change was to preface his condemnation of future opponents, the false teachers, by recalling that false prophets arose among the people, i.e., the people of Israel. This reference to false prophets created a chiastic relationship between 2 Pet 2:1–3 and 1:16–21. The false prophets of 2:1a correspond to the true prophets mentioned in 1:19–21; the false teachers of 2:1b–3 correspond to the apostolic teachers mentioned in 1:16–18.[49]

The author of 2 Peter also recast the main clause and final participial phrase of Jude 4 in 2 Pet 2:1; he refashioned the second participial phrase from Jude 4 in 2 Pet 2:2; and he rewrote the first participial phrase from Jude 4 in 2 Pet 2:3. Jude 5 may have suggested 2 Peter's reference to the people of Israel in 2:1 and its three references to destruction of the false teachers in 2:1, 3. Second Peter's revision of Jude served to connect the material adapted from Jude with the earlier part of 2 Peter, to predict the coming of false teachers, and to introduce the main things for which 2 Peter criticizes them.

The reference to false prophets among the people of Israel (v. 1) might remind the addressees of the occasional presentation of conflicting claims to be true prophets in the Jewish Scriptures. For example, 1 Kgs 22:5–28 recounts how Jehoshaphat, king of Judah, and Ahab, king of Israel, consulted prophets before attacking Aram. Many prophets predicted that they would be victorious, but Micaiah said this prediction was false; their attack would result in disaster for them. Ahab imprisoned Micaiah until he would return from the campaign in peace. Micaiah said, "If you return in peace, the Lord has not spoken by me" (v. 28). Cf. also Jer 28.

The following reference to false teachers seems to imply the existence of true teachers. There are other references in the New Testament to teachers among the early Christians: Acts 13:1; 1 Cor 12:28–29; Eph 4:11; Jas 3:1. In New Testament usage the word "teacher" designates one who indicates the way of God from the Torah to a group of students.[50] This includes repetition of the teaching of Jesus, proof from the Torah that Jesus is the Messiah, and deriving directions for Christian living from the Torah.[51] Eph 4:11 suggests

---

49. Bauckham, *Jude, 2 Peter*, 236; Watson, *Invention*, 106.
50. Rengstorf, "διδάσκω κτλ.," 153.
51. Ibid., 144–48.

that teaching is the responsibility of the pastor or leader of the community. Thus the false teachers mentioned in 2 Peter may be pictured as leaders of the community whose teaching does not correctly indicate the way of God to the members of their community.

Social-cultural texture. Since the testament often includes predictions of the last times, in New Testament examples including the appearance of false teachers,[52] this section continues the presentation of 2 Peter as a testament of Peter. Insofar as the addressees perceive this, the section would cause them once again to visualize Peter as writing this letter shortly before his death to make his teaching available to people after his death.

Inner texture. Several terms used in chapter 1 are repeated in 2:1–3 (see Appendix D). Other terms are introduced in 2:1–3 and used later in the letter.[53] Other terms are introduced and repeated in 2:1–3.[54]

The first chapter of 2 Peter was marked by alternation between "I" or "we" and "you." 2:1–3 is marked by alternation between "you" (2:1, 3) and "they" (2:1, 2, 3) as the author begins to warn the addressees against the false teachers.

The author of 2 Peter creates a literary parallel between the false prophets in Israel and the false teachers among the addressees in a number of ways. One of these is the repetition of ψευδο creating the paronomasia ψευδοπροφῆται (false prophets)—ψευδοδιδάσκαλοι (false teachers); the latter seems to have been newly coined by the author. In addition, the first two clauses of 2:1, which mention the false prophets and teachers, have almost the same number of syllables (isocolon). These two clauses are also arranged chiastically, with the prepositional phrase last in the first clause and first in the second.

The false teachers' secret introduction of their teaching leads them to destruction. The relationship between the two things is emphasized by the three-fold repetition of ἀπώλεια (twice in 2:1 and once in 2:3) in three different cases (polyptoton): their teaching is destructive and brings destruction upon them; this destruction does not sleep. It is also emphasized by the

---

52. Bauckham, *Jude, 2 Peter*, 237–38; Watson, *Invention*, 107; "Apocalyptic Discourse," 201.

53. ἐπάγοντες (bring on—2:1) is used later in 2:5.
ἀσελγείαις (lictentiousnesses—2:2) is used later in 2:7, 18.
βλασφημηθήσεται (slander—2:2) is used later in 2:10, 12; the cognate βλάσφημον (slanderous) is used in 2:11.
πλεονεξίᾳ (greed—2:3) is used later in 2:14.
κρίμα (judgment—2:3) is cognate to κρίσις (judgment) used four times later in the letter (2:4, 9, 11; 3:7) and to κατέκρινεν (to condemn) used in 2:6.

54. ψευδο (false) is an element of two different words in 2:1.
ἀγοράσαντα (purchase—2:1) is a synonym of ἐμπορεύσονται (to buy) used in 2:3.

paronomasia παρεισάξουσιν (secretly introduce)—ἐπάγοντες (bringing on), both compounds of the verb ἄγω (bring). Implicitly their teaching denies the master who bought them.

Sacred texture. The picture of Jesus as the master who bought the false teachers is quickly replaced by other pictures. However, it is notable as 2 Peter's most direct portrayal of the way Jesus functions as savior, a role frequently attributed to him by 2 Peter (see 1:1, 11; 2:20; 3:2, 18). Jesus saves by purchasing his followers from those to whom they are enslaved. Such purchase, a very common occurrence in the ancient world, is mentioned for example in Eccl 2:7 where Qoheleth says, "I bought male and female slaves." Purchase by Jesus might refer to setting free enslaved persons by purchase, something known both from the Old Testament (cf. Lev 25:47–55) and from Greek literature (cf. Diodorus Siculus *Hist.* 15.7.1; 36.2.2 and 1 Pet 1:18–19).[55] The sacral manumission practiced at Delphi is a particular form of freeing by purchase that might underlie 2 Peter; at Delphi Apollo purchased slaves for freedom.[56] However, for two reasons it is more likely that 2 Pet 2:1 refers to transferring ownership of slaves from one master to another. One is the use of the term δεσπότης (master) for Jesus, suggesting that Jesus is the new owner of his followers. The other is the verb ἀγοράζω (purchase), connoting purchase in the market. Paul uses this term in a similar way in 1 Cor 6:19-20. On the other hand, when Paul speaks of manumission in Gal 3:13; 4:5, he uses ἐξαγοράζω (set free).[57] Diodorus Siculus also uses ἐξαγοράζω in 15.7.1; 36.2.2. Thus 2 Peter probably presumes that Jesus has purchased his followers from their previous owner, and they have become Jesus' slaves. In line with this, the author of 2 Peter refers to himself as slave and apostle of Jesus Christ in 1:1. Like Paul, the author thinks it is better to be Jesus' slave than that of any other master, cf. Rom 6:16–23; 1 Cor 7:22–23.

Second Peter does not indicate how Jesus made this purchase. Rev 14:4 also uses the language of purchase without explaining how the purchase was made, and 1 Cor 6:20; 7:23 says only that a price was paid. Rev 5:9 says that the purchase price was the blood of Jesus. This may be presumed wherever the language of purchase is used. If so, the author of 2 Peter regards Jesus' death as the price he paid to buy his followers from their previous owner and make them his own slaves. Second Peter 2:1 does not specify the previous owner from whom Jesus purchased his followers. However, 2:19–20

---

55. Both the LXX of Lev 25:47–55 and 1 Pet 1:18–19 use the word λυτρόω.

56. On manumission of slaves see Bartchy, *Mallon Chresai,* 87–125. If this did refer to sacral manumission, it would be an element of *social-cultural texture.*

57. On this see Marshall, "Development of the Concept of Redemption," 156–57, especially n. 8.

implies that before being purchased by Jesus, his followers were slaves of corruption and the defilements of the world.

Inner texture. Returning to the pictures evoked by 2:2-3, we see that the false teachers are characterized by licentiousness and greed. Many will imitate their licentiousness, bringing the followers of Jesus into disrepute. In their greed, the false teachers will use counterfeit words to buy the addressees. The synonyms ἀγοράσαντα (purchase) and ἐμπορεύσονται (buy) are used in 2:1 and 3 respectively to express Jesus' saving activity and the false teachers' reversal of it via the same metaphor, i.e., that of purchase. Jesus saved by purchasing people from their former owner; the false teachers undo this salvation by purchasing people from Jesus. The relationship between others' slander of the way of truth and the false teachers' purchase of the addressees is emphasized by the homoeoteleuton of ending the last clause of 2:2 and the first clause of 2:3 with the same syllable (βλασφημηθήσεται [slander] in 2:2 and ἐμπορεύσονται [buy] in 2:3).

The judgment of the false teachers that was handed down long ago is not idle. The verb ἀργεῖ (is idle) is cognate to the adjective used in 1:8 to describe those who follow the author's exhortation as not idle, i.e., ἀργούς. Both those who act in accordance with the author's teaching and the judgment of those who do not are envisioned as not being idle. The synonymous character of the last two clauses of 2:3b is emphasized by two of their literary features. The two clauses have almost the same number of syllables (isocolon), and each of the clauses ends with a special verb creating the figure of speech disjunction.

The *argumentative* force of 2:1-3 may first of all be typological. The false prophets of the past are a type of the false teachers to come.[58] Secondly, the future appearance of false teachers and their destruction may be understood as a partial explication of the prophetic word's content. And finally, the author implies that the teachers are false because they incorrectly dismiss the prophecies of Jesus' second coming, not acknowledging the understanding of prophecy the author has articulated in 1:19-21.

Calling the teachers false implies an argument that they do not present reliable teaching. This argument is also expressed in the reference to their use of counterfeit words. The content of their false teaching is indicated by the statement that they deny the master who purchased them; they deny the second coming of Jesus.[59] The false teachers may also assert that escha-

---

58. Knoch, *Erste und Zweite Petrusbrief*, 259; Paulsen, *Zweite Petrusbrief*, 126.

59. Fornberg, *Early Church*, 36. Watson (*Invention*, 174) and Neyrey (*2 Peter, Jude*, 188-89) agree that the false teachers deny Jesus by denying his second coming. Bauckham argues that the opponents deny Jesus by teaching and practicing immorality (*Jude, 2 Peter*, 241; so also Davids, *2 Peter and Jude*, 221). Kelly thinks their denial took both

tological judgment is idle and the destruction consequent upon it sleeps, two things that the author of 2 Peter denies. The description of the false teachers as licentious and greedy attributes general moral failings to them. Likewise, those who follow them are licentious and bring the way of truth into disrepute. All of these descriptions undermine the false teachers' ethos and attempt to arouse the addressees' pathos against them, i.e., emotions of repugnance toward the false teachers, leading to rejection of them. The author of 2 Peter further develops this kind of argument in 2:10b–22.

Finally, the prediction that the false teachers will be destroyed in the future provides a basis for rejecting them. Insofar as the addressees accept destruction as the false teachers' destiny, they have reason not to follow them.

Insofar as the addressees of 2 Peter regard Jude as an authoritative text and perceive this section as dependent on it, the authority of Jude would accrue to 2 Peter.

Social-cultural texture. In speaking of the master who bought the false teachers, the author of 2 Peter again refers to the *social roles* of master and slave. In purchasing them Jesus also became their *patron*.[60] Speaking of the false teachers' purchase of the addressees may imply that the false teachers become their masters and patrons.

Denial of the master (2:1) *dishonors* him; reviling dishonors the way of truth (2:2).[61] The charge that the false teachers make use of counterfeit words (2:3) echoes the idea, rejected in 1:16, that the author of 2 Peter followed cleverly devised myths. As was noted above, the idea that the author followed cleverly devised myths may derive from the false teachers. If so, the author here charges them with a similar failing, offering a *riposte* to the *challenge* of 1:16.[62] The author accuses the false teachers of *impurity* by referring to their introduction of ruinous doctrines (2:1),[63] to their licentiousness (2:2), and to their greed (2:3).[64]

Accusations of licentiousness and greed were conventional elements of the Hellenistic polemical rhetoric used in disputes between rival philosophical schools, Jews and Gentiles, and rival groups of Jews.[65] Accusations

---

forms (*Peter and Jude*, 320).

60. Neyrey, *2 Peter, Jude*, 192.
61. Ibid., 189–90.
62. Ibid., 193.
63. Ibid., 190.
64. Ibid., 192.
65. On this see Johnson, "The New Testament's Anti-Jewish Polemic." On page 432, n. 47 Johnson lists love of pleasure, love of money, and love of glory as vices attributed to any opponent. See also du Toit, "Vilification," 408–9.

of being false, acting secretly, being a corrupting influence, slandering, and being liable to judgment were likewise conventional in early Christian polemical literature.[66] Thus almost all the elements of 2:1–3 may be conventional rather than particular to a specific situation.

Ideological social-cultural texture. The use of conventional vituperation[67] of the false teachers by the author of 2 Peter suggests that 2:1–3 derives from rivalry between the author and the false teachers for recognition as authentic leaders of the Christian movement. It also suggests that these accusations may not simply reflect the false teachers' behavior, but are mainly intended to communicate the author's negative evaluation of them, i.e., that they are false. The purpose is not to describe the false teachers, but to persuade the addressees to reject them. The author does this by presenting the false teachers in completely negative terms, making the choice between him and them clear and simple. As Andrie du Toit says, "Ideological literature works with contrasts; it does not seek the neutral middle-field. It creates heroes and villains."[68]

Rhetorical Force

In 2:1–3 the author continues his argument that the prophetic discourse of the Jewish Scriptures promises the apocalyptic second coming of Jesus by saying that false teachers will appear before Jesus comes again. These false teachers are like the false prophets that appeared in Israel. They and those who follow them will be destroyed when Jesus returns to destroy all evil. Therefore those who reject 2 Peter's interpretation of biblical prophecy are themselves a fulfillment of it and should themselves be rejected.

Similar views are expressed in Acts 20:29–30; 2 Tim 3:1–5; 4:3–4. This seems to reflect a development of apocalyptic discourse among Christians in which those who reject such discourse have been incorporated into it.

As we have seen, the negative portrayal of the false teachers in 2:1–3 is highly conventional. It would have been recognized by all segments of the Hellenistic world as the way in which one criticizes one's opponents.

C. Closing 2 Peter 2:4–10a

Prophecies of the Second Coming of Jesus

---

66. For this see du Toit, "Vilification," 405–10.
67. On this see Green, *Jude & 2 Peter*, 20–22.
68. du Toit, "Vilification," 411.

4 Εἰ γὰρ ὁ θεὸς ἀγγέλων ἁμαρτησάντων οὐκ ἐφείσατο ἀλλὰ σειραῖς[69] ζόφου ταρταρώσας παρέδωκεν εἰς κρίσιν τηρουμένους, 5 καὶ ἀρχαίου κόσμου οὐκ ἐφείσατο ἀλλὰ ὄγδοον Νῶε δικαιοσύνης κήρυκα ἐφύλαξεν κατακλυσμὸν κόσμῳ ἀσεβῶν ἐπάξας, 6 καὶ πόλεις Σοδόμων καὶ Γομόρρας τεφρώσας [καταστροφῇ][70] κατέκρινεν ὑπόδειγμα μελλόντων ἀσεβέ[σ]ιν[71] τεθεικώς, 7 καὶ δίκαιον Λὼτ καταπονούμενον ὑπὸ τῆς τῶν ἀθέσμων ἐν ἀσελγείᾳ ἀναστροφῆς ἐρρύσατο· 8 βλέμματι γὰρ καὶ ἀκοῇ ὁ δίκαιος ἐγκατοικῶν ἐν αὐτοῖς ἡμέραν ἐξ ἡμέρας ψυχὴν δικαίαν ἀνόμοις ἔργοις ἐβασάνιζεν· 9 οἶδεν κύριος εὐσεβεῖς ἐκ πειρασμοῦ ῥύεσθαι, ἀδίκους δὲ εἰς ἡμέραν κρίσεως κολαζομένους τηρεῖν, 10 μάλιστα δὲ τοὺς ὀπίσω σαρκὸς ἐν ἐπιθυμίᾳ μιασμοῦ πορευομένους καὶ κυριότητος καταφρονοῦντας.

4 For if God did not spare the angels who sinned but, having cast them into Tartarus, delivered them to chains of gloom, kept for judgment; 5 and if he did not spare the ancient world but guarded Noah, as an eighth, the herald of justice, having brought a deluge on the world of the impious; 6 and if he condemned the cities of Sodom and Gomorrah, having reduced them to ashes in a catastrophe, having made them an example of the things about to happen to the impious, 7 and he rescued just Lot, worn out by his life amidst the licentiousness of the lawless 8 for by means of seeing and hearing the just man dwelling among them day after day tortured his just soul with respect to their lawless works; 9 then the Lord knows how to rescue the pious from trial and how to keep the unjust confined for the day of judgment, 10 and especially those who go after the flesh in desire for defilement and despise dominion.

---

69. There is considerable uncertainty whether the original text of v. 4 read σειραῖς or σιροῖς. The former is found in P[72]; the latter in ℵ, A, and B. Fornberg argues that the latter is most likely to be original and further argues that σιροῖς is "religious vocabulary originally derived from the Eleusinian Mysteries" (Fornberg, *Early Church*, 53). Metzger argues that the latter is a correction of the former (Metzger, *A Textual Commentary*, 632). If Fornberg were correct, this would be an element of *social-cultural texture*.

70. There is considerable uncertainty whether the original text of v. 6 included καταστροφῇ or not. It is lacking in P[72] and B, and found in ℵ and A. Because καταστροφῇ and κατέκρινεν begin with the same three letters, the eye of the transcriber might have skipped to the second word, causing its omission (Metzger, *A Textual Commentary*, 632). The uncertainty about the original text in this case is indicated by the brackets that enclose καταστροφῇ.

71. There is similar uncertainty whether the original text of v. 6 read ἀσεβέσιν or ἀσεβεῖν. A σ has either been added to the text or fallen out of it. The σ is found in P[72] and B, and lacking in ℵ and A. The uncertainty about the original text in this case is indicated by the brackets that enclose the σ.

Rhetography

The author of 2 Peter now shows how the prophetic word predicts the apocalyptic power and coming of Jesus. He describes three occasions when the prophetic word says that God miraculously judged evildoers and, on two of these occasions, also rescued the upright. Because the prophetic word presents the past activity of God in this way, the author reasons that God obviously knows how to act in this way and presumably will do so in the future. He then describes God's characteristic activity as rescue of the pious and confinement of the unjust. The three descriptions of God's past activity and the description of God's typical activity each present God as judging creation. Taken together they present a vivid and detailed picture of God and God's activities, i.e., theography. Because the three past occasions when God judged the world inform the author's picture of God's future judgment, the entire passage can be seen as eschatography, a vivid picture of the end time.

Although the author of 2 Peter does not explicitly present them this way, the three past occasions he describes are often used in apocalyptic discourse to indicate some of the periods into which history has been divided by God.[72] This sequence of historical periods culminates in the end of the world.

The author's descriptions of these three occasions refer to stories told in the Jewish Scriptures. What we said above about the author's reference to the story of Jesus' transfiguration also applies to these references. These references would call the biblical stories to the minds of those who knew them. Those unfamiliar with the stories would only be aware of the features of the stories that the author mentions specifically. And even those familiar with the stories would be most aware of the details that are explicitly mentioned. Since the author uses the stories as instances of the prophetic word's prediction of the power and coming of Jesus, he probably presumes at least a general awareness that they are found in the Jewish Scriptures.

The first occasion was God's judgment of the sinful angels, probably referring to the story in Gen 6:1-4 in which the sons of God marry human women. The author evokes the picture of angels leaving their proper place in heaven and consorting with human women on earth. However, the author of 2 Peter says only that the angels sinned. If the addressees do not recognize the story to which this alludes, the picture presented is simply that of angels doing something wrong. Although the author does not describe the angels'

---

72. Sinful angels: *1 En.* 86-88; *2 Bar.* 56.10-14; Jude 6. Noah and the flood: *1 En.* 89.1-8; 93.4; *2 Bar.* 56.15-16; Matt 24:37-39/Luke 17:26-27. Sodom and Gomorrah: Matt 10:15/Luke 10:12; Luke 17:28-30, 32; Jude 7.

sin in any detail, he is more specific about their punishment. In consequence of their sin, God consigned the angels to Tartarus where they await final judgment, kept in chains of gloom. The author makes this vivid by using the rare word ταρταρόω (cast into Tartarus) and the metaphor "chains of gloom." The latter presents the angels as confined by darkness itself.

The second occasion was God's judgment of the world in the time of Noah, referring to the story told in Gen 6:5—9:29. Because of the wickedness of the human race God decided to destroy all the people and animals God had created. God told Noah to build an ark for himself, his wife, his three sons, and their wives, and two of every kind of animal. When Noah had built the ark and all its passengers were aboard, God sent a flood on the earth that blotted out every other living thing. When the floodwaters receded, God made a covenant with Noah and his descendants. In referring to the story of Noah, the author of 2 Peter mentions few details explicitly. He says only that God brought a deluge on the world of the impious, but guarded Noah, as one of eight, from that deluge. He describes Noah as a "herald of justice," picturing Noah as speaking out against the wickedness of his generation.

The third occasion was God's destruction of Sodom and Gomorrah after sending the righteous Lot out of Sodom. This refers to the story told in Gen 18–19. Because of Sodom and Gomorrah's bad reputation, God decided to investigate these cities and destroy them if they were as wicked as their reputation. Their reputation proved to be true, so God rained fire and brimstone on them and destroyed them, after first bringing Lot, his wife, and his daughters out to safety. Once again when the author of 2 Peter refers to the picture found in the biblical story, he mentions few details. He says only that God condemned Sodom and Gomorrah, reducing them to ashes in a catastrophe, and rescued Lot.

The author of 2 Peter emphasizes that Lot was oppressed by life among the wicked people of Sodom. The author pictures Lot as a just man who was afflicted by his life among the lawless. The author elaborates this by saying that this just man tortured his just soul day after day by what he saw[73] and heard living among them, evoking a mental image of Lot as seeing and hearing things. The expression "day after day" is the trope synechdoche, making the reader realize the whole from a part. It has the effect of emphasizing that Lot's suffering was constant. As the author evokes the picture of Lot as suffering from his contact with the wicked, he also summons a picture of the wicked as lawless and, specifically, licentious, i.e., sexually unrestrained. The biblical

---

73. Βλέμμα often means "appearance" but it denotes the activity of looking in Philo *Conf.* 11; *Contempl.* 77; *Spec.* 3.8; and *Virt.* 40.

account refers to the people of the cities as wicked in general. What most clearly indicates that their wickedness was sexual is the story of how the men of Sodom tried to force Lot to hand his guests over to them (Gen 19:4-11). The author of 2 Peter implies that this sort of thing happened repeatedly.

The author concludes from these three occasions that God knows how to rescue the pious and how to keep the unjust confined for the day of judgment. This conclusion is informed by the three occasions, and so the depictions of God's saving and punishing activity on these occasions are presumed in the conclusion. The conclusion itself, however, does not again describe this activity; it simply says that God knows how to do these things.

The author does provide some additional description of the unjust in his conclusion, indicating the nature of their injustice. He presents them as especially those who go after the flesh in desire for defilement and despise dominion. This description of the unjust also applies to the author's three descriptions of God's past activity, implying that the sinful angels, the generation of the flood, and the inhabitants of Sodom and Gomorrah were also guilty of these things. It is clear how the angels who married human women and the inhabitants of Sodom who wanted sexual relations with Lot's guests went after the flesh in desire for defilement; it can easily be supposed to apply to the generation of the flood. All despised dominion in at least the sense that they did not accept God as their Lord.

Not only does the conclusion use less pictorial language than the description of the three occasions, it is also a strikingly oblique demonstration of the author's thesis. The author concludes only that the prophetic word shows that God knows how to rescue the pious and punish the unjust, not that God will do so, though that is clearly presumed. At this point the author also refrains from any description of how God will do this. Both the direct assertion that God will bring the world to an end and the description of it are reserved for chapter 3.

Textural Analysis

Inner texture. Like 1:3-7, 2:4-10a is a conditional sentence, of which vv. 4-8 form the protasis and vv. 9-10a the apodosis.[74] Verses 4-7 consist of three parallel conditional clauses; the last is followed by a parenthetical explanatory clause in v. 8. In vv. 9-10a two infinitives depend on the main verb; the object of the second infinitive is modified by two participial phrases.

---

74. Gerdmar sees 2:4-7 as a protasis that lacks an apodosis (*Rethinking*, 33). Bigg (*St. Peter and St. Jude*, 274), Bauckham (*Jude, 2 Peter*, 253), Davids (*2 Peter and Jude*, 225) and Green (*Jude & 2 Peter*, 248) understand the syntax of 2:4-10a as I do above.

If the parenthetical clause in v. 8 is not counted, 2:4–10a consists of four clauses, of which the last is the longest. Each of the four clauses presents an antithesis, something especially appropriate for a period.[75] After 1:3–7 this is the most polished sentence in 2 Peter.

As is implied by the introductory γάρ (for), 2:4–10a supports the denial in 2:3b that the judgment of the false teachers is idle and their destruction is asleep. Thus it continues the apocalyptic discourse of 2:1–3. The *argument* is an induction from a series of examples.

> God has punished sinners in instance 'a'
>
> God has punished sinners and saved the righteous in instance 'b'
>
> God has punished sinners and saved the righteous in instance 'c'
>
> Therefore, God knows how to save the righteous and punish sinners.

All of these instances are found in Scripture; thus they explain how the prophetic word supports the author's presentation of the power and coming of Jesus. The argumentative force of the section derives from the succession of three pictures leading to the conclusion expressed in vv. 9–10a. These pictures are presented as parallel to one another and so as establishing a pattern of divine action on which the conclusion is based.

Several terms used in earlier in 2 Peter are *repeated* in 2:4–10a (see Appendix E). Other terms are introduced in 2:4–10a and used later in the letter (see Appendix F). Other terms are introduced and repeated in 2:4–10a, and in one case also used later in the letter.[76]

The parallelism of the three clauses in vv. 4, 5, and 6–7 is emphasized by various instances of repetition and *progression*. The first two conditional clauses, in vv. 4 and 5, each have two main verbs coordinated by ἀλλά (but). The third conditional clause, in vv. 6–7, also has two main verbs coordinated by καί (and). The second and third conditional clauses are linked to the first with καί. The first two conditional clauses are linked by use of the phrase οὐκ ἐφείσατο (did not spare) that ends the first clause of v. 4 and the first clause of v. 5; this constitutes epiphora and at the same time homoeoptoton, since the two verbs have the same ending. The second and third conditional clauses are linked by repetition of ἀσεβής (impious) in vv. 5–6 in two different cases (polyptoton). They are also linked by instances of paronomasia in vv. 5–7, namely, κατακλυσμὸν (deluge)—[καταστροφῇ] (catastrophe)—κατέκρινεν (condemned)—καταπονούμενον (worn out), [καταστροφῇ]—ἀναστροφῆς

---

75. Cf. Aristotle, *Rhetoric* 3.9.7–8; Demetrius, *On Style*, 22–24.

76. οὐκ ἐφείσατο (did not spare) is used in 2:4 and 5.
τηρουμένους (kept) is used in 2:4 and 9 and again in 2:17; 3:7.
ἐρρύσατο (save) is used in 2:7 and 9.

(life), and ἀσεβέ[σ]ιν (impious)—ἀθέσμων (lawless)—ἀσελγείᾳ (licentiousness). The third conditional clause and the parenthesis are linked by use of δίκαιος (just) and ἡμέρα (day) in different cases in vv. 7–8 (polyptoton).

The three conditional clauses present a chronological progression of events. They also represent a progression in the character of the events. The first clause (v. 4) refers only to God's punishment of the sinful. The second and third clauses (vv. 5 and 6–7) refer not only to this, but also to salvation of the righteous. The third clause is followed by a parenthetical clause (v. 8) that elaborates the description of the situation from which Lot was saved. Thus there is an increasing emphasis on salvation of the righteous.

There is also a noteworthy parallel between the three conditional clauses and the conclusion in vv. 9–10a; this helps establish that the conclusion truly follows from the conditional clauses.[77] The second and third conditional clauses are the basis for the conclusion that "the Lord knows how to rescue the pious from trial;" the verb ῥύεσθαι (rescue) is used in both v. 7 and v. 9 (transplacement). The first conditional clause is the basis for the conclusion that the Lord also knows how εἰς ἡμέραν κρίσεως κολαζομένους τηρεῖν (to keep confined for the day of judgment), since the sinful angels are explicitly said to be εἰς κρίσιν τηρουμένους (kept for judgment) in v. 4.[78] There is thus a chiastic relationship between the three conditional clauses and the conclusion; the author first draws a conclusion from the second and third clauses and then from the first clause. This brings the entire period back to its starting point. The author also sees the second part of the conclusion as based on the second and third conditional clauses, however. This is explicit in the comment that what happened to Sodom and Gomorrah was an example of what will happen to the impious. The author's explicit reference to the licentiousness of Sodom and Gomorrah grounds the conclusion that the unjust that God especially knows how to confine for the day of judgment are those who go after the flesh in desire for defilement.

Virtually all interpreters understand κολαζομένους to mean "being punished" and discuss whether it refers to punishment that occurs on the day of judgment, or punishment that precedes it.[79] Although "punish" is the most common meaning of κολάζω, in this context I understand the word

---

77. There are also links between the parenthetical clause (v. 8) and the conclusion. Verses 8 and 9 are linked by the paronomasia δίκαιος—ἀδίκους and the figure of speech adjunction, i.e., the verb comes at the end of v. 8 and at the beginning of v. 9.

78. In order to create this parallel, the author may describe God's treatment of the unjust too narrowly. While God kept the sinful angels for judgment, this does not seem to describe God's treatment of the generation of the flood or Sodom and Gomorrah; nor does it seem to describe what will happen at the end according to 3:10–12.

79. See for example Bauckham, *Jude, 2 Peter*, 253–54.

as meaning "restrain" or "confine." Plutarch uses the word this way when he says it is a great achievement for someone τὰ μοχθηρὰ καὶ ἀγεννῆ καὶ πανοῦργα πάθη κολάζειν καὶ ταπεινὰ ποῖειν (to repress and put down base, ignoble, and knavish propensities—*Moralia* 91D).[80] Understood this way, κολαζομένους expands the meaning of τηρεῖν (to keep), somewhat as the phrase ἡμέραν κρίσεως (day of judgment) expands the meaning of κρίσιν (judgment).

The author implies that the false teachers of 2:1–3 are among the unjust whom the Lord knows how to keep confined for the day of judgment by repeating some of the terms used to describe the false teachers. 2:7 mentions the licentiousness of the inhabitants of Sodom, and in 2:10a the unjust are further described as "especially those who go after the flesh in desire for defilement and despise dominion." These echo the references in 2:2 to the licentiousness of the false teachers, and in 2:1 to the denial of their master. In saying that they "despise dominion" the author refers to their eschatological skepticism and consequent ethical laxity; they doubt that God (and Jesus?) will act as Lord by bringing the world to an end, and do not now acknowledge God (and Jesus?) as Lord by their way of life.

In this section the author *elaborates* the importance of the virtue of justice. In 1:1 he spoke of the justice of "our God and savior Jesus Christ," and in 1:13 he described himself as just. In this section he calls Noah the herald of justice (v. 5), describes Lot as just (vv. 7–8), and speaks of those who will be punished as unjust (v. 9).

Insofar as the addressees of 2 Peter regard the Jewish Scriptures and the letter of Jude as authoritative texts and perceive 2:4–10a as dependent on them, the authority of these texts would accrue to 2 Peter.

Intertexture. Second Peter 2:4–10a *recontextualizes* Jude 5–8a. Passing over Jude 5,[81] 2 Peter incorporated Jude 6–8a into the long conditional sentence described above. The author of 2 Peter fashioned the historical precedents cited in Jude 6–7 into two conditional clauses (vv. 4, 6–7), and added a third clause of his own (v. 5). In this way 2 Peter created a list of precedents to support the conclusion that God both punishes the unrighteous and rescues the godly. Second Peter used the first part of Jude 8 to describe the unrighteousness of the false teachers it opposes.

The author begins by describing God's judgment of the sinful angels. This probably refers to the story in Gen 6:1–4 about sons of God marrying

80. For other examples see Plutarch *Moralia* 89C; 452C; 1008B; Plato *Gorgias* 491E; and possibly Philo *Jos.* 220; Acts 4:21.

81. Perhaps he does this partly in order to replace an example drawn from the history of Israel, i.e., the Exodus generation, with one having more directly universal significance, i.e., the story of Noah.

human women. This story does not say that the sons of God were angels, or that their marriage to human women was sinful, or that God punished them for it, though the second of these may be implied by Gen 6:5. However, when 1 *Enoch* retells the story, it includes all three elements; the first can be seen in 1 *En.* 6.2; 10.7, the second and third in 12.4–6. These three elements are also included in Jude 6 on which the author of 2 Peter depends at this point: "And the angels who did not keep their own position, but left their proper dwelling, [God] has kept in eternal chains in deepest darkness for the judgment of the great Day." Here the second element, the sin of the angels, is indicated somewhat obliquely as a matter of leaving their proper place.

The author goes on to describe God's judgment of the world in the time of Noah, alluding to the story told in Gen 6:5—9:29. In referring to the story of Noah, the author of 2 Peter mentions few details. The author does not say that God guarded Noah by means of an ark, nor does he say anything about animals or a covenant. He does, however, include one detail not found in the biblical account, namely the description of Noah as a "herald of justice." Although this detail is not part of the biblical account, it is found in other versions of the story of Noah. Josephus says that the angels who consorted with human women begot children who were disdainful of all good (*Ant.* 1.73). Noah urged them to come to a better understanding and to change their actions (74). Josephus then observes that God loved Noah for his justice (75).

Finally the author describes God's destruction of Sodom and Gomorrah after sending the righteous Lot out of Sodom. This evokes the story told in Gen 18–19. Once again when the author of 2 Peter refers to the picture found in the biblical story (and in Jude 7 on which the author depends here), he mentions few details. One of these few details, namely the reduction of Sodom and Gomorrah to ashes, is not found in the biblical account or in Jude 7; however, it is found in Philo *Abr.* 139 where Philo says that in one day the cities became the tomb of their inhabitants, and buildings of stone and wood became ashes (τέφρα) and thin dust. To this the author adds that in treating Sodom and Gomorrah this way, God made them an example of what is about to happen to the impious. Even more significantly, the author of 2 Peter emphasizes that Lot was oppressed by life among the wicked people of Sodom.

Social-cultural texture. Second Peter 2:4–10a is a *riposte* to the *challenge* implied by 2:3b.[82] The challenge to God's *honor* is also mentioned in v. 10a which refers to the unjust's despising dominion. Those who are judged by God are described as *impure*. They are impious (vv. 5, 6), licentious, law-

---

82. Neyrey, *2 Peter, Jude,* 195–96, 199–200.

less (v. 7), and they desire defilement (v. 10).[83] On the other hand those who will be saved are pious (v. 9).

By referring to the underworld as Tartarus in v. 6, the author invokes the picture of Zeus's consignment of the Titans to Tartarus after they rebelled against him. Hesiod describes this by saying that the Titan gods have been hidden in Tartarus under gloom (ζοφερόεντι) by the will of cloud-driving Dis (= Zeus) in a dank place at the ends of the huge earth (*Theogony* 729–31). Other elements of 2 Peter's presentation, especially use of the word "angels," make it seem very probable that the author subordinates this picture to the one derived from the Jewish Scriptures and the tradition based on them. Perhaps because of the parallel between God's punishment of the angels and Zeus's punishment of the Titans, the author of 2 Peter uses the name for the Titans' place of punishment. This integration of Tartarus into the picture of divine judgment in Judaism was probably already familiar to the author and addressees.[84]

Judgment by water and fire, such as is described in vv. 5–6, is found among the Greeks as well as the Jews.[85] As with the reference to Tartarus, if the author has such ideas in view, they seem subordinate to the descriptions of these things in the Jewish Scriptures.

Sacred texture. This passage has much to say about God: God did not spare the sinful angels, but sent them to Tartarus (2:4); God did not spare the ancient world, but saved Noah (2:5); God condemned Sodom and Gomorrah, reducing them to ashes and making them a sign of what will happen to the impious (2:6), but saved Lot (vv. 7–8); God knows how to save the pious and punish the wicked (2:9), a general conclusion from the particular cases mentioned in 2:4–8.

Rhetorical Force

The author concludes his argument that the prophetic discourse of the Jewish Scriptures promises the apocalyptic second coming of Jesus by showing how it does so. He pictures God's judgment of the sinful angels, destruction of the world by flood and rescue of Noah, and destruction of Sodom and Gomorrah and rescue of Lot as revealing a pattern of divine activity that will issue in a day of judgment when Jesus comes again. In this way the author concludes his argument with eschatography, a vivid picture of the end of the

---

83. Ibid., 200–201.

84. Bauckham, *Jude, 2 Peter*, 249. See also Neyrey, *2 Peter, Jude*, 202; Davids, *2 Peter and Jude*, 226; and Green, *Jude & 2 Peter*, 250–51.

85. Neyrey, *2 Peter, Jude*, 203.

world. It is notable, however, that the author implies, rather than explicitly states, that God will judge the world at the second coming of Jesus. At this point he only shows that judgment is a characteristic activity of God; later (in 3:4–13) he will directly assert that God will judge the world when Jesus comes again.

This argument reconfigures the argumentation typical of apocalyptic discourse. The latter usually conceives of history as a sequence of events that unfold by divine plan, culminating in the end of the world. Recognition of this plan and one's place in it allows one to realize that the final period of world history has arrived. There is an emphasis on the time of the end in order to show that it is near. The author of 2 Peter instead sees past events as precedents that show how God will act in the future, but not as a sequence of events, fore-ordained by God, unfolding in history. This eschatography preserves a more prophetic character than is found in more common apocalyptic discourse. Second Peter puts less emphasis on the precise time of the end, but focuses instead on the certainty that it will come. Later the author emphasizes the need to have a lively expectation of the coming end of the world (3:11–13).

It is striking that none of 2 Peter's precedents are drawn from the history of Israel, i.e., from the time of Abraham onward. All are taken from the Jewish Scriptures, but from that part of them that concerns the history of the human race before the existence of the Jewish people. This seems likely to be intentional and to be another indication that the author principally addresses Gentile Christians. Here and elsewhere he interprets the Jewish Scriptures in such a way that they also speak to Gentiles.

The picture of the end of the world described by the author of 2 Peter is intended to replace the different picture of world history presented by the false teachers. It also provides an alternative to other non-apocalyptic pictures of world history to be found in the Greco-Roman world.

Appendix A: Terms Mentioned in 1:1–15 and Repeated in 1:16–18

γάρ (for—1:16, 17) was used earlier in 1:8, 9, 10, 11.

ἐγνωρίσαμεν (make known—1:16) is cognate to ἐπίγνωσις (full knowledge) mentioned earlier in 1:3, 8; and γνῶσις (knowledge) mentioned earlier in 1:5, 6; and a synonym of οἶδα (to know) mentioned earlier in 1:12, 14.

ὑμῖν (you—1:16 [twice]) was mentioned earlier in 1:5, 8, 10, 11, 12, 13, 15 τοῦ κυρίου ἡμῶν Ἰησοῦ Χριστοῦ (our Lord Jesus Christ—1:16) was used earlier in 1:8, 14; and all of the elements of the phrase were used earlier additional times.

δύναμιν (power—1:16) was used earlier in 1:3.

λαβών (received—1:17) was used earlier in 1:9.

θεός (God—1:17) was used earlier in 1:1, 2.

τιμήν (honor—1:17) is cognate to ἰσότιμον (equal in honor) used earlier in 1:1 and τίμια (precious) used earlier in 1:4.

δόξαν (glory—1:17 [twice]) was used earlier in 1:3.

μου (my—1:17 [twice]) was used earlier in 1:14.

ἀγαπητός (beloved—1:17) is cognate to ἀγάπη (love) used ealier in 1:7.

ταύτην (this—1:18) was used earlier in 1:4, 5, 8, 9, 10, 12, 13, 15.

αὐτῷ (him—1:18) was used earlier in 1:3, 5, 9.

Appendix B: Terms mentioned in 1:1–18 and repeated in 1:19–21

ἔχομεν (have—1:19) was used earlier in 1:15.

βεβαιότερον (more secure—1:19) was used earlier in 1:10.

ποιεῖτε (do—1:19) was used earlier in 1:10 (twice), 15.

ὑμῶν (your—1:19) was used earlier in 1:1, 2, 5, 8, 10, 11, 12, 13, 15, 16.

τοῦτο (this—1:20) was used earlier in 1:4, 5, 8, 9, 10, 12, 13, 15, 17, 18.

γινώσκοντες (knowing—1:20) is cognate to the following words used earlier: ἐπίγνωσις (full knowledge) found in 1:2, 3, 8; γνῶσις (knowledge) found in 1:5, 6; γνωρίζω (to make known) found in 1:16; it is synonymous with οἶδα (to know) found in 1:12, 14.

πᾶσα (all—1:20) was used earlier in 1:3, 5.

ἰδίας (one's own—1:20) was used earlier in 1:3.

γάρ (for—1:21) was used earlier in 1:8, 9, 10, 11, 16, 17.

ποτέ (ever—1:21) was used earlier in 1:10.

θεοῦ (God—1:21) was used earlier in 1:1, 2, 17.

126 Acknowledging the Divine Benefactor

Appendix C: Terms Introduced in 1:19-21 and Repeated Later in 2 Peter

λόγον (word) is used in 1:19 and three times later in the letter (2:3; 3:5, 7).

ἡμέρα (day) is used in 1:19 and ten times later in the letter (2:8 [twice], 9, 13; 3:3, 7, 8, 10, 12, 18).

καρδία (heart) is used in 1:19 and again in 2:14.

πρῶτον (first) is used in 1:20; 2:20; 3:3.

τοῦτο πρῶτον γινώσκοντες (first knowing this) is used in 1:20 and again in 3:3.

γραφῆς (Scripture) is used in 1:20 and again in 3:16; the cognate verb γράφω (to write) is also used in 3:1, 15.

ἐλάλησαν (spoke) is used in 1:21 and again in 3:16.

Appendix D: Terms Used in Chapter 1 and Repeated in 2:1-3

ψευδοπροφῆται (false prophets—2:1) is cognate to προφητικόν (prophetic) used in 1:19 and προφητεία (prophecy) used in 1:20, 21.

ὑμῖν (you—2:1, 3) was used earlier in 1:5, 8, 10, 11, 12, 13, 15, 16, 19.

ἀπωλείας (destruction—2:1 [twice], 3) is a synonym of φθορά (corruption) used in 1:4.

αὐτούς (them—2:1, 2, 3) was used earlier in 1:3, 5, 9, 17, 18.

δεσπότην (master—2:1) is a synonym of κύριος (lord) used earlier in 1:8, 11, 14, 16.

ταχινήν (imminent—2:1) was used earlier in 1:14.

ἐξακολουθήσουσιν (follow—2:2) was used earlier in 1:16.

ὁδός (way—2:2) is cognate to εἴσοδος (entrance) used in 1:11 and its antonym ἔξοδος (departure) used in 1:15.

ἀληθείας (truth—2:2) was used earlier in 1:12.

λόγοις (words—2:3) was used earlier in 1:19.

ἔκπαλαι (long ago—2:3) is cognate to πάλαι (past) used in 1:9.

ἀργεῖ (be idle—2:3) is cognate to ἀργούς (idle) used in 1:8.

Appendix E: Terms Used in Earlier in 2 Peter and Repeated in 2:4–10a

γάρ (for—2:4, 8) was used earlier in 1:8, 9, 10, 11, 16, 17, 21.

θεός (God—2:4) was used earlier in 1:17, 21.

ἁμαρτησάντων (to sin—2:4) is cognate to ἁμαρτιῶν (sins) used earlier in 1:9.

κρίσιν (judgment—2:4, 9) is cognate to κρίμα (judgment) used earlier in 2:3, as is κατέκρινεν (to condemn—2:6).

κόσμου (world—2:5 [twice]) was used earlier in 1:4.

δικαιοσύνης (justice—2:5) was used earlier in 1:1; its cognate δίκαιος (just—2:7, 8 [twice]) was used earlier in 1:13; another cognate ἀδίκους (unjust) is found in 2:9.

ἀσεβῶν (impious—2:5, 6) is cognate to εὐσέβεια (piety) used earlier in 1:3, 6, 7; another cognate εὐσεβεῖς (pious) is found in 2:9.

ἐπάξας (bring on—2:5) was used earlier in 2:1.

μελλόντων (about to—2:6) was used earlier in 1:12.

ἀσελγείᾳ (licentiousness—2:7) was used earlier in 2:2.

αὐτοῖς (them—2:8) was used earlier in 1:3, 5, 9, 17, 18; 2:1, 2, 3.

ἡμέραν (day—2:8 [twice], 9) was used earlier in 1:19.

οἶδεν (know—2:9) was used earlier in 1:12, 14; it is related in meaning to ἐπίγνωσις (full knowledge) used earlier in 1:1, 3, 8; γνῶσις (knowledge) used earlier in 1:5, 6; γνωρίζω (to make known) used earlier in 1:16; and γινώσκω (to know) used earlier in 1:20.

κύριος (lord—2:9) was used earlier in 1:2, 8, 11, 14, 16; the synonym δεσπότην (master) was used in 2:1; the cognate κυριότητος (dominion) is found in 2:10.

ἐπιθυμίᾳ (desire—2:10) was used earlier in 1:4.

Appendix F: Terms Introduced in 2:4–10a and Used Later in 2 Peter

ἀγγέλων (angels) is used in 2:4 and again in 2:11.

ζόφου (gloom) is used in 2:4 and again in 2:17.

παρέδωκεν (hand over) is used in 2:4 and again in 2:21.

ἐφύλαξεν (guarded) is used in 2:5 and again in 3:17.

ἀθέσμων (lawless) is used in 2:7 and again in 3:17.

ἀναστροφῆς (life) is used in 2:7 and again in 3:11; the cognate verb ἀναστρεφομένους (to live) is used in 2:18.

ψυχήν (soul) is used in 2:8 and again in 2:14.

ἔργοις (works) is used in 2:8 and again in 3:10.

σαρκός (flesh) is used in 2:10 and again in 2:18.

πορευομένους (go) is used in 2:10 and again in 3:3.

Section 3: 2 Peter 2:10b–22

Letter Body, Part 2
Prophetic Denunciation of the False Teachers

This second part of the body of 2 Peter (i.e., 1:16—3:13) is a critique of those who deny that Jesus will come again. In the first part of this middle section (i.e., 1:16—2:10a), the author makes two arguments that Jesus will come again. In the section that follows the author presents an *ad hominem* attack on his opponents, developing themes stated more briefly in 2:1–3.

Second Peter 2:10b–22 is primarily prophetic discourse. In this section the author functions as a prophet who criticizes the behavior of the false teachers and warns the addressees against adhering to them.

This section also includes admixtures of apocalyptic, priestly, miracle, and wisdom discourse. Apocalyptic and priestly discourse are blended into the entire passage. Apocalyptic discourse is found in the statement that the false teachers will be destroyed (v. 12), the reference to the darkness reserved for them (v. 17), and the identification of Jesus as savior (v. 20).[1] Priestly discourse is present in the descriptions of the false teachers as corrupt (vv. 13–14, 19), the addressees (and the false teachers) as having escaped the defilements of the world (vv. 18, 20), and the commandment as holy (v. 21). Miracle discourse blends into this passage in the reference to Balaam's being rebuked by his donkey (v. 16). The latter verses of this passage (vv. 20–22) are primarily wisdom discourse. Here the author makes it clear that one escapes the defilements of the world through knowledge of Jesus Christ.

---

1. Watson ("Apocalyptic Discourse," 212) speaks of vv. 17–21 as apocalyptic discourse.

UNIT 1: 2 PETER 2:10B–17

Prophetic Denunciation of the False Teachers' Moral Failings

10b Τολμηταί αὐθάδεις,[2] δόξας οὐ τρέμουσιν βλασφημοῦντες, 11 ὅπου ἄγγελοι ἰσχύϊ καὶ δυνάμει μείζονες ὄντες οὐ φέρουσιν κατ' αὐτῶν[3] παρὰ κυρίου[4] βλάσφημον κρίσιν. 12 οὗτοι δέ ὡς ἄλογα ζῷα γεγεννημένα φυσικὰ εἰς ἅλωσιν καὶ φθοράν ἐν οἷς[5] ἀγνοοῦσιν βλασφημοῦντες, ἐν τῇ φθορᾷ αὐτῶν[6] καὶ φθαρήσονται 13 ἀδικούμενοι[7] μισθὸν ἀδικίας, ἡδονὴν ἡγούμενοι τὴν ἐν ἡμέρᾳ τρυφήν, σπίλοι καὶ μῶμοι ἐντρυφῶντες ἐν ταῖς ἀπάταις[8] αὐτῶν συνευωχούμενοι ὑμῖν, 14 ὀφθαλμοὺς ἔχοντες μεστοὺς μοιχαλίδος καὶ ἀκαταπαύστους ἁμαρτίας,[9] δελεάζοντες ψυχὰς ἀστηρίκτους, καρδίαν γεγυμνασμένην πλεονεξίας ἔχοντες, κατάρας τέκνα: 15 καταλείποντες[10] εὐθεῖαν ὁδὸν

2. Τολμηταί is a noun; αὐθάδεις is an adjective modifying it (Bigg, *St. Peter and St. Jude*, 279).

3. αὐτῶν refers to the false teachers; so Davids, *2 Peter and Jude*, 236; and Green, *Jude & 2 Peter*, 274. Bigg (*St. Peter and St. Jude*, 280); Schelkle (*Die Petrusbriefe*, 211); Bauckham (*Jude, 2 Peter*, 261) and Harrington ("Jude and 2 Peter," 268–69) think it refers to the glories.

4. There is considerable uncertainty whether the original text read παρὰ κυρίου or παρὰ κυρίῳ. The former is found in P[72], the latter in ℵ and B; A omits the prepositional phrase. The former might be considered original on the basis that it is the most difficult reading; it might have been altered or omitted to avoid the difficulty. The ECM regards παρὰ κυρίῳ as most likely to be original; Metzger seems to agree (*A Textual Commentary*, 633), as does Kraus ("Παρὰ κυρίου, παρὰ κυρίῳ oder *omit* in 2Petr 2,11").

5. ἐν οἷς = ἐν τούτοις ἅ or possibly ἐν τούτοις οὕς or even τὰ ἐν οἷς. In the first two cases, ἐν τούτοις is the object of βλασφημοῦντες; in the last case ἐν οἷς indicates that with respect to which the false teachers are ignorant.

6. The antecedent of αὐτῶν is unclear; the most likely possibilities are that it refers to the irrational animals, or that it refers to the ones slandered by the false teachers. I take it to be the former. According to Bauckham (*Jude, 2 Peter*, 263–64) this is the majority view. Davids (*2 Peter and Jude*, 238) and G. Green (*Jude & 2 Peter*, 276) also advocate it.

7. There is some uncertainty whether the original text read ἀδικούμενοι or κομιούμενοι. The former is found in P[72], the original text of ℵ, and B; the latter in the correction of ℵ and A. The former is probably to be preferred as the more difficult reading (Metzger, *A Textual Commentary*, 634).

8. There is also some uncertainty whether the original text read ἀπάταις or ἀγάπαις. The former is found in P[72], ℵ, and the original text of A; the latter in the correction of A and B. The latter might have been an assimilation of the text of 2 Peter to that of Jude 12 on which 2 Peter depends at this point (Metzger, *A Textual Commentary*, 634), perhaps facilitated by the similarity of the letters Γ, Π, and Τ.

9. ἀκαταπαύστους, like μεστοὺς, modifies ὀφθαλμοὺς; both adjectives are followed by a dependent noun in the genitive case.

10. It is uncertain whether the original text read καταλείποντες or καταλίποντες. The former is found in ℵ, A, and the original text of B; the latter in P[72] and the second correction of B. The latter may have been a correction of the original text intended to

ἐπλανήθησαν, ἐξακολουθήσαντες τῇ ὁδῷ τοῦ Βαλαὰμ τοῦ Βοσόρ, ὃς μισθὸν ἀδικίας ἠγάπησεν 16 ἔλεγξιν δὲ ἔσχεν ἰδίας παρανομίας· ὑποζύγιον ἄφωνον ἐν ἀνθρώπου φωνῇ φθεγξάμενον ἐκώλυσεν τὴν τοῦ προφήτου παραφρονίαν. 17 οὗτοί εἰσιν πηγαὶ ἄνυδροι καὶ ὁμίχλαι ὑπὸ λαίλαπος ἐλαυνόμεναι, οἷς ὁ ζόφος τοῦ σκότους τετήρηται.

10b Stubborn bold ones, they do not tremble, slandering the glories, 11 where angels, being greater in strength and power, do not bear against them a slanderous judgment from (the side of) the Lord. 12 But these, like irrational animals begotten naturally for capture and corruption, slandering things of which they are ignorant, will also be corrupted in their corruption, 13 being wronged as the reward of wrongdoing, considering luxuriousness during the day a pleasure, spots and blemishes luxuriating in their deceits while feasting together with you, 14 having eyes full of an adulteress and not ceasing from sin, enticing unstable souls, having a heart trained in greed, children of a curse. 15 Abandoning the straight way, they have gone astray, having followed in the way of Balaam, son of Bosor, who loved the reward of wrongdoing. 16 And he received a rebuke of his own lawbreaking. A voiceless donkey having spoken with a human's voice prevented the madness of the prophet. 17 These are waterless springs and mists driven by a storm for whom the gloom of darkness has been kept.

Rhetography

In 2:10b-17 the author of 2 Peter prophetically denounces the false teachers by using a rather large number of briefly evoked negative images, somewhat as he had earlier in 2:1-3. He begins by picturing them as recklessly self-confident of their false teaching and contrasting them with the angels (vv. 10b-11); he then likens them to irrational animals (v. 12). Both of these comparisons picture the false teachers as misbehaving with their mouths (i.e., slandering) in a way that will lead to their destruction.

In v. 10b the primary mental image the author summons is that of the false teachers speaking. These teachers speak as stubborn, bold people. He also summons an alternative picture of the false teachers trembling when they do something audacious in order to deny that they do this; they do not display fear when it would be appropriate to do so. What they are doing that does not arouse fear, though it should, is slandering the glories. This probably refers to the false teachers' skepticism that Jesus will return and that God will bring this world to an end.

---

align the tense of the participle with that of the following verb and participle.

In v. 11 the author contrasts the inappropriately audacious behavior of the false teachers with the behavior of the angels. Although the angels are greater in strength and power than the false teachers,[11] and so have better reason for audacity, they do not bring a defamatory judgment against the false teachers from the side of the Lord. As he did in v. 10b, the author summons a picture for the purpose of rejecting it. In this case he pictures the angels moving from the presence of the Lord, i.e., probably God, to bring a judgment against the false teachers, in order to deny that the angels do this. The restraint of the angels heightens the reckless impropriety of the false teachers' own behavior.

The author begins v. 12 with a similitude comparing the false teachers ("these") to irrational animals that are begotten naturally for capture and corruption. He pictures them as less than human, lacking reason, and simply part of the natural world of birth, death, and decomposition. Since he specifically mentions capture, the author seems to be comparing the false teachers to wild animals rather than domesticated ones, wild animals that are hunted for food or sport. He does not make explicit whether he envisions, and wants the addressees to envision, humans hunting animals, or animals hunting each other.

The author proceeds to say that the false teachers slander things of which they are ignorant, repeating in somewhat different words what he said in v. 10b–11, where he also mentioned the angels' avoidance of slanderous judgment. This slander is apparently the main evidence of the false teachers' irrationality. The slander is probably the same as that of v. 10b, i.e., eschatological skepticism. Once again this is a mental image of the false teachers as expressing skepticism in speech.

The author then says that the false teachers will undergo corruption in the corruption of the irrational animals who, the author has said, were begotten for this. Both the false teachers and the irrational animals will die and decompose; this is the main way in which the two are alike. Both will die and decompose and cease to exist. This happens at their individual deaths and will happen to all at the end of the world. At the beginning of v. 13, the author describes the false teachers' corruption as a matter of being wronged as a reward for wrongdoing. The fate of the false teachers will be commensurate with their behavior. At the end of the world people will be treated (by God?) in a way corresponding to their actions.

---

11. So Grundmann, *Brief des Judas und zweite Brief des Petrus*, 95. Schelkle (*Die Petrusbriefe*, 210), Kelly (*Peter and Jude*, 338), Fornberg (*Early Church*, 54) and Bauckham (*Jude, 2 Peter*, 262) think the angels are said to be greater in strength and power than the glories.

In the remainder of v. 13 and v. 14, the author uses a series of brief critical pictures to describe the false teachers. These verses particularly resemble 2:1–3. All of these brief pictures may portray the false teachers as misbehaving at meals; they are pictured as misbehaving with eyes and heart, and as having a negative effect on the souls of others.

The first picture in the series presents the false teachers as considering luxuriousness during the day a pleasure. This directly describes the thoughts of the false teachers;[12] however, it implies that their behavior is in line with these thoughts. This behavior may consist of holding lavish meals during the day rather than properly in the evening. It is possible that the author develops this picture of misbehavior at meals in the rest of vv. 13-14; he explicitly does so at the end of v. 13. His other descriptions do not explicitly advert to the setting of meals, but can be understood in that context.

The author goes on to describe the false teachers as spots and blemishes. This pictures the false teachers as stains on a fabric or defects of body such as might disqualify an animal from being a sacrificial victim.[13] The author probably pictures them as flaws in the Christian community. If the author continues to envision the setting of meals, he sees them as flaws in the Christian community as it gathers to eat. Specific ways in which they constitute such flaws are indicated in the series of pictures that follows.

The first two of these present the false teachers as luxuriating in their deceits while feasting together with the addressees. This repeats the just-made connection of the false teachers with luxuriousness. In this case the author describes them as luxuriating in their deceits, i.e., in things about which they have been deceived or about which they deceive others. This probably refers to their idea that Jesus will not come again, which is the foundation for their immoral behavior. In this case the author also specifies that their misbehavior occurs at the common meals of the Christian community.

The author next (in v. 14) pictures the false teachers as having eyes full of an adulteress and not ceasing from sin, i.e., they are always looking for opportunities to engage in adulterous sexual relations. The author might mean this literally or be using adultery as a metaphor for infidelity to God. This description evokes the mental image of the false teachers as using the sense of sight. It is striking that the eyes of the false teachers are said to sin without ceasing, not merely that their eyes cause them to sin.

The author proceeds to describe the false teachers as enticing unstable souls. This metaphor pictures the false teachers as using bait to catch those

---

12. This continues the emphasis on the cognitive found throughout 2 Peter.
13. Cf. Lev 1:3 where the sacrificial victim is required to be ἄμωμος.

who follow them, as fishermen use bait to catch fish. These followers are unstable (ἀστήρικτος, a rare word), making them vulnerable to capture in this way.[14] The author then describes the false teachers as having a heart trained in greed. This metaphor pictures them as having engaged in disciplined training of their hearts to make them excel in greed. The author might mean greed literally, but probably understands greed metaphorically to mean the false teachers' desire to gain control of the addressees, as in 2:3.

The final description of the false teachers in v. 14 is that they are children of a curse. This probably makes use of the Semitic idiom in which "child of" indicates a wide range of relationships. Here it means that the false teachers are under a curse. The author does not indicate who cursed them, or the circumstances in which this occurred, or the effect of the curse. The two presentations that precede it and this final description are not explicitly related to behavior at meals, but the author may have this in mind.

The author then compares the false teachers to Balaam (vv. 15–16), picturing their feet as walking the same wrong road Balaam took. While a voiceless donkey prevented the lawbreaking and madness of Balaam, presumably there has not been a similar check on the false teachers. The author ends by describing them as waterless springs and mists driven by a storm (v. 17).

In comparing the false teachers to Balaam, the author evokes the story told in Num 22–24. Balak, king of Moab, sent for Balaam, offering to pay him for cursing the Israelites. In obedience to God, Balaam both refused Balak's first summons and accepted the second. As Balaam was on his way, the donkey he was riding three times saw an angel of the Lord and either turned aside or stopped. When Balaam struck the donkey, it asked why he did so. Then Balaam too saw the angel of the Lord. Balaam offered to return home, but was told to continue his journey, but to say only what the angel of the Lord told him to say. Balaam did so and then several times blessed the Israelites instead of cursing them.

The author does not repeat this story in detail. As with all of the author's allusions to biblical stories, what he does say would call this story to the minds of those who knew it. Those unfamiliar with the story of Balaam would only be aware of what the author mentions explicitly. And even those who are familiar with the story would be most aware of the details that are specifically mentioned.

The author begins the comparison with Balaam by saying that the false teachers, abandoning the straight way,[15] have gone astray, having followed

---

14. Their instability is the antithesis of the security encouraged in 1:10, 12, 19.
15. The straight way is the same as the way of truth mentioned in 2:2.

in the way of Balaam. The author pictures the false teachers as people on a journey who have taken the wrong route, the same wrong route Balaam took as he journeyed to curse the Israelites (see Num 22:22–35). Balaam literally traveled; in the case of the false teachers, taking the wrong route is a metaphor for moral failure.

The author implicitly specifies the false teachers' moral failure by saying that Balaam loved the reward of wrongdoing. In v. 13 the author had said that the false teachers would receive the reward of wrongdoing, visualizing this as punishment for wrongdoing; now he says that Balaam, whom they imitate, loved the reward of wrongdoing. He did wrong in order to gain something desirable. This probably pictures Balaam as motivated by greed, and implies the same regarding the false teachers, as the author has already said explicitly in 2:3 and 14.

The author suggests that the false teachers, who imitate Balaam, also imitate his lawbreaking and madness. The author calls Balaam a prophet. Balaam may be one of the false prophets among the people to which the author referred in 2:1, who are a type of the false teachers whom the author opposes.[16]

Following this portrayal of the false teachers as like Balaam, in v. 17 the author continues to criticize the false teachers using two metaphors. He first describes them as waterless springs. They are like springs to which one would go for water that do not supply any water. This depicts the false teachers as essentially worthless. They seem to be sources of something necessary for life, but actually do not provide it.[17] The author then describes the false teachers as mists driven by a storm. This depicts them as insubstantial and as under the control of powerful forces outside themselves. Finally the author says that the gloom of darkness has been kept for them. Just as the sinful angels have been delivered to chains of gloom, being kept for judgment (2:4; cf. also 2:9), so the same gloom is being kept for the false teachers. The gloom is the gloom of Tartarus.

Textural Analysis

Intertexture. Second Peter 2:10b–17 *recontextualizes* Jude 8b–13. This includes a verbatim recitation of Jude 13b in 2 Pet 2:17b, omitting only the words εἰς αἰῶνα (forever).

---

16. Grundmann, *Brief des Judas und zweite Brief des Petrus*, 99. Both Balaam and the false prophets are contrasted with the true prophets mentioned in 1:20–21.

17. According to Watson, this is a traditional metaphor; he cites Jer 2:13 (*Invention*, 120).

Jude 13b οἷς ὁ ζόφος τοῦ σκότους εἰς αἰῶνα τετήρηται

2 Pet 2:17b οἷς ὁ ζόφος τοῦ σκότους τετήρηται

In 2 Pet 2:10b-11 the author separated the final clause of Jude 8 from the preceding two clauses and joined to it a revised version of Jude 9. In 2 Pet 2:12 the author followed Jude 10 more closely, though still making substantial changes. The author of 2 Peter added 2:13-14, making some use of Jude 12. In 2 Pet 2:15 the author used one of the three elements of Jude 11. He expanded upon it and developed it further by the addition of 2 Pet 2:16.

Second Peter's comparison of humans to irrational animals has parallels in many other writings, but no other author says that the two are alike while specifying that irrational animals are begotten naturally for capture and corruption.[18] The closest parallel is found in Ps 49:12 and 20: "Mortals cannot abide in their pomp; they are like the animals that perish." In the Greek translation of this psalm, though not in the Hebrew text, the animals are explicitly described as irrational (τοῖς κτήνεσιν τοῖς ἀνοήτοις—Ps 48:13, 21).

Criticism of the false teachers for misbehavior at meals (2:13b-14) derives from Jude 12, which refers to the opponents as "blemishes on your love-feasts (ἀγάπαις), while they feast with you (συνευωχούμενοι) without fear, feeding themselves." Of this 2 Peter has only retained the idea that the false teachers feast with the addressees (συνευωχούμενοι); perhaps the author did not want to say explicitly that the misbehavior he describes occurs at the official gatherings of the community (ἀγάπαις). One example of such misbehavior is the conduct for which Paul criticizes the Corinthians in 1 Cor 11:17-22;[19] similar misbehavior might be in view in Jude and 2 Peter. In 1 Cor 11:21 Paul describes the problematic behavior of the Corinthians in this way:

> For when the time comes to eat, each of you goes ahead with your own supper, and one goes hungry and another becomes drunk.

Even if the author of 2 Peter does not refer explicitly to ἀγάπαις, it is clear that the behavior being criticized occurs at meals that involve both the false teachers and those the author warns against them.

The author of 2 Peter has replaced Jude's references to misbehavior with several others. He first suggests that holding lavish meals during the day is problematic. This is regarded negatively by Eccl 10:16-17 (cf. also Isa 5:11):

18. Callan, "Comparison of Humans to Animals," 101-5.
19. Grundmann, *Brief des Judas und zweite Brief des Petrus*, 97.

> Alas for you, O land, when your king is a servant, and your princes feast in the morning!
> Happy are you, O land, when your king is a nobleman, and your princes feast at the proper time—for strength, and not for drunkenness!

Later he says that the false teachers have eyes full of an adulteress and not ceasing from sin. This is reminiscent of the teaching of Jesus in Matt 5:27 that everyone who looks at a woman to desire her has already committed adultery with her in his heart. Meals were a setting often associated with adultery.[20] Ovid describes the behavior of an adulterous couple at a banquet in *Amores* 1.4. The speaker asks his paramour to interact with him covertly:

> Watch me and my nods, and loquacious expression:
> pick up their secret messages and yourself reply.
> Voiceless, I'll speak eloquent words with eyebrows (lines 17-19):
> *me specta nutusque meos vultumque loquacem;*
> *excipe furtivas et refer ipsa notas.*
> *verba superciliis sine voce loquentia dicam;*

Later he asks her not to make love to her husband at the banquet saying

> Often my girl and I, with quick pleasure,
> completed the sweet work, the cloth covering us (lines 47-48).[21]
> *saepe mihi dominaeque meae properata voluptas*
> *veste sub iniecta dulce peregit opus.*

In 2 Pet 2:15-16 the author depends not only on Jude 11, but also on Num 22-24, on which Jude also depends. In saying that Balaam loved the reward of wrongdoing the author of 2 Peter probably sees him as motivated by greed. In the biblical account, Balaam is not motivated by greed, but this is how he was seen in post-biblical Jewish tradition.[22] For example, when Philo tells the story of Balaam in *Mos.* 1.263-99, he says that Balak, after a first set of envoys did not succeed in bringing Balaam to him, sent a second set

> who brought more money and promised more abundant gifts. Enticed by those offers present and prospective, and in deference to the dignity of the ambassadors, [Balaam] gave way. (*Mos.* 1.267-68)

---

20. On this see Green, *Jude & 2 Peter*, 281-82.

21. Translation by A. S. Kline at http://www.poetryintranslation.com/PITBR/Latin/AmoresBkI.htm#_Toc520535259. Accessed May 28, 2013.

22. Bauckham, *Jude, 2 Peter*, 260, 268.

Balaam's greed is literal; as we have seen, that of the false teachers is probably metaphorical.

The exact nature of the wrongdoing whose reward Balaam loved is not clear. The author may be thinking of Balaam's advice to the Moabites (Num 31:16) to have their women lead the Israelites into idolatry (see Num 25). The author may imply that the false teachers lead people astray through sexual misconduct; he has already accused the false teachers of sexual misbehavior in 2:1 and 14. In 2:13 the author looked forward to the false teachers' receiving the reward of wrongdoing. Here he may be thinking that Balaam's ultimate reward for his behavior was to be killed by the Israelites along with the Midianites (Num 31:8); if so, the reference to Balaam's love for the reward of wrongdoing would be ironic.[23] The false teachers' reward will be similar to that of Balaam.

The author continues the story of Balaam by saying that he received a rebuke of his own lawbreaking when a voiceless donkey having spoken with a human's voice prevented the madness of the prophet. The author of 2 Peter has taken this from Num 22:28–30. These verses tell how the Lord opened the mouth of Balaam's donkey to reproach Balaam for beating the donkey. It is possible that this beating is what the author of 2 Peter means by Balaam's lawbreaking and his madness. However, it seems more likely that the author understands lawbreaking and madness more broadly. The reference to the donkey's rebuke of Balaam evokes a mental image of the donkey as speaking. The author probably presumes the elaboration of the story of Balaam that is found in non-biblical sources. One such elaboration is found in Targum Neofiti. In the targum to Num 22:30, the donkey reproaches Balaam in these words:

> You lack understanding! What! If you are not able to curse me who am an unclean beast, and die in the world and do not enter the world to come, how much less are you able to curse the sons of Abraham, of Isaac and Jacob, on whose account the world was created from the beginning, and for whose merits it is remembered before them?[24]

Here Balaam's lawbreaking consists of cursing the Israelites as he intends, and his madness consists of his failure to understand that it is impossible for him to do so.

---

23. The wrongdoing mentioned in 2:13, 15 echoes the reference to the unjust in 2:9, and is the antithesis of the justice mentioned in 1:1, 13; 2:5, 7, 8, and that will be mentioned in 2:21.

24. Translation taken from *Targum Neofiti 1*, 127–28. The donkey's speech in *Targum Pseudo-Jonathan* is quite similar (ibid., 254).

Another indication that the author of 2 Peter depends on non-biblical elaboration of the Balaam story is that the author of 2 Peter uses the word ὑποζύγιον for Balaam's donkey as does Philo (*Mos.* 1.269); the LXX uses ὄνος (as does Josephus; see *Ant.* 4.109-10).

Second Peter 2:17 recontextualizes Jude 12-13. Second Peter 2:17 used the opening words of Jude 12, modified one of the five descriptions of the opponents in Jude 12-13 (namely one found in v. 12), and used the final clause of v. 13. From a rhetorical point of view, one can say that here and in the following section of 2 Peter (vv. 18-22), the author reworked a portion of Jude that attempted to prove Jude's thesis, into a digression in which the author of 2 Peter denounced his opponents.[25]

Inner texture. This rather lengthy denunciation begins with a noun and an adjective (Τολμηταί αὐθάδεις) naming the false teachers as stubborn, bold people, using single words (comma) without connecting particles (asyndeton) to increase their impact. The author makes similarly terse and direct identifications of the false teachers twice more in what follows. In v. 13 he calls them spots and blemishes (σπίλοι καὶ μῶμοι) and at the end of v. 14, children of a curse (κατάρας τέκνα). In v. 17 the author describes the false teachers somewhat more elaborately as waterless springs and mists driven by a storm (πηγαὶ ἄνυδροι καὶ ὁμίχλαι ὑπὸ λαίλαπος ἐλαυνόμεναι).

In between these nouns that identify the false teachers, the false teachers are described using eleven participles. This greatly augments the negative description of the false teachers. Together with the six nouns already mentioned, these participles present the false teachers as persons whose negative character is overwhelming. Nine of the eleven participles are present, active participles. This emphasizes the active character of the false teachers' bad behavior and its persistence. (This dependence on participles to describe the false teachers continues in the following section of 2 Peter in vv. 18-19.)

The first two participles (v. 10b, 12) speak of the false teachers as slandering (βλασφημοῦντες). In between them (in v. 11) the author refers to a slanderous (βλάσφημον) judgment. These three references exhibit *progression.* The author first says that the false teachers slander the glories (δόξας). "Glories" is usually interpreted as referring to church[26] or secular[27] leaders or to angels, either good[28] or evil.[29] These explanations may be too much in-

25. Watson, *Invention*, 48-49, 114-15.
26. Bigg, *St. Peter and St. Jude*, 279-80.
27. Reicke, *James, Peter and Jude*, 167.
28. Neyrey, *2 Peter, Jude*, 213-14; Harrington, "Jude and 2 Peter," 268; Davids, *2 Peter and Jude*, 234-36; Green, *Jude & 2 Peter*, 270-71.
29. Windisch, *Katholische Briefe*, 95; Schelkle, *Die Petrusbriefe*, 210; Kelly, *Peter and Jude*, 337; Bauckham, *Jude, 2 Peter*, 261; Knoch, *Erste und zweite Petrusbrief*, 266;

fluenced by the way Jude uses the word. In the context of 2 Peter, the glories are most likely to be God and Jesus, since they are the ones 2 Peter has said have glory—God in 1:17; Jesus in 1:3, 17 (and later in 3:18).

In v. 11 the author contrasts the inappropriately audacious behavior of the false teachers with that of the angels who do not bring a slanderous judgment against the false teachers from the side of the Lord. This suggests that the false teachers' slander of the glories is specifically a slanderous judgment against them. It is not clear on what basis the author asserts that the angels refrain from bringing judgment in this way. Perhaps he assumes that this would be public and well known to those he addresses if it had happened. Since it is not known to have happened, the author says that it has not.

In v. 12 the author says that the false teachers resemble irrational animals when they slander things of which they are ignorant. This suggests that the slanderous judgment of the false teachers proceeds from ignorance. The false teachers' lack of the knowledge whose benefits the author has emphasized repeatedly throughout 2 Peter, has led to their slanderous judgment against God and Jesus. This slanderous judgment is probably their doubt that Jesus will return and God will bring this world to an end, i.e., their eschatological skepticism.

In 2:2 the author had said that following the licentiousnesses of the false teachers would result in slander of the way of truth. In vv. 10b–12 he indicates that others' slander of the way of truth parallels the false teachers' slander of the glories. "Slander" is the first of a number of terms used in 2:1–3 that are repeated in vv. 10b–17, showing the close connection between the two sections of the letter. Other terms include "destruction" (2:1 [twice], 3) a synonym of "corruption" (2:12 [three times]); "greed" (2:3, 14); "way" (2:2, 15 [twice]); and "follow" (2:2, 15).

Second Peter 2:12–14 constitutes a single long sentence. The subject is οὗτοι (these); the verb is φθαρήσονται (will be corrupted). The subject is modified by one participial phrase in v. 12, and by two more in v. 13a. A relative clause depends on the first of these three. In v. 13b–14 two nouns in apposition to the subject are modified by five more participial phrases. Verse 14 ends with a phrase in apposition to the subject. This period consists of two clauses. The sentence comprises a series of brief critical pictures that are presented with few connecting particles (asyndeton), emphasizing the movement from one to the next. This sentence includes ten of the eleven

---

Paulsen, *Zweite Petrusbrief*, 138–39; Vögtle, *Der Judasbrief/Der 2. Petrusbrief*, 197–99. Grundmann (*Brief des Judas und zweite Brief des Petrus*, 95) cannot decide whether the author refers to good or evil angels. Spicq (*Épitres de Saint Pierre*, 234–35) says that the glories are fallen angels, but entertains the possibility of a reference to Christ.

participles discussed above. Thus it is primarily in this sentence that the accumulation of participles has its effect.

The three references to corruption in the first verse of this sentence (v. 12) exhibit progression. The author begins the sentence by comparing the false teachers ("these") to irrational animals that are begotten naturally for capture and corruption (φθοράν). Death, decomposition, and ceasing to exist are the natural end of irrational animals. The author then says that the false teachers slander things of which they are ignorant; this slander is apparently the main evidence of the false teachers' irrationality. Of course, irrational animals do not slander anything, but the irrationality of slandering something (or someone) of which one is ignorant is comparable to the irrationality that animals display in other ways. The main clause of the sentence then says that the false teachers will undergo corruption (φθαρήσονται) in the corruption (φθορά) of the irrational animals. The false teachers' slander reduces them to the level of irrational animals and ensures that the false teachers will share the fate of these animals. Corruption as the destiny of the irrational animals is underscored by the use of φθορά in two different cases (polyptoton); the relationship between the false teachers and irrational animals is underscored by use of the cognate verb to describe the destiny of the former (paronomasia).

In v. 13 using another participial phrase that modifies the false teachers, the author describes their corruption as a matter of being wronged (ἀδικούμενοι) as the reward of wrongdoing (μισθὸν ἀδικίας). This paronomasia (ἀδικούμενοι—ἀδικίας) emphasizes the correspondence between the behavior of the false teachers and the way they will be treated (by God?) at the end of the world.[30] The false teachers' wrongdoing will result in their suffering the same thing in the end. In v. 15 the author again mentions wrongdoing. He says that the false teachers imitate Balaam, who loved (ἠγάπησεν) the reward of wrongdoing (μισθὸν ἀδικίας); this suggests that the false teachers also loved the reward of wrongdoing. As v. 13 says, the reward of wrongdoing is being wronged; surely the false teachers did not love this. They loved what they thought was the reward of wrongdoing, but they were mistaken about its real reward. They were motivated by misplaced love. The author has previously referred to love as a positive value (see 1:7, 17), but love of the wrong thing is obviously problematic.

In the remainder of v. 13 and v. 14, the author further describes the wrongdoing of the false teachers in another participial phrase, followed by two nouns in apposition to the false teachers that are modified by five more participial phrases, and ending with a phrase in apposition to the false

---

30. A similar, but positive, correspondence is expressed in 1:5 and 11.

teachers. The first of these participial phrases describes the false teachers as considering luxuriousness during the day a pleasure (ἡδονὴν ἡγούμενοι τὴν ἐν ἡμέρᾳ τρυφήν) using alliteration. The next participial phrase describes the false teachers as luxuriating (ἐντρυφῶντες) in their deceits while feasting together with the addressees. The paronomasia τρυφήν (luxuriousness)—ἐντρυφῶντες (luxuriating) exhibits progression. The author first mentions luxuriousness during the day and then speaks of luxuriating in their deceits, i.e., in things about which they have been deceived or about which they deceive others. This probably refers to their idea that Jesus will not come again, which is the foundation for their immoral behavior.

In v. 14 the statement that the false teachers are always seeking adultery is periphrastic and probably hyperbolic, and is expressed using the rare word ἀκατάπαυστος (not ceasing). All of these emphasize this aspect of the false teachers' behavior. The statement that the false teachers have trained their hearts in greed is also periphrastic and hyperbolic, emphasizing this aspect of their behavior.

After the long, kaleidoscopic description of the false teachers in vv. 12–14, in vv. 15–16 the author continues his critical description of them by comparing them to Balaam. The author begins the comparison with Balaam by saying that the false teachers, abandoning the straight way, have gone astray, having followed in the way of Balaam. The references to "leaving the straight way" and "going astray" constitute the figure of thought refining, i.e., dwelling on the same thought yet seeming to say something new. Repetition of the word "way" (ὁδός) in different cases (polyptoton) exhibits progression. What is first identified as leaving the straight way is later explicated as following Balaam's way.[31]

The author continues his presentation of the false teachers as imitators of Balaam by saying that Balaam received a rebuke of his own lawbreaking (παρανομία) when a voiceless donkey having spoken with a human voice prevented the madness (παραφρονία) of the prophet. The author describes the wrongdoing of Balaam as lawbreaking and madness, coining a new word for madness and using a word similar to it (paronomasia) for lawbreaking. He implies that the same can be said of the false teachers. In 2:12 the author compared the false teachers to irrational animals; the implication that the false teachers imitate Balaam's madness further develops this idea. His donkey's restraint of Balaam is an instance in which an irrational animal behaved better than a human being; insofar as the false teachers are like Balaam, they are actually inferior to this irrational animal.

---

31. The image of "following" was previously evoked in 1:16 and 2:2.

Here the author describes the donkey not as irrational, but rather as lacking a voice. The donkey that lacked a voice spoke with a human voice; the author underlines this contrast by the paronomasia of using the antonyms ἄφωνον (voiceless) and φωνῇ (voice).[32]

The *argumentative* force of 2:10b–17 consists mainly in establishing the negative ethos, or moral character, of the false teachers, and at the same time attempting to arouse the pathos of the addressees, their emotional rejection of the false teachers. This is implicitly an argument that the addressees of 2 Peter should reject the false teachers because they are bad.

Once again, insofar as the addressees of 2 Peter regard Jude as an authoritative text and perceive this section as dependent on it, the authority of Jude would accrue to 2 Peter. In vv. 15–16 the author of 2 Peter elaborates a comparison of the false teachers to Balaam that he took from Jude 11. Both Jude and 2 Peter derive their information about Balaam at least partly from the book of Numbers. If the addressees are aware of this, the authority of this source might lend support to the author's argument.

Social-cultural texture. In this section the author defends the *honor* of God by *shaming* the false teachers.[33] The false teachers dishonor God by reviling the glories (v. 10b), which is a matter of reviling things of which they are ignorant (v. 12). The author shames the false teachers by contrasting their behavior with that of the angels; though greater in power than the false teachers, the angels do not revile them (v. 11).

The author shames the false teachers in 2:10b–17 principally by presenting them as *impure*. The author presents the false teachers as impure by saying that they suffer the penalty for wrongdoing (v. 13), i.e., they lack the piety recommended in 1:3, 6, 7; 2:9 and are instead unjust (cf. 2:9) or impious (cf. 2:5, 6). They seek pleasure and are blots and blemishes (v. 13). Their mouths (vv. 10b–12) and eyes (v. 14) are uncontrolled. The author also shames the false teachers by further developing topics introduced earlier. Corruption, mentioned in 1:4 as something the addressees have escaped, is mentioned again in 2:12 as the destiny of the false teachers. The accusation of greed, introduced in 2:3, is repeated in 2:14, 15. Lawlessness, in 2:7 said to characterize the people of Sodom and Gomorrah, is also mentioned as a characteristic of Balaam, whom the false teachers follow, in 2:16.

I noted above in discussing 2:1–3 that accusations of slander, being liable to judgment, licentiousness, being a corrupting influence, and greed are conventional elements of vituperation of opponents. Another conventional

---

32. On the contrast between the false teachers and Balaam's donkey see Callan, "Comparison of Humans to Animals," 105–6.

33. Neyrey, *2 Peter, Jude*, 212–13, 221–23.

accusation that is used in 2:10b–17 is that of association with dubious historical characters, in this case, Balaam.[34]

Ideological social-cultural texture. As is the case with 2:1–3 the author's use of conventional vituperation probably reflects rivalry between the author of 2 Peter and the false teachers for recognition as authentic leaders of the Christian movement. This portrayal of the false teachers creates a stark contrast between them and the author of 2 Peter, supporting the author's appeal to reject them as evil.

Rhetorical Force

Like 2:1–3, vv. 10b–17 make use of conventional topics of vituperation to picture the false teachers in strikingly negative ways. This can be seen as a reconfiguration of the prophetic denunciation of foes in Hellenistic terms. In the Jewish Scriptures prophets denounce both the nations of the world (e.g. Amos 1:3—2:3) and the Jewish people (e.g. Amos 2:4–16), the latter for such things as mistreating the poor and afflicted (as in Amos 2:6–7). The author of 2 Peter uses Greco-Roman vituperation to denounce the false teachers. One element of this is the comparison of the false teachers to Balaam that summarizes some of the main themes of his denunciation.

In the prophetic discourse of the Jewish Scriptures, denunciation often ends with a prediction of destruction (e.g., Amos 1:7–8). The author of 2 Peter has reconfigured this into a description of the false teachers as destined for corruption (v. 12; cf v. 17), which he understands as eschatological destruction, as is typical of apocalyptic discourse. In this way the author's portrayal of the false teachers becomes eschatography, a vivid picture of bad behavior that will receive its reward at the end of the world.

The vituperation of 2 Pet 2:10b–17 is broadly similar to other instances of vituperation. The simplest form of this is a list of vices such as that found in Rom 1:29–31, which includes 21 vices. Such a catalog of bad behavior is frequently elaborated in various ways. One example is found in Wis 14:22–28. This passage describes the people it criticizes in a series of sentences (vv. 22, 23–24, 25–26, 27–28) that incorporate three participial phrases (vv. 22, 23, 24) and two lists of vices. A smaller list of three vices is the object of the participle in v. 23, and a longer list of 15 vices is the object of the verb in vv. 25–26. This passage accuses people of things such as being deceived about knowledge of God (v. 22) and not keeping their lives or marriages clean (v. 24).

---

34. du Toit, "Vilification," 410.

Another elaborate catalog of bad behavior is found in Matt 23. This passage criticizes the scribes and Pharisees as people who do not practice what they teach (v. 3) and consists mainly of 7 woes against them beginning in vv. 13, 15, 16, 23, 25, 27, and 29 respectively. Each of these woes except the third begins by calling the scribes and Pharisees "hypocrites," an epithet that summarizes the accusation that they do not practice what they teach. Each woe statement is followed by a circumstantial description of the scribes and Pharisees' bad behavior. The passage criticizes them for things such as locking people out of the kingdom of heaven (v. 13) and neglecting justice, mercy, and faith (v. 23).

Neither of these elaborate examples of vituperation is very similar to 2 Pet 2:10b-17 in content, and they are even less similar in form. I have not been able to find any other example of elaboration by an accumulation of participles such as we find in 2 Pet 2:10b-17. This seems to be a way of expressing vituperation that is unique to the author of 2 Peter.

Another somewhat novel element of this section is the author's emphasis on the false teachers' misbehavior at meals (v. 13). This points to the importance of common meals in the life of the Christian community and the consequent danger presented by improper behavior at such meals.

UNIT 2: 2 PETER 2:18-22

Prophetic Analysis of the False Teachers' Destructive Effect on Others

18 ὑπέρογκα γὰρ ματαιότητος φθεγγόμενοι δελεάζουσιν ἐν ἐπιθυμίαις σαρκὸς ἀσελγείαις τοὺς ὀλίγως³⁵ ἀποφεύγοντας τοὺς ἐν πλάνῃ ἀναστρεφομένους 19 ἐλευθερίαν αὐτοῖς ἐπαγγελλόμενοι, αὐτοὶ δοῦλοι ὑπάρχοντες τῆς φθορᾶς· ᾧ γάρ τις ἥττηται, τούτῳ³⁶ δεδούλωται. 20 εἰ γὰρ ἀποφυγόντες³⁷ τὰ μιάσματα

---

35. There is some uncertainty whether the original text read ὀλίγως or ὄντως. The former is found in P⁷², A, and B; the latter in ℵ. The latter is the more familiar word and may have been substituted for the former, with the aid of the similarity between ΛΙΓ and ΝΤ (Metzger, *A Textual Commentary*, 635).

36. There is some uncertainty whether the original text included καί between τούτῳ and δεδούλωται. The καί is omitted by P⁷², ℵ, and B; all other manuscripts include it. It is perhaps somewhat more likely that καί has been added than that it has been omitted.

37. It is somewhat unclear whether ἀποφυγόντες (and αὐτοῖς in vv. 20-22) refers to the false teachers or to those deceived by them. I take it to refer primarily to those deceived by the false teachers (as does Kelly, *Peter and Jude*, 347-48), but also to apply to the false teachers themselves; they entice others to follow the path they have already taken themselves. Other interpreters understand these words as referring primarily to the false teachers; for this view see Schelkle, *Die Petrusbriefe*, 217; Bauckham, *Jude, 2 Peter*, 277; Knoch, *Erste und zweite Petrusbrief*, 269-70; Harrington, "Jude and 2 Peter,"

τοῦ κόσμου ἐν ἐπιγνώσει τοῦ κυρίου [ἡμῶν] καὶ σωτῆρος Ἰησοῦ Χριστοῦ,[38] τούτοις δὲ πάλιν ἐμπλακέντες ἡττῶνται, γέγονεν αὐτοῖς τὰ ἔσχατα χείρονα τῶν πρώτων. 21 κρεῖττον γὰρ ἦν αὐτοῖς μὴ ἐπεγνωκέναι τὴν ὁδὸν τῆς δικαιοσύνης ἢ ἐπιγνοῦσιν ὑποστρέψαι ἐκ τῆς παραδοθείσης αὐτοῖς ἁγίας ἐντολῆς. 22 συμβέβηκεν αὐτοῖς τὸ τῆς ἀληθοῦς παροιμίας, Κύων ἐπιστρέψας ἐπὶ τὸ ἴδιον ἐξέραμα, καὶ ὗς λουσαμένη εἰς κυλισμὸν[39] βορβόρου.

18 For speaking boastful words of futility they entice with the desires of the flesh, with licentiousnesses, those who are just escaping from the people who live in error, 19 promising them freedom while being themselves slaves of corruption. For by whatever someone has been overcome, to this he has been enslaved. 20 For if, having escaped the defilements of the world by full knowledge of our Lord and savior Jesus Christ, and again having been implicated in them, people are overcome, for them the last things have become worse than the first. 21 For it was better for them not to have fully known the way of justice than, having fully known it, to turn away from the holy commandment delivered to them. 22 The meaning of the true proverb has applied to them: a dog having turned back to his own vomit, and a sow, having been washed, to wallowing in the mud.

Rhetography

In 2:18–22 the author of 2 Peter completes his prophetic denunciation of the false teachers by describing their negative impact on those who follow them in terms that also apply to the false teachers themselves. He pictures the false teachers as speaking empty words that entice recent converts to follow them by saying that they may indulge the desires of the flesh (v. 18). Once again this is a mental image of the false teachers as speaking. They are pictured as enticing recent converts by using bait to catch them as a fisherman catches fish. Their empty words promise freedom, but do so falsely because the false teachers themselves are slaves, not free, slaves of corruption (v. 19). Here the author uses slavery as an image for being under the control of corruption,

---

277; Davids, *2 Peter and Jude*, 249 n. 67; Green, *Jude & 2 Peter*, 300.

38. There is also uncertainty whether the original text read κυρίου [ἡμῶν] καὶ σωτῆρος Ἰησοῦ Χριστοῦ or lacked ἡμῶν. The former is found in P[72], ℵ, and A; B lacks ἡμῶν. It is easy to suppose that scribes would add ἡμῶν to complete this stereotypical expression, but the evidence for it seems greater than that against it. The uncertainty about the original text in this case is indicated by the brackets that enclose ἡμῶν.

39. There is uncertainty whether the original text read κυλισμὸν or κυλισμά. The former is found in P[72] and B; the latter in ℵ and A. The latter may have arisen from assimilation to ἐξέραμα.

picturing the false teachers as owned by it. At the same time corruption is personified as the master of the slaves.

The author pictures the false teachers' followers, and the false teachers themselves, as having earlier escaped defilement and then been entangled in it again; their last state is worse than the first (v. 20). The author also describes this as having fully known the way of justice and then turning away from the holy commandment (v. 21).

In vv. 20–21 the author presumes that, but does not explain why, it is worse to have returned to slavery to corruption after having escaped it, than never to have escaped at all. It is obvious that in such a case the last things are at least as bad as the first, but not immediately obvious why they should be worse. In saying that the last things have become worse than the first, the author quotes Matt 12:45/Luke 11:26. In the gospels this is the conclusion to a brief story about a person from whom an unclean spirit has been exorcised. The unclean spirit returns and brings along with it seven other spirits more evil than itself. This story makes clear why the last state of the person is worse than the first. Perhaps the author has this story in mind, expects the addressees to have it in mind, and presumes that one who returns to slavery after having escaped from it is more thoroughly enslaved than before.[40]

The author concludes his warning against returning to the defilements from which the addressees have escaped with two vivid pictures. He compares the false teachers' followers, and the false teachers themselves, to a dog who eats what he has vomited and a sow who has been washed and rolls in the mud again (v. 22).

Textural Analysis

Intertexture. In 2:18 the author *recontextualizes* Jude 16. 2:20 includes a *recitation* and recontextualization of Matt 12:45/Luke 11:26.[41]

> Matt 12:45/Luke 11:26 γίνεται τὰ ἔσχατα τοῦ ἀνθρώπου ἐκείνου χείρονα τῶν πρώτων
>
> 2 Pet 2:20 γέγονεν αὐτοῖς τὰ ἔσχατα χείρονα τῶν πρώτων

---

40. Schelkle (*Die Petrusbriefe*, 218–19), Kelly (*Peter and Jude*, 349) and Davids (*2 Peter and Jude*, 250) suggest that the author presumes what Heb 6:4-6 and 10:26 say explicitly, i.e., that there is no remedy for apostasy. Bauckham suggests that the author presumes those in the initial state of slavery to corruption were ignorant, but they would return to slavery after having gained full knowledge of Christ; thus the last state would be worse than the first. This argument is explicit in *Hermas Sim.* 9.17.5–18.2 (*Jude, 2 Peter*, 277–78).

41. Gilmour, *Significance of Parallels*, 98.

In speaking of "not fully knowing the way of justice" in 2:21, the author of 2 Peter recites Job 24:13.

Job 24:13 οὐκ ἐπέγνωσαν ὁδὸν δὲ δικαιοσύνης

2 Pet 2:21 μὴ ἐπεγνωκέναι τὴν ὁδὸν τῆς δικαιοσύνης

"The way of justice" is also mentioned in Prov 21:16, 21; Matt 21:32. Second Peter 2:22 cites a proverb made up of two maxims. The first of the two maxims derives from Prov 26:11; the second part seems to come from *The Story of Ahikar* 8:15, 18.

Comparison of humans to dogs and pigs in order to present humans negatively is common in the cultural context of 2 Peter.[42] Humans are frequently compared with dogs as a way of criticizing their aggressiveness, eating habits, or sexual behavior. Apart from 2 Pet 2:22, however, it is only in Prov 26:11 that people are said to be like dogs specifically in that they return to their own vomit: "Like a dog that returns to its vomit is a fool who reverts to his folly."[43] Humans are frequently compared with pigs, as with dogs, to criticize their aggressiveness, eating habits, or sexual behavior. They are also compared with pigs to criticize them for wanting to live in the dirt. It is only in *The Story of Ahiqar* 8.15/18, however, that the preference for dirt is contrasted with having first been washed clean:

> O my son! thou hast been to me like the pig who went into the hot bath with people of quality, and when it came out of the hot bath, it saw a filthy hole and it went down and wallowed in it.[44]

Humans are also compared with dogs and pigs together, as they are in 2 Pet 2:22, to criticize their behavior. The best known example is the saying of Jesus in Matt 7:6:

> Do not give what is holy to dogs; and do not throw your pearls before swine, or they will trample them under foot and turn and maul you.

Here the people referred to as dogs and swine are seen as like those animals in their aggressive behavior. Closer to the comparison in 2 Peter is

---

42. On this see Callan, "Comparison of Humans to Animals," 106–12. The same comparison is also used to present humans positively.

43. This is similar to 2 Pet 2:22 in thought but not in language—ὥσπερ κύων ὅταν ἐπέλθῃ ἐπὶ τὸν ἑαυτοῦ ἔμετον.

44. Translation of 8.15 in the Arabic version taken from Charles, *Apocrypha and Pseudepigrapha* 2:772. Ahiqar 8.18 in the Syriac version parallels this but is not as close to the text of 2 Peter.

the statement in Horace, *Epistles* 1.2.26 that Ulysses, if he had drunk from Circe's cup, would have lived like a filthy dog or a hog delighting in mire.

Inner texture. The two references to escaping in vv. 18, 20 exhibit progression. In v. 18 the author speaks of those who are just escaping (ἀποφεύγοντας) those who live in error. In v. 20 the author speaks of having escaped (ἀποφυγόντες) the defilements of the world. The latter makes it clear that escaping those who live in error is a matter of escaping their condition, i.e., living in error and so being defiled, not just their proximity. In 1:4 the author had spoken of having escaped (ἀποφυγόντες) the corruption in the world by desire. The author probably understands the error mentioned in v. 18 as embracing desire, and the defilements mentioned in v. 20 as equivalent to corruption.

The references in v. 19 to the false teachers' promise of freedom while being themselves slaves of corruption because a person is enslaved to whatever has overcome him also display progression. Freedom (ἐλευθερία) is the opposite of the condition of slaves (δοῦλοι). By describing the content of the false teachers' message as freedom and the teachers themselves as slaves, the author of 2 Peter presents an extreme contrast between their condition and their message. And this in turn makes it impossible to take their message at face value. If the false teachers promise freedom, but are not free themselves, it seems impossible that they can truly offer freedom to others. Their message, apparently offering freedom, actually offers slavery. The false teachers' promise is thus very different from the promises of Jesus that lead to sharing divine nature (1:4).

The false teachers are slaves of corruption. This recalls the author's statement in 2:12 that the false teaches will suffer corruption. In v. 19 the author says that whatever has overcome someone has enslaved (δεδούλωται) him. Since the false teachers have been overcome by corruption, i.e., will suffer corruption, they have been enslaved by it. This will also be the lot of those who believe their promise of freedom.

There is also a progression in the two references to being overcome in vv. 19, 20. As we have just seen, v. 19 articulates the general rule that whatever overcomes (ἥττηται) someone enslaves him. In v. 20 the author applies this rule to a specific case. He speaks of again having been implicated in the defilements of the world and being overcome (ἡττῶνται) by them.

The three references to full knowledge in vv. 20–21 also exhibit progression. In v. 20 the author says that full knowledge (ἐπιγνώσει) of "our Lord and savior Jesus Christ" is the means by which one escapes the defilements of the world. In v. 21 he says it is better not to have fully known (ἐπεγνωκέναι) the way of justice than, having fully known (ἐπιγνοῦσιν) it, to turn away from the holy commandment. These three references suggest that full knowledge of Jesus is equivalent to full knowledge of the way of justice, and that turning away from the holy commandment is equivalent to deviating from the way of justice. The author again uses the image of being on a journey as in 1:11, 15; 2:2, 15. The holy commandment is the commandment to follow the way of justice, i.e., persisting in the life of holiness begun through one's full knowledge of Jesus. "Holy commandment" is a synecdoche for a complete description of Christian living.

There is also progression in the use of the cognates ὑποστρέψαι (turn away) and ἐπιστρέψας (turn back) in vv. 21 and 22 (paronomasia). The two words are antonyms; turning away is the opposite of turning back. However, in vv. 21–22 the "turning away" is equivalent to "turning back." Turning away from the holy commandment is substantially the same as the behavior comparable to the dog's turning back to his vomit and the sow's to wallowing in the mud; turning away from the holy commandment is turning back to one's situation before beginning to follow the holy commandment.

The *argumentative* texture of vv. 18–21 is very marked, as is signaled by the repetition of γάρ (for) in vv. 18, 19, 20, 21; these verses consist of a series of *enthymemes*. Verses 17–19a form an enthymeme in which vv. 18–19a support the assertions of v. 17. The argument can be restated:

> One who entices with licentious desires of the flesh those who are escaping those who live in error, etc. is a waterless spring, etc.
>
> The opponents of the author of 2 Peter do entice with licentious desires of the flesh those who are just escaping those who live in error, etc.
>
> Therefore, the author's opponents are waterless springs, etc.

Thus in v. 18 the author begins to explain why he says that the false teachers are waterless springs—they speak boastful words of futility. Like Balaam's donkey they speak; the connection is emphasized by use of the same verb meaning "speak" (φθεγξάμενον—φθεγγόμενοι—transplacement). But their speech does not rebuke lawbreaking and prevent madness, as the donkey's did. Rather, their speech is inflated and empty. Its purpose is to entice those to whom they speak. This repeats the metaphor used to criticize the false teachers in v. 14, namely that they entice unstable souls using bait to catch them as a fisherman uses bait to catch fish. Their teaching seems to be a source of wisdom, but like a waterless spring, it does not provide any wisdom. It offers bait that will draw those who follow their teaching away from wisdom.

The false teachers entice those who are just escaping from the people who live in error. This describes recently converted Christians who are now in the process of leaving their former life behind. ὀλίγως (just) might emphasize that this has happened recently, or that it has happened by a small margin. This is why the author called them unstable in v. 14; they are not firmly established in Christian life. These recent converts resemble Lot who was surrounded in Sodom by people living very differently than he did (vv. 7–8). Until recently they lived the same way as those around them; now they are escaping from this way of living. The false teachers use bait to catch these people. The bait is the desires of the flesh, licentiousnesses.

In v. 19 the author further describes this as promising them freedom, making explicit the content of the false teachers' boastful words of futility.[45] This suggests that the false teachers try to attract adherents by saying that those who follow them can indulge their appetites. They persuade people to abandon eschatological hope by presenting it as an opportunity to give free rein to their appetites.

The author may presume that the false teachers simply criticize expectation of Jesus' second coming and say that since there will be no final judgment, there is no need to be concerned about behavior. This is possible but hardly seems in itself to be a recognizably Christian view. Another possibility is that the false teachers understand salvation as fully accomplished in such a way that behavior no longer matters. This seems to have been the view of some of the Corinthian Christians addressed by Paul (see e.g., 1 Cor 6:12–20) and that of some Gnostics. The Corinthians' views seem to have been based on misunderstanding of Paul's teaching, and the same may be true of the false teachers; the author of 2 Peter refers to their misinterpretation of Paul in 3:16.[46] The author does not describe the views of the false teachers at any length. He only makes it clear that they deny the second coming of Jesus and do not prohibit licentiousness.

After saying that the false teachers entice people by promising them freedom in the first part of v. 19, the author contrasts this promise with the antithetical condition of the false teachers themselves in the remainder of v. 19. They are slaves of corruption, having been overcome by it. In this way the author develops the image of the false teachers as mists driven by a storm. The author implies that they claim to be free, presumably because they enjoy the same freedom they promise their followers. However, they are not actually free; they have been overcome by corruption and are slaves

---

45. Their promise contrasts with the promises given by Christ mentioned in 1:4.
46. Bauckham, *Jude, 2 Peter*, 275–76; Knoch, *Erste und zweite Petrusbrief*, 269; Green, *Jude & 2 Peter*, 297.

to it. Corruption is the powerful external force that controls the false teachers as a storm drives mist. The author implies that this will also be true for those who take the bait and follow the false teachers.

Verse 19 is a second *enthymeme* in which v. 19b supports the assertion of v. 19a. The argument:

> One is enslaved to whatever masters that person.
>
> The opponents of the author of 2 Peter are mastered by corruption.
>
> Therefore, the author's opponents are slaves of corruption even though they promise freedom to others.

The connection between v. 19a and 19b is emphasized by the paronomasia δοῦλοι (slaves)—δεδούλωται (enslaved). Verse 19b is a maxim. Its force is underlined by having the verbs of its two clauses, ἥττηται (has been overcome) and δεδούλωται, come at the end of the clause (adjunction) and end the same way (homoeoteleuton).

Social-cultural texture. The author has previously referred to the *master-slave* relationship in 1:1 and 2:1. Both of these refer to being a slave of Jesus Christ. 2:1 also implies previous slavery to some other owner, probably the owner mentioned here. Like Paul, the author may presume that one has a choice of masters, but cannot be without some master; cf. Rom 6:15–23.[47]

In picturing the false teachers as slaves to corruption, the author says two distinct but related things about them. They are slaves to corruption understood metaphorically because they are slaves to their own appetites, to licentiousness, the same condition to which they entice their adherents (v. 18). They are slaves to literal corruption because their metaphorical corruption will ultimately lead to their being destroyed along with the present heaven and earth when Jesus comes again (v. 12).

Inner texture. In vv. 20–21 the author continues to explain why the teaching of the false teachers constitutes "boastful words of futility" (v. 18) and implicitly to criticize them as followers of their own teaching. According to v. 20 the initial state of those enticed by the false teachers (as well as that of the false teachers themselves and probably all human beings) is that of involvement in the defilements of the world, i.e., slavery to corruption; the author does not explain how they came to be in that state. Those enticed by the false teachers (and the false teachers themselves) have escaped from this state "by full knowledge of our Lord and savior Jesus Christ."[48] The false

---

47. Schelkle also sees connections with the thought of Paul at this point (*Die Petrusbriefe*, 217).

48. As in 1:11 the author combines three titles for Jesus that he uses elsewhere.

teachers, who themselves have now returned to slavery, tempt others to return to it. The author says, "For them the last things have become worse than the first."

Verses 18 and 20 form a third *enthymeme*, with v. 20 supporting the assertion in v. 18 that the false teachers speak "boastful words of futility." The argument:

> Instruction that worsens one's situation is futile.
>
> The author's opponents are worsening the situation of the addressees by enticing them to return to the defilement they have escaped.
>
> Therefore, the false teachers offer futile instruction.

This enthymeme is connected to the enthymeme in v. 19 by the repetition ἥττηται—ἡττῶνται (overcome—transplacement). In v. 20 the antithesis between having escaped the defilements of the world and being subject to them sharpens the argument. The final clause of v. 20 is a maxim derived from Matt 12:45/Luke 11:26. If the addressees recognize the source of the maxim, the authority of the gospels may support the author's argument at this point.

In v. 21 the author elaborates the idea that the last things have become worse than the first by stating it positively, saying in effect that the first things are better than the last. The author says, "It was better for them not to have fully known the way of justice than, having fully known it, to turn away from the holy commandment delivered to them."

Verses 20b–21 form a fourth *enthymeme* in which v. 21 supports the conclusion of v. 20, namely that the last state of those deceived by the false teachers (and of the false teachers themselves) is worse than the first. The argument:

> Returning to a bad situation from which one has been delivered is worse than simply being in the bad situation.
>
> The author's opponents are enticing those who have known the way of righteousness to turn aside from it.
>
> Therefore, their last state is worse than the first.

Verse 21 repeats and refines the thought of v. 20, including the antithesis found in it. In v. 21 the antithesis is sharpened by the repetition ἐπεγνωκέναι—ἐπιγνοῦσιν (fully know—transplacement).

In v. 22 the author concludes his explanation of the danger posed by the false teachers and his implicit critique of them by comparing those who have returned to slavery after having escaped from it to two animals: "a dog having turned back to his own vomit, and a sow, having been washed, to wallowing in the mud." The author connects the two parts of his illustration together by the ellipsis of omitting ἐπιστρέψας from the second part. This resumes the unflattering comparison with animals begun in 2:12 and continued in v. 16. The behavior of the dog and sow parallels the backsliding the author criticizes. Having expelled something noxious from his body, the dog returns to it. The author makes this more vivid by using the rare word ἐξέραμα (vomit). Having been washed clean, the sow muddies herself again. "Washing" may summon the picture of baptism.[49] Comparing the behavior of the false teachers' followers to that of the dog and the sow graphically illustrates the author's claim that those who follow the false teachers (and the false teachers themselves) are not improving their situation but rather returning to a worse situation from which they have escaped. It also arouses emotions of revulsion at this behavior.

As before, if the addressees regard Jude as an authoritative text and perceive this section of 2 Peter as dependent on it, the authority of Jude might be transferred to 2 Peter. If the addressees recognize the dependence of v. 22 on Proverbs, the authority of this text may lend support to the author's argument.

Social-cultural texture. Verse 22 returns to the type of argument found in vv. 10b–17, describing those deceived by the false teachers (and the false teachers themselves) in negative terms, criticizing their ethos and trying to arouse pathos against them. Comparison with dogs and pigs *shames* them because dogs and pigs are unclean in both Jewish and Greek culture.[50] This kind of argument is also present in vv. 18–21 as the author shames the false teachers for having uncontrolled mouths (vv. 18–19) and being subject to corruption (vv. 19–20), and their followers as having uncontrolled genitals (v. 18) and turning away from holiness (v. 21).[51]

I noted above, in discussing 2:1–3 and 10b–17, that accusations of being a corrupting influence and licentiousness are conventional elements of vituperation of opponents. Another conventional accusation used in 2:18–22 is that of inflated self-esteem; this appears in the reference to the false teachers as speaking boastful words (v. 18).[52]

Ideological social-cultural texture. As is the case with 2:1–3 and 10b–17 the author's use of conventional vituperation probably reflects rivalry between the author of 2 Peter and the false teachers for recognition

---

49. Grundmann, *Brief des Judas und zweite Brief des Petrus*, 101.
50. Neyrey, *2 Peter, Jude*, 224–25.
51. Ibid., 221–23.
52. du Toit, "Vilification," 407–8.

as authentic leaders of the Christian movement. In 2:18–22, however, the author explains exactly how the false teachers constitute a corrupting influence and so goes beyond simple vilification.

Sacred texture. In the course of making the arguments found in vv. 20–21, the author finally makes explicit why ἐπίγνωσις (full knowledge), to which he has referred a number of times earlier, is so important. As we have noted above, 2 Pet 2:19–20 strongly suggests that before they were purchased by Jesus, his followers were enslaved to corruption and the defilements of the world.[53] In this passage the author describes the false teachers he opposes as promising freedom although they themselves are slaves of corruption (φθορᾶς). He proceeds to explain that someone is enslaved by whatever overcomes that person (v. 19), clearly presuming that corruption has overcome the false teachers. The author says this directly in 2:12. The false teachers are like irrational animals, born for capture and corruption. When the animals undergo corruption, the false teachers will undergo corruption (φθαρήσονται) along with them. In 2:20 the author says, in reference to the false teachers and any who might follow them, that if those who have escaped the defilements (μιάσματα) of the world by recognizing Jesus, are again overcome by them, their last state is worse than the first.

It is full knowledge (ἐπίγνωσις) of Jesus that saves one from slavery to corruption and the defilements of the world. In commenting on the rhetography of 2:1 above, I suggested that the verse portrays Jesus as having purchased his followers from their previous owner. In light of 2:19–20 we can see that this previous owner was corruption and the defilements of the world. I also suggested that the author of 2 Peter understands Jesus as having purchased his followers by his death; death was the price Jesus paid to transfer human beings from enslavement to corruption to his own service. However, the author's emphasis on the importance of full knowledge implies that this transfer does not take effect until it is known to have occurred. Prior to such knowledge, human beings continue to serve their previous master because they do not know they have a new one. In this way the author of 2 Peter regards full knowledge of Jesus as absolutely crucial.

The specification of slavery to corruption and the defilements of the world as that from which Jesus saves people also indicates what salvation means for the author of 2 Peter. The basic meaning of φθορά is destruction, with a strong implication that the destruction results from the kind of disintegration that occurs in decay, or even digestion (see Philo *Aet.* 5). In addition to its use to mean physical destruction/disintegration, φθορά

---

53. Philo uses σωτηρία as the opposite of φθορά in *Mos.* 1.146; *Praem.* 22; *Aet.* 37 and *QG* 2.22.

can also be used to mean metaphorical destruction/disintegration (like the English word "corruption"). Second Peter 2:12 clearly shows that the author of 2 Peter uses φθορά to mean physical corruption. There are two indications that the author uses the term in 2:19 to mean metaphorical as well as physical corruption. First, in 2:20 he implies that enslavement to φθορά is the same as being overcome by the defilements of the world. Second, in 2 Pet 2:18 the author implies that enslavement to φθορά is the same as living in error (πλάνη) and involvement in licentious desires of the flesh.[54]

The author of 2 Peter may understand enslavement to corruption to mean "subject to corruption," i.e., mortal. In line with this, the author of 2 Peter mentions frequently that destruction (ἀπώλεια) is the destiny of those enslaved to corruption. The false teachers introduce heresies of destruction and by denying the Master who bought them, bring destruction on themselves (2:1). Their destruction does not sleep (2:3). However, the author of 2 Peter also understands enslavement to corruption as meaning being overcome by the defilements of the world, living in error and being subject to licentious desires. In 2:10 the author describes those whom the Lord will punish as going after the flesh in the desire for defilement (μιασμοῦ). The basic meaning of μίασμα is "stain," e.g., a color imparted to a fabric. However, it is used almost exclusively in a figurative and pejorative sense to mean wrongful behavior of various kinds. Enslavement to this metaphorical corruption leads to literal corruption.

In light of this we can see that for the author of 2 Peter salvation means freedom from metaphorical corruption now and freedom from literal corruption at the end of the world. In commenting on the rhetography of 1:4, I suggested that the author understands sharing in divine nature as a matter of becoming incorruptible.

Finally, 2:18 suggests an explanation of how slavery to corruption and the defilements of the world came to be. This verse says that the false teachers tempt those who have escaped those who live in error; the false teachers tempt them by speaking bombast of futility (ματαιότητος) and appealing to licentious desires of the flesh. Speaking of escape from those who live in error is probably equivalent to speaking of freedom from slavery to corruption. Because the false teachers tempt them with futile speech and an appeal to desire, it seems likely that this is how they originally became slaves to corruption. Futility is the opposite of knowledge (see Philo *Conf.* 141 and especially 159); it is easy to see how futile speech would lead people into error and thus into slavery to corruption. The causal role of desire is

---

54. Corruption and desire are also connected in 1:4. Desire is also presented negatively in 2:10; 3:3.

confirmed by 1:4 which refers to the addressees of 2 Peter as ones who have escaped the corruption in the world by desire. Thus the author of 2 Peter does not understand enslavement to corruption as intrinsic to the human condition, but rather as due to error, futility, and the desires of the flesh.[55] We can probably see yet another reference to Jesus' followers' escape from slavery in 1:9 which mentions the cleansing of past sins. This suggests that enslavement to corruption is the result of sin.

Rhetorical Force

The author of 2 Peter concludes his *ad hominem* critique of the false teachers by arguing that following them is a matter of abandoning the benefits received through faith in Christ and further arguing that doing so is not simply a return to one's former state, but rather to a worse condition. No doubt the false teachers themselves would agree that one should not reject the benefits bestowed by Christ, but would deny that they teach people to do so. The author of 2 Peter is not concerned to present the teaching of his opponents, but he does say that they promise their followers freedom. It is the author of 2 Peter who interprets their teaching as a rejection of Christ's benefits.

This rhetorical strategy is similar to that of Paul in the letter to the Galatians, though applied to a very different situation. The Galatians presumably thought they could combine observance of the Torah with faith in Christ. Paul, however, argues that attempting to keep the Torah is a rejection of Christ. Both the author of 2 Peter and Paul in Galatians argue that more is involved in the choice confronting those they address than the addressees realize. Insofar as they succeed in convincing the addressees of their analysis, they also succeed in persuading them not to follow the course they are considering. In analyzing the destructive impact of the false teachers, the author of 2 Peter presents more clearly than anywhere else the exact character of the present benefits bestowed by Christ as he understands it, and the way the behavior promoted by the false teachers constitutes a rejection of these benefits.

In Galatians Paul argues against Gentile Christians' keeping the Torah; the author of 2 Peter argues against licentious behavior proceeding from denial that Jesus will come again. Galatians is an argument against a certain way of combining Judaism with faith in Jesus. Second Peter can be seen as an argument against a certain combination of Greco-Roman thought and behavior with faith in Jesus. This can also be seen as argument for the

55. Bauckham, *Jude, 2 Peter*, 182–84.

retention of Jewish elements as part of faith in Jesus. Second Peter insists on the belief, derived from Jewish apocalyptic thinking, that the world will come to an end when Jesus returns. And 2 Peter rejects the morality that characterized much of Greco-Roman culture in the eyes of Jews. This rejection parallels the Jewish critique of that culture, reflected for example in Wis 14:12–31.

The persuasiveness of 2:18–22 owes much to its rhetography. Picturing the false teachers and their followers as returning to the slavery from which they were freed graphically portrays the hidden significance of the false teaching. Comparison with the behavior of a dog and a sow portrays following the false teachers as disgusting, evoking a mental picture of something that is immediately rejected.

Appendix A: Terms Used Earlier in 2 Peter and Repeated in 2:10b–17

δόξας (glories—2:10) was used earlier in 1:3, 17.

βλασφημοῦντες (slandering—2:10, 12) was used earlier in 2:2; the cognate adjective βλάσφημον is used in 2:11.

ἄγγελοι (angels—2:11) was used earlier in 2:4.

δυνάμει (power—2:11) was used earlier in 1:13, 16.

φέρουσιν (bear—2:11) was used earlier in 1:17, 18, 21 (twice).

αὐτῶν (them—2:11, 12, 13) was used earlier in 1:3, 5, 9, 17, 18; 2:1, 2, 3, 8.

κυρίου (lord—2:11) was used earlier in 1:2, 8, 11, 14, 16; 2:9; the cognate κυριότητος (dominion) was used in 2:10; the synonym δεσπότην (master) was used in 2:1.

κρίσιν (judgment—2:11) was used earlier in 2:4, 9; the cognate κρίμα (judgment) was used in 2:3.

οὗτοι (these—2:12, 17) was used earlier in 1:4, 5, 8, 9, 10, 12, 13, 15, 17, 18, 20.

φθοράν (corruption—2:12 [twice]) was used earlier in 1:4; the cognate verb φθαρήσονται (to be corrupted) is also used in 2:12; the synonym ἀπώλεια (destruction) was used earlier in 2:1 (twice), 3.

ἀγνοοῦσιν (be ignorant—2:12) is a verbal antonym of ἐπίγνωσις (full knowledge) used earlier in 1:2, 3, 8, and of γνῶσις (knowledge) used earlier in 1:5, 6, and of the cognate verbs γνωρίζω (to make known) and γινώσκω (know) used in 1:16 and 1:20 respectively, and of the synonym οἶδα used in 1:12, 14; 2:9.

ἀδικούμενοι (being wronged—2:13) is cognate to δικαιοσύνη (justice) used earlier in 1:1; 2:5, to δίκαιος (just) used earlier in 1:13; 2:7, 8, and to ἄδικος (unjust) used earlier in 2:9; the cognate noun ἀδικία (wrongdoing) is used in 2:13, 15

ἡγούμενοι (considering—2:13) was used earlier in 1:13.

ἡμέρᾳ (day—2:13) was used earlier in 1:19; 2:8 (twice), 9.

ὑμῖν (you—2:13) was used earlier in 1:2, 5, 8, 10, 11, 12, 13, 15, 16, 19; 2:1, 3.

ἔχοντες (having—2:14 [twice], 16) was used earlier in 1:15, 19.

ἁμαρτίας (sin—2:14) was used earlier in 1:9; the cognate verb ἁμαρτησάντων (to sin) was used in 2:4.

ἀστήρικτος (unstable—2:14) is cognate to ἐστηριγμένους (to establish) used earlier in 1:12.

ψυχάς (souls—2:14) was used earlier in 2:8.

καρδίαν (heart—2:14) was used earlier in 1:19.

πλεονεξίας (greed—2:14) was used earlier in 2:3.

ὁδόν (way—2:15 [twice]) was used earlier in 2:2; it is cognate to εἴσοδος (entrance) used in 1:11 and its antonym ἔξοδος (departure) used in 1:15.

ἐξακολουθήσαντες (having followed—2:15) was used earlier in 1:16; 2:2.

ἠγάπησεν (loved—2:15) is cognate to ἀγάπη (love) used in 1:7 and ἀγαπητός (beloved) used in 1:17.

ἰδίας (his—2:16) was used earlier in 1:3, 20.

ἀνθρώπου (human being—2:16) was used earlier in 1:21 (twice).

φωνῇ (voice—2:16) was used earlier in 1:17, 18; the cognate ἄφωνον (voiceless) is also found in 2:16.

προφήτου (prophet—2:16) is cognate to προφητικόν (prophetic) used earlier in 1:19, to προφητεία (prophecy) used earlier in 1:20, 21, and to ψευδοπροφῆται (false prophets) used earlier in 2:1.

ζόφος (gloom—2:17) was used earlier in 2:4.

τετήρηται (kept—2:17) was used earlier in 2:4, 9.

Appendix B: Terms Used Earlier in 2 Peter and Repeated in 2:18–22

γάρ (for—2:18, 19, 20, 21) was used earlier in 1:8, 9, 10, 11, 16, 17, 21; 2:4, 8).

φθεγγόμενοι (speaking—2:18) was used earlier in 2:16.

δελεάζουσιν (entice—2:18) was used earlier in 2:14.

ἐπιθυμίαις (desires—2:18) was used earlier in 1:4; 2:10.

σαρκός (flesh—2:18) was used earlier in 2:10.

ἀσελγείαις (licentiousnesses—2:18) was used earlier in 2:2, 7.

ἀποφεύγοντες (escape—2:18, 20) was used earlier in 1:4.

πλάνῃ (error—2:18) is cognate to ἐπλανήθησαν (to go astray) used in 2:15.

ἀναστρεφομένους (live—2:18) is cognate to ἀναστροφῆς (life) used in 2:7.

ἐλευθερίαν (freedom—2:19) is opposite to the condition of a δοῦλος (slave) mentioned earlier in 1:1; δοῦλος is also used in 2:19 as is the cognate verb δεδούλωται (to enslave).

αὐτοῖς (them—2:19 [twice], 20, 21 [twice], 22) was used earlier in 1:3, 5, 9, 17, 18; 2:1, 2, 3, 8, 11, 12, 13.

ἐπαγγελλόμενοι (promise—2:19) is cognate to ἐπαγγέλματα (promises) used in 1:4.

ὑπάρχοντες (being—2:19) was used earlier in 1:8.

φθορᾶς (corruption—2:19) was used earlier in 1:4; 2:12 (twice); the cognate verb φθαρήσονται (to be corrupted) was also used in 2:12; the synonym ἀπώλεια (destruction) was used in 2:1 (twice), 3.

τούτῳ (this—2:19, 20) was used earlier in 1:4, 5, 8, 9, 10, 12, 13, 15, 17, 18, 20; 2:12, 17.

κόσμου (world—2:20) was used earlier in 1:4; 2:5.

ἐπιγνώσει (full knowledge—2:20) was used earlier in 1:2, 3, 8; as were the cognate noun γνῶσις (knowledge) in 1:5, 6; the cognate verbs γνωρίζω (to make known) and γινώσκω (to know) in 1:16 and 1:20 respectively; the synonym οἶδα (to know) in 1:12, 14; 2:9; and the antonym ἀγνοοῦσιν (to be ignorant) in 2:12; the cognate verb ἐπιγινώσκω (to know fully) is used twice in 2:21.

τοῦ κυρίου [ἡμῶν] καὶ σωτῆρος Ἰησοῦ Χριστοῦ (our Lord and savior Jesus Christ—2:20) was used earlier in 1:11; κυρίου (lord) was also used in 1:2, 8, 14, 16; 2:9, 11; the cognate κυριότητος (dominion) was used in 2:10; the synonym δεσπότην (master) was used in 2:1; ἡμῶν (our) was also used in 1:1 (twice), 2, 3 (twice), 4, 8, 14, 16, 18; σωτῆρος (savior) was also used in 1:1; Ἰησοῦ Χριστοῦ (Jesus Christ) was also used in 1:1 (twice), 8, 14, 16; and Ἰησοῦ alone was also used in 1:2.

πρώτων (first—2:20) was used earlier in 1:20.

ὁδόν (way—2:21) was used earlier in 2:2, 15 (twice); it is cognate to εἴσοδος (entrance) used in 1:11 and its antonym ἔξοδος (departure) used in 1:15.

δικαιοσύνης (justice—2:21) was used earlier in 1:1; 2:5; the cognate adjective δίκαιος (just) was used earlier in 1:13; 2:7, 8; as was ἄδικος (unjust) in 2:9; the cognate noun ἀδικία (wrongdoing) 2:13, 15; and the cognate verb ἀδικούμενοι (to be wrong) in 2:13.

παραδοθείσης (hand over—2:21) was used earlier in 2:4.

ἁγίας (holy—2:21) was used earlier in 1:18, 21.

ἀληθοῦς (true—2:22) is cognate to ἀλήθεια (truth) used earlier in 1:12; 2:2.

ἴδιον (his—2:22) was used earlier in 1:3, 20; 2:16.

Section 4: 2 Peter 3:1–13

Letter Body, Part 3

Restatement of Letter's Purpose and Resumption of Its Argument

After the digression of 2:10b–22, this third part of the body of 2 Peter (i.e., 1:16—3:13) restates the letter's occasion and purpose, and resumes in vv. 1–3 the direct argument against the doctrine of the false teachers. This passage begins as prophetic discourse blended with wisdom discourse, but it then becomes mainly apocalyptic discourse. It restates the occasion of the letter as reminding the addressees of the beneficial knowledge mentioned in the letter opening, and is thus prophetic discourse blended with wisdom discourse. However, the content of this knowledge is apocalyptic discourse: Jesus is savior (v. 2); these are the last days (v. 3); the promise of the παρουσία (v. 4), the day of judgment (vv. 7, 8–13), is secure.[1]

Miracle discourse is blended into the apocalyptic discourse in that the flood is presented as a precedent for the day of judgment (vv. 5–6). Priestly discourse is blended into the entire passage in the statements that the addressees should be sincere (v. 1) and should live lives of holiness and piety (v. 11), that what they should remember derives partly from the holy prophets (v. 2), and in statements that the false teachers indulge their own lusts (v. 3) and are impious (v. 7).

---

1. Once again Watson simply treats 3:1–13 as apocalyptic discourse ("Apocalyptic Discourse," 203–10).

UNIT 1: 2 PETER 3:1-4

Peter's Prophetic Reminder of Beneficial Teaching

1 Ταύτην ἤδη, ἀγαπητοί, δευτέραν ὑμῖν γράφω ἐπιστολήν, ἐν αἷς[2] διεγείρω ὑμῶν ἐν ὑπομνήσει τὴν εἰλικρινῆ διάνοιαν 2 μνησθῆναι τῶν προειρημένων ῥημάτων ὑπὸ τῶν ἁγίων προφητῶν καὶ τῆς τῶν ἀποστόλων ὑμῶν ἐντολῆς τοῦ κυρίου καὶ σωτῆρος, 3 τοῦτο πρῶτον γινώσκοντες ὅτι ἐλεύσονται ἐπ' ἐσχάτων τῶν ἡμερῶν [ἐν] ἐμπαιγμονῇ[3] ἐμπαῖκται κατὰ τὰς ἰδίας ἐπιθυμίας αὐτῶν πορευόμενοι 4 καὶ λέγοντες, Ποῦ ἐστιν ἡ ἐπαγγελία τῆς παρουσίας αὐτοῦ; ἀφ' ἧς[4] γὰρ οἱ πατέρες ἐκοιμήθησαν, πάντα οὕτως διαμένει ἀπ' ἀρχῆς κτίσεως.

1 Beloved, I now write this second letter to you, in which I arouse in your remembrance the pure understanding 2 to remember the words spoken beforehand by the holy prophets and the commandment of your apostles of our Lord and savior, 3 first knowing this, that in the last days scoffers will come with scoffing, going according to their own desires 4 and saying: "Where is the promise of his coming? For since the fathers have fallen asleep all things continue thus from the beginning of creation."

Rhetography

This restatement of the letter's occasion and resumption of its argument pictures Peter as prophetically writing a second letter to the addressees to remind them of the words of the prophets and commandment of their apostles. In speaking of the addressees as beloved in v. 1 the author of 2 Peter pictures them as people with whom he has a very intimate, affectionate relationship. It is like the relationship between God the Father and Jesus made known by the heavenly voice (1:17). In this section the author refers again to the picture evoked by the letter as a whole, namely the picture of Peter as writing a testamentary letter near the end of his life so that people can remember his teaching in the future.

The resumption of this picture, however, does not repeat all of the elements mentioned earlier and introduces some new details. The author does

---

2. ἐν αἷς is elliptical, used in place of a phrase that explicitly makes reference to the present letter and a previous one.

3. There is uncertainty whether the original text read [ἐν] ἐμπαιγμονῇ or lacked ἐν. The former is found in ℵ, A, and B; P[72] lacks ἐν. However, P[72] uses the spelling ἐνπεγμονη, suggesting that ἐν might have been omitted from that manuscript as the scribe's eye skipped over it to the same letters at the beginning of the next word. The uncertainty about the original text in this case is indicated by the brackets that enclose ἐν.

4. ἀφ' ἧς instead of ἀπὸ τῆς ἡμέρας ἧ is ellipsis.

not again explicitly refer to the imminence of his own death or to making it possible to remember his teaching in the future, though he surely presumes the addressees will continue to have these things in mind. On the other hand, he refers to the present letter as the second one he has written, probably thinking of 1 Peter as the first.[5] The purpose of both is to arouse in the memory of the addressees a pure understanding so that they remember the words spoken beforehand by the holy prophets and the commandment given by the apostles of Jesus.

This evokes a picture in which this teaching has previously been delivered to the addressees. As in 1:20 the author probably presumes that the words of the prophets have come to them by means of the Bible. In referring to the commandment of the addressees' apostles ("your apostles"), the author may evoke a picture in which apostles presented this commandment to the addressees either orally or by means of writings like the earlier letter of the author and the letters of Paul. Second Peter 3:15 makes it clear that the author regards Paul as having written to the addressees of 2 Peter. Perhaps "your apostles" are, or at least include, Peter and Paul. The teaching of the prophets is presumed to be apocalyptic; it concerns what will happen in the last days and is directed especially to those who will live at that time. The commandment of the apostles is probably the holy commandment mentioned in 2:21,[6] i.e., the commandment to live a holy life in expectation of Jesus' return. Thus the author evokes the basic apocalyptic picture of the world under the rule of God who is about to bring this world to an end and replace it with another.

This section also portrays Peter as making the apocalyptic prediction that there will be scoffers in the last days who will question belief in the second coming of Jesus. The scoffers doubt that they are living in the last days because they doubt that there will be any last days. They doubt this because they follow their own desires. This pictures the doubters as ones who reject expectation of the end of the world because it allows them to indulge their appetites.

The scoffers argue that Jesus will not come again to bring the world to an end because nothing like that has ever happened before. The author presents them as asking the rhetorical question, "Where is the promise of his coming?" and supporting the doubt this expresses by saying, "For since

---

5. So Bigg, *St. Peter and St. Jude*, 288–89; Kelly, *Peter and Jude*, 352–53; Bauckham, *Jude, 2 Peter*, 286; Green, *Jude & 2 Peter*, 310–11. Davids (*2 Peter and Jude*, 257–59) rejects this view. Lapham ("Second Epistle of Peter," 154–58) argues that 2 Pet 3:1 refers to the first two chapters of 2 Peter as the author's first letter.

6. Kelly, *Peter and Jude*, 354; Bauckham, *Jude, 2 Peter*, 288; Watson, *Invention*, 126; Green, *Jude & 2 Peter*, 313.

the fathers have fallen asleep all things continue thus from the beginning of creation." The author paints a vivid picture of the scoffers by using the figure of thought dialogue. Their statement uses sleep as a metaphor for death.

The scoffers' argument evokes the anti-apocalyptic picture of world history as an uninterrupted continuum. Perhaps they see the world as eternal.[7] The author of 2 Peter presents the appearance of those who doubt apocalyptic expectation as an element of that expectation, which is ironic. In these ways the author begins to develop a vivid picture of the last days, i.e., eschatography.

Textural Analysis

Intertexture. This passage continues and concludes the *recontextualization* of Jude 4-18 in 2 Pet 2:1—3:3. Second Peter 3:1-3 recontextualizes Jude 17-18. Second Peter 3:1 does not derive from Jude, but 2 Pet 3:2-3 is virtually a *recitation* of Jude 17-18. However, the author of 2 Peter made many small changes in this material to make it better serve his purpose and to reflect his stylistic preferences.

> Jude 17-18 μνήσθητε τῶν ῥημάτων τῶν προειρημένων ὑπὸ τῶν ἀποστόλων τοῦ κυρίου ἡμῶν Ἰησοῦ Χριστοῦ 18 ὅτι ἔλεγον ὑμῖν [ὅτι] Ἐπ' ἐσχάτου [τοῦ] χρόνου ἔσονται ἐμπαῖκται κατὰ τὰς ἑαυτῶν ἐπιθυμίας πορευόμενοι τῶν ἀσεβειῶν.

> 2 Pet 3:2-3 μνησθῆναι τῶν προειρημένων ῥημάτων ὑπὸ τῶν ἁγίων προφητῶν καὶ τῆς τῶν ἀποστόλων ὑμῶν ἐντολῆς τοῦ κυρίου καὶ σωτῆρος, 3 τοῦτο πρῶτον γινώσκοντες ὅτι ἐλεύσονται ἐπ' ἐσχάτων τῶν ἡμερῶν [ἐν] ἐμπαιγμονῇ ἐμπαῖκται κατὰ τὰς ἰδίας ἐπιθυμίας αὐτῶν πορευόμενοι

Second Peter 3:1-2 *refers* to a previous letter of Peter and can be seen as a recitation of 1 Peter that summarizes a span of text. We previously noted that the first five words of the greeting in 2 Pet 1:2 are the same as the first five words of the greeting in 1 Pet 1:2. This is the most obvious evidence that 2 Peter depends on 1 Peter. Michael J. Gilmour discusses other similarities between the two, including:[8]

1. Use of ἀρετή (virtue) in reference to God in 1 Pet 2:9 and 2 Pet 1:3;

---

7. Bigg, *St. Peter and St. Jude,* 292; though many agree, Bauckham doubts this (*Jude, 2 Peter,* 294). Neyrey (*2 Peter, Jude,* 231) and Green (*Jude & 2 Peter,* 318) seem to disagree with Bauckham.

8. See Gilmour, *Significance of Parallels,* 91-95.

2. Use of χορηγεῖ in 1 Pet 4:11 and ἐπιχορηγήσατε (supply) in 2 Pet 1:5 (its use in 1:11—not mentioned by Gilmour—is an even closer parallel);

3. Use of ἐποπτεύω in 1 Pet 2:12; 3:2 and ἐπόπτης (eyewitness) in 2 Pet 1:16;

4. Use of ἀμώμου καὶ ἀσπίλου in 1 Pet 1:19 and σπίλοι καὶ μῶμοι (spots and blemishes) in 2 Pet 2:13 along with ἄσπιλοι καὶ ἀμώμητοι (spotless and unblemished) in 2 Pet 3:14; and

5. Both mention the fallen angels along with Noah and those saved with him (1 Pet 3:18-20; 2 Pet 2:4-5).

Bauckham and Watson argue that 2 Pet 3:4-13 makes use of a Jewish apocalypse that was also used by *1 Clem* 23.3-4; *2 Clem* 11.2-4; 16.3 and perhaps *1 Clem* 23.5 and 27.4.[9] And Watson suggests that the question in v. 4, introduced by ποῦ ἐστιν (where is), is modeled on mocking questions in the Old Testament that begin this way. For example, in Mal 2:17 those who have wearied the Lord with their words are presented as asking, ποῦ ἐστιν ὁ θεὸς τῆς δικαιοσύνης (Where is the God of justice?).[10]

Inner texture. 3:1-4a constitutes an *elaborate* sentence whose main clause is found in v. 1a. A relative clause (v. 1b) depends on it, and an infinitive phrase (v. 2) depends on the relative clause. In v. 3a a participial phrase, continuing the infinitive with an imperatival meaning,[11] introduces a noun clause (v. 3b), whose subject ἐμπαῖκται (scoffers) is modified by two participles, the second of which introduces a direct quotation in v. 4. This period consists of four clauses.

Several terms used earlier in 2 Peter are *repeated* in 3:1-4 (see Appendix A). Another term is introduced in 3:1-4 and repeated later in the letter; ἐπιστολήν (letter) is used in 3:1 and again in 3:16. Other terms are introduced and repeated in 3:1-4.[12]

A number of the terms repeated from earlier parts of 2 Peter serve the author's restatement of the letter's occasion and resumption of its argument. The author stated the letter's occasion in 1:12-15. As in 1:12-15 the author

---

9. Bauckham, *Jude, 2 Peter*, 283-85; Watson, "Apocalyptic Discourse," 203-4.

10. Watson, "Apocalyptic Discourse," 205-6.

11. BDF § 468; Kraus, *Sprache, Stil*, 271; Green, *Jude & 2 Peter*, 315. Mayor (*St. Jude and St. Peter*, liv-lv) analyzes 3:2 as an accusative-infinitive construction, and the participle in 3:3a as modifying the implied subject. On this analysis the case of the participle is wrong, nominative instead of accusative. Bigg (*St. Peter and St. Jude*, 290) and Gerdmar (*Rethinking*, 34-35) agree.

12. προειρημένων (spoken beforehand) and its cognate ῥημάτων (words) are both used in 3:2. ἐμπαιγμονῇ (scoffing) and its cognate ἐμπαῖκται (scoffers) are both used in 3:3.

twice uses first person singular verbs in 3:1 and speaks of the addressees as "you" in 3:1-2. Here he also addresses them as "beloved." In 1:12-15 the author spoke of his intention διεγείρειν ὑμᾶς ἐν ὑπομνήσει (to arouse you by remembrance—1:13); here he uses almost the same words to say that in this letter and a previous one, διεγείρω ὑμῶν ἐν ὑπομνήσει (I arouse in your remembrance—3:1). As was true in 1:13, this constitutes the trope periphrasis because this idea could be expressed more simply. This periphrasis emphasizes reminding as the author's purpose.

Just as the author mentioned remembering several times in 1:12-15, here he mentions it a second time in 3:2, using the paronomasia ὑπομνήσει (remembrance)—μνησθῆναι (to remember) in vv. 1-2. In 3:1 the author speaks of arousing in the addressees' remembrance the pure understanding they have had in the past; in 3:2 remembering this pure understanding is further specified as remembering the words of the prophets and the commandment of the apostles. The author's purpose is cognitive, as it is throughout 2 Peter; he wants the addressees to have knowledge. The danger he wants to avert is that of forgetting or misunderstanding. At least in part, his teaching is not unique to him, but is an endorsement of the words of the prophets and the commandment of the addressees' apostles.

The author's repeated statement that his purpose is reminding the addressees of what they already know is a renewal of his effort to win the addressees' good will and receptivity to his message and to establish his own ethos.

The author's second argument that Jesus will come again was an appeal to the prophetic word in 1:19-2:10a. The author repeats several terms from that argument in 3:1-4. Cognates of προφητῶν (prophets—3:2) were used in 1:19, 20, 21. The description of prophets as ἁγίων (holy—3:2) is repeated from 1:21. The phrase τοῦτο πρῶτον γινώσκοντες (first knowing this—3:3) is repeated from 1:20. Although there are no verbal similarities, the prediction in 3:3 that there will be scoffers in the last days is similar to the prediction of the rise of false teachers in 2:1-3. The description of the scoffers as going according to their own desires (3:3) repeats the words πορευόμενοι (going) and ἐπιθυμίας (desires) from 2:10.

Finally, the scoffers' question, "Where is the promise of his coming?" (3:4) repeats παρουσίας (coming) from 1:16 where the author introduced his first argument that Jesus will come again (1:16-18) by denying that he and others had followed cleverly devised myths in making known the coming of Jesus.

As a resumption of the main message of the letter, 3:1-4 is an example of two figures of thought, namely, aphodos and transitio.

The paronomasia προειρημένων ῥημάτων (words spoken beforehand) in v. 2 emphasizes the predictive character of prophecy. Use of the word ἐντολῆς (commandment) repeats the synecdoche found in 2:21; it is shorthand for a complete description of Christian living.

The author says that in the last days there will be scoffers. He emphasizes this scoffing by coining the new word ἐμπαιγμονῇ (scoffing) in 3:3 and by the paronomasia of pairing this word with ἐμπαῖκται (scoffers). Presenting the appearance of these scoffers as an element of the last days that was predicted to occur implicitly undermines their scoffing. Except as a sign that the last days have arrived, their scoffing can be ignored.

The words of the scoffers quoted in 3:4 constitute an *enthymeme*, the presence of which is signaled by use of the word γάρ (for). This enthymeme can be restated:

> One can only affirm the promise of Jesus' coming if something similar has happened previously
>
> But since the fathers have fallen asleep all things continue thus from the beginning of creation.
>
> Therefore, the promise of Jesus' coming is false.

The identity of "the fathers" mentioned by the scoffers is not clear. Bigg argues that the fathers are the patriarchs of Israel.[13] Kelly and others argue that they are the first Christian generation that has now died,[14] i.e., the fathers of the scoffers.[15] Neither of these interpretations agrees very well with the parallel specification of time later in the verse, i.e., "from the beginning of creation." Since the beginning of creation antedates the death of the fathers, referring to the death of the fathers seems to add nothing to the argument. An interpretation that diminishes, but does not eliminate, this problem is to see the fathers as the ancestors of the human race.[16] Then the death of the fathers and the beginning of creation are roughly commensurate ways of referring to the beginning of the world's history.

If the addressees perceive 2 Pet 3:1–2 as referring to 1 Peter, the awareness underlines the identity of the author as Peter. As before, if the addressees regard Jude as an authoritative text and perceive this section of 2 Peter as dependent on it, the authority of Jude might be transferred to 2 Peter.

---

13. Bigg, *St. Peter and St. Jude,* 291; so also Davids, *2 Peter and Jude,* 265–67.

14. Kelly, *Peter and Jude,* 355–56; Bauckham, *Jude, 2 Peter,* 290–91; Paulsen, *Der Zweite Petrusbrief,* 157.

15. Schelkle, *Die Petrusbriefe,* 224.

16. Cf. Green, *Jude & 2 Peter,* 317–18.

Social-cultural texture. Second Peter 3:4 reports a *challenge* to which vv. 5–13 are the *riposte*.[17] The author invokes the value of *purity* by referring to sincerity (v. 1) and holiness (v. 2) on one hand, and desire (v. 3) on the other. In this way the author calls the addressees to purity and accuses the false teachers of impurity.

Rhetorical Force

As the author restates the occasion of the letter in 3:1–4 in order to resume its argument, he provides the clearest description of his opponents. The letter opened (1:1–15) without any explicit reference to people who might disagree with the content of the letter. In the following sections (1:16—2:22) the author first adverted to the existence of ideas he rejected and then to the false teachers who advanced them, whose deficiencies of character he described at some length. Now the author describes his opponents as scoffers destined to appear in the last days and allows the addressees to see them clearly by quoting their words.

In 3:1–4 the author makes explicit what he implied in 2:1–3, namely, that the appearance of false teachers, here called scoffers, is itself an element of the apocalyptic expectation he advocates. The rise of the false teachers is a sign that these are the last days. The author's vivid description of the scoffers, who are presumably already active among the addressees, makes the implication that the addressees are living in the last days more forceful.

Recognition that the scoffers are themselves a sign of the last days in itself implicitly undermines their opposition to expectation of the end of the world; their opposition need not be regarded as a serious threat because it is itself part of the chain of events by which God will bring the world to an end. Nevertheless, the author goes on to respond to the arguments of the false teachers.

UNIT 2: 2 PETER 3:5-13

Renewed Argument that Jesus Will Come Again

---

17. Neyrey, *2 Peter, Jude,* 227–29, 236–37.

5 λανθάνει γὰρ αὐτοὺς τοῦτο θέλοντας¹⁸ ὅτι οὐρανοὶ ἦσαν ἔκπαλαι καὶ γῆ ἐξ ὕδατος καὶ δι' ὕδατος συνεστῶσα¹⁹ τῷ τοῦ θεοῦ λόγῳ, 6 δι' ὧν²⁰ ὁ τότε κόσμος ὕδατι κατακλυσθεὶς ἀπώλετο· 7 οἱ δὲ νῦν οὐρανοὶ καὶ ἡ γῆ τῷ αὐτῷ λόγῳ τεθησαυρισμένοι εἰσὶν πυρὶ τηρούμενοι εἰς ἡμέραν κρίσεως καὶ ἀπωλείας τῶν ἀσεβῶν ἀνθρώπων. 8 Ἓν δὲ τοῦτο μὴ λανθανέτω ὑμᾶς, ἀγαπητοί, ὅτι μία ἡμέρα παρὰ κυρίῳ ὡς χίλια ἔτη καὶ χίλια ἔτη ὡς ἡμέρα μία. 9 οὐ βραδύνει κύριος τῆς ἐπαγγελίας, ὥς τινες βραδύτητα ἡγοῦνται, ἀλλὰ μακροθυμεῖ εἰς ὑμᾶς,²¹ μὴ βουλόμενός τινας ἀπολέσθαι ἀλλὰ πάντας εἰς μετάνοιαν χωρῆσαι. 10 Ἥξει δὲ ἡμέρα κυρίου ὡς κλέπτης, ἐν ᾗ οἱ οὐρανοὶ ῥοιζηδὸν παρελεύσονται στοιχεῖα δὲ καυσούμενα λυθήσεται καὶ γῆ καὶ τὰ ἐν αὐτῇ ἔργα εὑρεθήσεται.²² 11 τούτων οὕτως²³ πάντων λυομένων²⁴ ποταποὺς δεῖ ὑπάρχειν [ὑμᾶς]²⁵ ἐν ἁγίαις ἀναστροφαῖς καὶ εὐσεβείαις, 12 προσδοκῶντας καὶ σπεύδοντας τὴν παρουσίαν τῆς τοῦ θεοῦ ἡμέρας δι' ἣν οὐρανοὶ πυρούμενοι λυθήσονται καὶ στοιχεῖα καυσούμενα τήκεται. 13 καινοὺς δὲ οὐρανοὺς καὶ γῆν καινὴν κατὰ τὸ ἐπάγγελμα αὐτοῦ προσδοκῶμεν, ἐν οἷς δικαιοσύνη κατοικεῖ.

---

18. λανθάνει γὰρ αὐτοὺς τοῦτο θέλοντας = For they wish this unaware. The antecedent of τοῦτο is πάντα οὕτως διαμένει ἀπ' ἀρχῆς κτίσεως (3:4). θέλοντας is a supplementary participle depending on λανθάνει and modifying αὐτοὺς. Thus the translation "For this they wilfully fail to see" (Bigg, *St. Peter and St. Jude*, 292) is not possible. Kelly and Bauckham also reject this interpretation, but not as completely (Kelly, *Peter and Jude*, 357; Bauckham, *Jude, 2 Peter*, 297).

19. συνεστῶσα = fem. sg. pf. act. ptc. συνίστημι. It is in agreement with γῆ, but probably only as a result of attraction to the nearest noun; it probably refers to both heavens and earth because the two are treated together in what follows (Kelly, *Peter and Jude*, 357-58; Bigg [*St. Peter and St. Jude*, 293] takes the opposite view).

20. The antecedents are ὕδατος and λόγῳ (Bigg, *St. Peter and St. Jude*, 293-94; Kelly, *Peter and Jude*, 359-60; Bauckham, *Jude, 2 Peter*, 298).

21. There is some uncertainty whether the text read εἰς ὑμᾶς or δι' ὑμᾶς. The former is found in P⁷² and B; the latter in ℵ and A. The latter may have arisen from the unusual usage represented by the former.

22. There is considerable uncertainty whether the text read εὑρεθήσεται or something else. εὑρεθήσεται is the reading of ℵ and B. P⁷² adds λυόμενα after εὑρεθήσεται, which seems to be an attempt to explain the meaning of εὑρεθήσεται, as do the various readings of other manuscripts (see Bauckham, *Jude, 2 Peter*, 316-21; Metzger, *A Textual Commentary*, 636-37).

23. There is uncertainty whether the text read οὕτως or οὖν. The former is found in P⁷² and B; the latter in ℵ and A. The latter may be a correction intended to make the text easier to understand.

24. τούτων οὕτως πάντων λυομένων is a genitive absolute.

25. There is also uncertainty whether or not the text included [ὑμᾶς], as is indicated by the brackets enclosing it. The word is found in A, but lacking from P⁷² and B; ℵ reads ἡμᾶς, perhaps a mistake for ὑμᾶς arising from the similar sound of the two words (Metzger, *A Textual Commentary*, 637).

5 For it escapes the notice of those maintaining this that there were heavens long ago and an earth constituted from water and through water by the word of God, 6 through which [water and word] the world of that time was destroyed, having been deluged with water. 7 And the present heavens and the earth are treasured up by the same word, kept for fire on the day of judgment and destruction of impious human beings. 8 And let this one thing not escape your notice, beloved, that one day with the Lord is like a thousand years and a thousand years like one day. 9 For the Lord of the promise does not delay, as some consider delay, but he is patient toward you, not wishing that any be destroyed, but that all come to repentance. 10 And the day of the Lord will come like a thief, on which the heavens will pass away with a rushing noise, and the elements, set on fire, will be dissolved, and the earth and the works on it will be discovered. 11 Since all these things are thus being dissolved, what sort of people is it necessary that you be with holy lives and pieties, 12 awaiting and eagerly seeking the coming of the day of God on account of which the heavens, burning, will be dissolved and the elements, set on fire, are melted. 13 And we await new heavens and a new earth according to his promise, in which justice dwells.

Rhetography

As the author of 2 Peter confirms the truth of his apocalyptic teaching by refuting the skepticism of the scoffers, he invokes a series of pictures. He briefly describes the creation of the world, its destruction by the flood, and the future destruction of the present world by fire.

In referring to God's destruction of the world in the time of Noah, the author again evokes the story told in Gen 6:5—9:29, as he did in 2:5. Here he makes no reference to the salvation of Noah and those with him; he speaks only of God's destruction of the world at that time.

However, in 3:5 the author puts this destruction in the context of creation, evoking the story told in Gen 1:2, 6-9. God created the world with a word, first dividing the primeval waters with the dome of the heavens and then gathering the waters below the dome into one place so that dry land appeared.[26] At the time of Noah, God destroyed the world by water and word. At God's word the waters above and below the dome were released from their boundaries. Gen 7:11 describes the beginning of the flood in this way: "on that day all the fountains of the great deep burst forth, and the windows of the heavens were opened."

---

26. See Kelly, *Peter and Jude*, 358–59; Bauckham, *Jude, 2 Peter*, 297; Paulsen, *Zweite Petrusbrief*, 160–61; Davids, *2 Peter and Jude*, 268–70.

The author of 2 Peter describes creation only by saying that long ago there were heavens and an earth constituted from water and through water by the word of God. Someone who did not recognize the allusion to Genesis might have difficulty understanding exactly what that means; however, the author of 2 Peter probably presumes that those he addresses will recognize the allusion. He describes the destruction of the world at the time of Noah as having taken place through water and the word. For those who recognized the author's allusion to Genesis, this would imply that the destruction resulted from God's undoing the work of creation. The author describes the destruction itself as a matter of the world's having been deluged with water. This is the same picture presented earlier in 2:5.

Just as the world was destroyed in the time of Noah, so the present heavens and earth are being treasured up by the same word, kept for fire on the day of judgment and destruction of impious human beings. The expression is periphrastic, making the picture more elaborate. This repeats the picture presented in 2:4 and 9 of sinners and the unjust as being kept for judgment (see also 2:17). Here the author makes it clear that the judgment involves the entire world and will take place by fire. This evokes a mental picture like that depicted in the words of God in Deut 32:22, "For a fire is kindled by my anger, and burns to the depths of Sheol; it devours the earth and its increase, and sets on fire the foundations of the mountains."

In v. 8 the author again calls the addressees beloved, reverting a second time to the picture of them as people with whom he has an intimate relationship first evoked in 3:1. The author then says that for God one human day is like a thousand years and a thousand human years like one day. The author thus calls attention to a fundamental difference between God and human beings. This pictures God as being outside the human world in a situation where something as basic as time is different than it is in the human world. A short time in the human world may correspond to a long time in God's situation, and a long time in the human world may correspond to a short time in God's situation.

The author's denial in v. 9 that the Lord of the promise delays evokes the picture of the Lord's delaying in order to deny that he does so. This rejected picture may derive from the scoffers the author opposes. The author makes a distinction between delay and patience. Saying that God is patient portrays God as benevolent, wishing only the good of human beings. The author's picture of God as patient and benevolent makes it impossible to think that God has simply neglected to fulfill the promise of Jesus' return.

In v. 10 the author says that the day of the Lord will come like a thief, i.e., unexpectedly. The author evokes the picture of a thief secretly approaching the person he plans to rob and taking his victim by surprise. The vivid picture of the return of Jesus as analogous to a totally unexpected theft eliminates any possibility that its time could be known.

Verse 10 continues with a description of the day of the Lord; this description is repeated in v. 12, where the day of the Lord is called the day of God. On that day the heavens will pass away with a rushing noise (v. 10) or will be dissolved by fire (v. 12). The picture underlying the first of these may be that of destruction of the heavens by fire, which is explicit in the second; the rushing noise with which the heavens pass away may be the noise of a roaring fire.[27] The author uses the rare word ῥοιζηδόν for "rushing noise;" this is onomatopoeia since the sound of the word expresses its meaning. An eschatological fire will also dissolve or melt the elements of which the world is composed. The author uses the rare word καυσόω (be on fire) metaphorically in vv. 10 and 12, implying that the heat that dissolves the universe is like the fever that accompanies disease.

At the end of v. 10 the author observes that when the world ends, the earth and the works on it will be discovered. In saying this, the author may evoke a picture like that presented explicitly in 1 Cor 3:12–15. In this passage Paul says that the nature of the work a person has done in building on the foundation of Christ will be revealed by fire on the last day. Good work will survive the fire; poor work will be burned up.

> Now if anyone builds on the foundation with gold, silver, precious stones, wood, hay, straw—the work of each builder will become visible, for the Day will disclose it, because it will be revealed with fire, and the fire will test what sort of work each has done. If what has been built on the foundation survives, the builder will receive a reward. If the work is burned up, the builder will suffer loss; the builder will be saved, but only as through fire.

In 3:11 the author of 2 Peter envisions the addressees as living holy and pious lives. He expresses this by means of an exclamation that begins by picturing the addressees living in a different way than those among whom Lot lived (2:7) and among whom they previously lived (2:18), living holy and pious lives instead of licentious ones.[28] This artful exclamation is the figure of thought exclamation.[29] At the beginning of v. 12 the author further

---

27. Bauckham, *Jude, 2 Peter*, 315.

28. The author uses ἀναστροφή in 3:11 and 2:7 and the cognate verb in 2:18, linking the three passages.

29. According to Watson this exclamation can also be seen as an epiphoneme, an exclamation attached to the close of a proof or statement as a climax (*Invention*, 134), whose use, according to Demetrius, produces grandeur of style (*On Style* 106–11).

describes their way of life as one of awaiting and eagerly seeking the coming of the day of God, which he then goes on to describe for a second time in the remainder of v. 12, as we have seen.

As was the case in the time of Noah, the heavens and earth that have been destroyed will be replaced by new heavens and earth (v. 13). This will be God's third creation of heaven and earth. God destroyed the first heaven and earth in the time of Noah and then recreated them; on the day of the Lord, God will destroy the second heaven and earth and then recreate them. The author pictures the new heavens and earth as the fulfillment of the promise made (probably) by the Lord of the promise mentioned in 3:9. Justice will dwell in this third heaven and earth. Justice is pictured as a person that lives in the new creation. This evokes a mental picture like that depicted in Isa 32:16, "Then justice will dwell in the wilderness, and righteousness abide in the fruitful field."

Taken together these pictures provide the author's most detailed description of the end of the world, his eschatography.

Textural Analysis

Intertexture. 3:5–6 are a *recitation* that summarizes a span of text that includes various episodes, namely Gen 1–7.

The statement that the world is being kept for judgment by the word of God probably means that it is predicted in the Bible. The author sees it as predicted by the scriptural accounts of the events he has mentioned in 2:4–8. In 2:5 he presented the reduction of Sodom and Gomorrah to ashes (by fire) as a sign of what will happen to the impious. He may also see the judgment of the world by fire predicted by passages such as Deut 32:22; Mal 3:19; Isa 66:15–16; Zeph 1:18. And he may be thinking that it is predicted by 1 Cor 3:13–15.

In 3:8 the author *recites* Ps 90:4 (LXX 89:4).

Ps 90:4 χίλια ἔτη ἐν ὀφθαλμοῖς σου ὡς ἡ ἡμέρα

2 Pet 3:8 χίλια ἔτη ὡς ἡμέρα μία

Watson suggests that Hab 2:3 may underlie 2 Pet 3:9.[30] The phrase ἡμέρα κυρίου ὡς κλέπτης (day of the Lord like a thief) in 3:10 is probably

---

30. Watson, "Apocalyptic Discourse," 207.

recited from 1 Thess 5:2;[31] the basic idea, however, is also found in several other places.[32]

1 Thess 5:2 ἡμέρα κυρίου ὡς κλέπτης

2 Pet 3:9 ἡμέρα κυρίου ὡς κλέπτης

Watson sees a combination of Mal 3:19 and Isa 34:4 as underlying 2 Pet 3:10, 12, possibly with some influence of Hab 2:3.[33]

In 3:13 the promise of new heavens and earth is probably that found in Isa 65:17; 66:22, since 3:13 is a recitation of these passages.[34]

Isa 65:17; 66:22 ὁ οὐρανὸς καινὸς καὶ ἡ γῆ καινή

2 Pet 3:13 καινοὺς δὲ οὐρανοὺς καὶ γῆν καινὴν

The depiction of justice as a person that lives in the new creation is adapted from Isa 32:16.

Inner texture. Several terms used earlier in 2 Peter are *repeated* in 3:5–13 (see Appendix B). Other terms are introduced in 3:5–13 and repeated later in the letter.[35] Other terms are introduced and repeated in 3:5–13 and in one case later in the letter (see Appendix C).

The false teachers argue that everything remains as it has from the beginning (3:4). There is no precedent for the coming of Jesus and the end of the world and thus no reason to think it will happen. The author refutes this argument in vv. 5–6 by describing again (as in 2:5) the flood in the time of Noah. These verses form an *enthymeme*,[36] signaled by the use of γάρ (for), whose *argument* can be restated:

> One can only maintain that all things have remained as they are since the beginning of creation if the world has not previously been destroyed.

---

31. Fornberg, *Early Church in Pluralistic Society*, 25; Neyrey, *2 Peter, Jude*, 242; Davids, *2 Peter and Jude*, 282. Bauckham (*Jude, 2 Peter*, 306) disagrees and Green is uncertain (*Jude & 2 Peter*, 329). Gilmour (*Significance of Parallels*, 103–4) argues that "the day of the Lord will come like a thief" is widely used and cannot be traced to a specific source with confidence.

32. Matt 24:43–44/Luke 12:39–40; Rev 3:3; 16:15.

33. Watson, "Apocalyptic Discourse," 208–9.

34. Bauckham, *Jude, 2 Peter*, 326; Davids, *2 Peter and Jude*, 292; Green, *Jude & 2 Peter*, 334–35.

35. νῦν (now—3:7) is used again in 3:18. μακροθυμεῖ (be patient) is used in 3:9 and its cognate μακροθυμίαν (patience) is used in 3:15. εὑρεθήσεται (find—3:10) is used again in 3:14

36. Watson, *Invention*, 129.

But the world was destroyed previously by the flood.

Therefore, all things have not remained as they are since the beginning of creation (and one can maintain that the world will be destroyed again).

The picture of the world's destruction in the time of Noah powerfully contradicts the view that all things have remained the same since the beginning of creation. The author links creation and destruction by repeating the word ὕδωρ (water) three times in two different cases (polyptoton).

The author says that the picture of creation and destruction he evokes escapes the notice of the scoffers. He emphasizes this by putting the verb λανθάνει (escapes the notice of) at the beginning of v. 5 (adjunction). He uses the same verb again in v. 8 as he admonishes the addressees not to let something escape their notice. These references to the danger of not noticing or forgetting continue the emphasis on the cognitive found throughout 2 Peter.

Having argued in vv. 5–6 that all things have not remained unchanged since the beginning of creation, the author concludes in v. 7 that the present heavens and earth are treasured up for destruction by fire. As the author had described past judgment by water and fire in 2:5–6, he now links that same past judgment by water with a future judgment by fire. This future judgment will occur by means of the same word that was operative in the creation and destruction of the first heavens and earth. The author links the creation of the world and its final destruction by repeating the words οὐρανοί (heavens), γῆ (earth), and λόγῳ (word) in vv. 5 and 7 (transplacement). He links the destruction in the time of Noah and the final destruction of the world by the paronomasia of pairing ἀπώλετο (be destroyed) with the cognate noun ἀπωλείας (destruction) in vv. 6–7.

Verse 8 is connected with v. 7 by repetition of the word ἡμέρα (day). Verse 7 refers to the day of judgment; v. 8 comments on the meaning of "day" for God. However, v. 8 does not seem to be a direct comment on the meaning of "day" in the phrase "day of judgment." Instead the author takes up a different, but related topic, namely the time when the day of judgment will occur. In v. 9 the author clearly responds to an argument that he has not explicitly attributed to the scoffers, namely, the argument that the return of Jesus has been delayed. It seems likely that he is already addressing this argument in v. 8. Apparently the scoffers' skepticism is partly based on the idea that the return of Jesus should have already occurred by their time if it was going to happen at all. Since it has not, they view the expectation as unfounded. The author responds to this in two ways.

He first addresses the perception that the return of Jesus to end the world has been delayed by saying that time is different for God than for human beings. He begins by telling the addressees not to let this escape their notice. They should not make the mistake made by the scoffers (v. 5), by not having important information in mind. Since time has different meanings for human beings and for God, it is not possible to say that what seems like a long time to human beings is actually a long time for God. Thus human perceptions of time cannot be the basis for saying that God has delayed some action; the divine perception of time is completely different.

The author has taken this picture from Ps 90:4 (LXX 89:4). His main point in citing Ps 90:4 seems to be that a long time for humans ("a thousand years") is like a short time ("one day") for God. This directly refutes the suggestion that the return of Jesus has been delayed, and this is what the author recites from Ps 90:4. However, instead of simply saying this, the author has prefaced it with the statement that what is a short time for humans ("one day") is like a long time ("a thousand years") for God.

The recitation and the author's prefaced statement (μία ἡμέρα παρὰ κυρίῳ ὡς χίλια ἔτη καὶ χίλια ἔτη ὡς ἡμέρα μία—one day with the Lord is like a thousand years and a thousand years like one day) have five words in common, but in the opposite order, creating a chiastic pattern. These two clauses exhibit two figures of speech—antimetabole and antithesis. The former consists of expressing two different thoughts one after the other so that the latter follows from the former though contrary to it; thus it includes antithesis.

Since the author does not make explicit from whose perspective the "day" and "thousand years" are being reckoned, it is possible that he has prefaced the recitation from Ps 90:4 with the statement that what is a short time for God is a long time for humans. In this case he would have said exactly the same thing as the words from the psalm but in reverse order, presumably repeating himself for the sake of emphasis. However, this would mean that the prefaced statement adds no content to his communication. More significantly it would require the addressees to understand the statement as first speaking about time from God's perspective as compared to time from the human perspective and then the reverse, i.e., time from the human perspective as compared to God's, without any explicit indication of this. It seems more natural to understand the two statements as speaking about the two perspectives in the same order.

On this understanding, the author has prefaced the psalm recitation with the statement that what is a short time for God is a long time for humans in order to indicate that time is simply different for God than for humans. The most important implication of this is that humans cannot conclude that the return of Jesus has been delayed. But that is not because a thousand human years constitute one divine day; it is because no conclusions about divine time are possible on the basis of human time.[37]

Although the author does not explicitly say that he is reciting the psalm in v. 8, he presumably expects the addressees to recognize that he is. And the recognition that he is restating the teaching of an authoritative text is a reason for accepting the teaching.

The author makes a second response to the idea that the return of Jesus has been delayed in v. 9. He connects it with the objection of the scoffers in 3:4 by repeating the word ἐπαγγελίας (promise). This argument that God has not delayed to keep the promise of Jesus' return presumes that "delay" means simple procrastination. If God has a reason for sending Jesus at one time rather than another, this is not delay. This *enthymeme*[38] can be restated:

> One can say that the Lord is slow to keep his promises only if there is no sufficient reason for delay in keeping them.
>
> But the Lord delays out of patience, giving all the opportunity for repentance.
>
> Therefore, the Lord is not slow to keep his promises.

The Lord of the promise is the one who determines its fulfillment; the promise is probably the promise of Jesus' coming mentioned in v. 4. By putting the verb οὐ βραδύνει (does not delay) first in the sentence (adjunction), the author emphasizes his rejection of the picture of the Lord as delaying. He also emphasizes this by the paronomasia of pairing this verb with a cognate noun (βραδύνει—βραδύτητα [delay]). The author says that rather than delaying, the Lord of the promise is patient, not wishing that any be destroyed, but that all come to repentance.

In v. 10 the author offers a final response to the argument that the return of Jesus has been delayed. He says that the day of the Lord will come

---

37. The Venerable Bede offers a similar interpretation in his commentary on 2 Peter; see also Schelkle, *Die Petrusbriefe*, 226–27; Spicq, *Épitres de Saint Pierre*, 250–51; Kelly, *Peter and Jude*, 361–62; Neyrey, *2 Peter, Jude*, 238; Paulsen, *Zweite Petrusbrief*, 163–64; Knoch, *Erste und zweite Petrusbrief*, 279–80; Harrington, "Jude and 2 Peter," 288; Davids, *2 Peter and Jude*, 277. Käsemann presumes this interpretation and argues that it robs apocalyptic expectation of all meaning ("Apologia," 193–94; see also Windisch, *Katholische Briefe*, 102; Grundmann, *Brief des Judas und zweite Brief des Petrus*, 115–16; Fornberg, *Early Church*, 68). Bauckham (*Jude, 2 Peter*, 310) and Green (*Jude & 2 Peter*, 326) reject both the interpretation and Käsemann's inference from it. I agree that Käsemann's inference is wrong but not his interpretation of v. 8; I regard v. 8 is a way of saying that the time of the end is unknown, a prominent theme of apocalyptic expectation.

38. Watson, *Invention*, 130–31.

like a thief, i.e., unexpectedly. Since no one knows when it will come, it is impossible to say that is has been delayed. By putting the verb (ἥξει—will come) first in the sentence (adjunction) the author emphasizes his assertion that the day of the Lord will come like a thief. Use of κύριος (Lord) in vv. 8, 9, and 10 connects these three verses. Verse 8 speaks of the meaning of time for the Lord; v. 9 denies that the Lord of the promise delays; and v. 10 speaks about the coming day of the Lord.

Although the author has not explicitly indicated that he is reciting 1 Thessalonians in v. 10, he may presume that the addressees will recognize that he is and that the authority of 1 Thessalonians will be a reason to accept this teaching. In the remainder of v. 10 the author describes the coming of the day of the Lord. And he repeats the description in v. 12.

10 Ἥξει δὲ ἡμέρα κυρίου ὡς κλέπτης,	12 προσδοκῶντας καὶ σπεύδοντας τὴν παρουσίαν τῆς τοῦ θεοῦ ἡμέρας
ἐν ᾗ οἱ οὐρανοὶ ῥοιζηδὸν παρελεύσονται	δι' ἣν οὐρανοὶ πυρούμενοι λυθήσονται
στοιχεῖα δὲ καυσούμενα λυθήσεται	καὶ στοιχεῖα καυσούμενα τήκεται.

The four clauses (cola) that describe the dissolution of the heavens and earth all have the same grammatical structure (parisosis) and all end with the same syllable, namely ται (homoeoteleuton and homoeoptoton).[39] The words οὐρανοί (heavens), λύω (dissolve), στοιχεῖα (elements), and καυσούμενα (burning) are all repeated (transplacement). οὐρανοί is used with the article in v. 10 and without it in v. 12. λύω is used in two different forms in vv. 10 and 12 and a third form in v. 11 (λυθήσεται—λυομένων—λυθήσονται). There are other differences in vocabulary between the two descriptions. This combination of differences and similarities emphasizes the details of the day of the Lord by repeating them in an interestingly varied way. Verse 12 speaks of the coming (παρουσίαν) of the day of God. This repeats the word used in 1:16 and 3:4 to speak of the coming of Jesus. The coming of Jesus is also the coming of the day of God.

At the end of v. 10 the author observes that when the world ends, the earth and the works on it will be discovered. They will be discovered because the false teachers and their followers will be destroyed on the day of the Lord, and only the upright will remain. Because this is the case, the addressees should live holy and pious lives. The slavery to corruption of the earth and some of its inhabitants will be clear when they undergo corruption at the end. Likewise, the freedom from corruption of those who do not

---

39. The final clause (colon) of v. 10 ("and the earth and the works on it will be discovered") is parallel to the earlier two cola of v. 10 that are paralleled in v. 12. It continues the parisosis, homoeoteleuton, and homoeoptoton found in the earlier two clauses and their parallels in v. 12.

will be clear. The dissolution of the universe at the end is thus a motive for living virtuously. The same argument is made, in completely different terms, in 1 Thess 5:3-11. This passage says in part (vv. 4-8)

> But you, beloved, are not in darkness, for that day to surprise you like a thief; for you are all children of light and children of the day; we are not of the night or of darkness. So then let us not fall asleep as others do, but let us keep awake and be sober; for those who sleep sleep at night, and those who are drunk get drunk at night. But since we belong to the day, let us be sober, and put on the breastplate of faith and love, and for a helmet the hope of salvation.

In 3:11 the author of 2 Peter summarizes the description of the end in v. 10 by speaking of "all things being thus dissolved," using the verb from v. 10 that he will use again in v. 12. The author then envisions the addressees as living holy and pious lives. Most interpreters understand σπεύδοντας as meaning "hasten" rather than "eagerly seeking."[40] However, in view of the author's frequent references to the need for eagerness (1:5, 10, 15; 3:14), "eagerly seeking" seems better.

In v. 13 the author speaks of awaiting new heavens and a new earth. The author connects the end of this world and its replacement by a new one by using the word προσδοκῶντες (await) in vv. 12 and 13. He and the addressees await both the end of the old and the beginning of the new. He also connects the two by using οὐρανοί (heavens) in vv. 10, 12, and 13, and γῆ (earth) in vv. 10 and 13. He emphasizes the newness of the new world by using the adjective καινούς (new) twice in v. 13.

The author connects his description of the destruction of the present world and its replacement by a new one in vv. 10-13 with his description of the first creation and destruction of the world in vv. 5-6 by repeating the words οὐρανοί (heavens) and γῆ (earth) from v. 5. These words are also used in v. 7, making it clear that the destruction predicted there is the same one described in vv. 10, 12.

The descriptions of the destruction of the present world in v. 7 and vv. 10-12 are also connected by a number of other repetitions. In vv. 5-7 the creation of the world, its destruction in the time of Noah, and its future destruction are all said to be the work of the word of God; in v. 12 this future destruction is called the day of God. πυρί (fire) is used in v. 7 and the cognate verb πυρούμενοι (burn) in v. 12; ἡμέρα (day) is used in v. 7 and

---

40. See Bigg, *St. Peter and St. Jude*, 298; Schelkle, *Die Petrusbriefe*, 229; Kelly, *Peter and Jude*, 367; Bauckham, *Jude, 2 Peter*, 325; Davids, *2 Peter and Jude*, 290-91; Green, *Jude & 2 Peter*, 333-34.

again in vv. 10, 12; and ἀσεβῶν (impious) is used in v. 7, and a noun with an opposite meaning εὐσεβείαις (pieties) is used in v. 11. Since the day of judgment will yield the destruction of the impious (v. 7), the addressees are urged to be pious (v. 11).

The new heavens and earth will appear in accordance with his (probably God's) promise (ἐπάγγελμα—3:13). The word for promise used here is a synonym of the word used in 3:9 to speak of the Lord of the promise (ἐπαγγελίας). The latter is the same word used in 3:4 where the scoffers ask about the promise of his coming. The promise of Jesus' coming, of which God is Lord, includes the promise of new heavens and earth. The word used in 3:13 was used earlier in 1:4 to speak of the promises Jesus gave the author and addressees through which the addressees become sharers of divine nature having escaped the corruption in the world. In the new heavens and earth, people will share divine nature. In 2:19 the cognate verb was used to say that the false teachers promise (ἐπαγγελλόμενοι) freedom while being slaves of corruption themselves. True freedom from corruption comes from the promise of Jesus' coming which includes new heavens and earth in which one shares divine nature.

Justice will dwell in the new heavens and earth. One must be just if one hopes to dwell in the new creation along with justice. Here the author mentions for the last time one of the main topics of the letter. In 1:1 the author said the addressees received faith by the justice of God. In 2:5 Noah, one of those rescued by God, is described as a herald of justice, and in 2:21 Christian life is called the way of justice. The author describes himself as just (δίκαιον) in 1:13. He describes Lot, another of those rescued by God, as just in 2:7, 8 (twice). Those whom God condemns are described as unjust (ἄδικος) in 2:9. In 2:15 the author applies the cognate noun ἀδικία (wrongdoing) to Balaam, role model of the false teachers; in 2:13 he applies it and the cognate verb ἀδικούμενοι (being wronged) to the false teachers themselves.

Social-cultural texture. As we have noted in discussing 2 Pet 2:5–6 above, judgment by water and fire (3:5–7) is found among the Greeks as well as the Jews. In addition to invoking biblical predictions of the judgment of the world by fire, the author's picture might also remind the addressees of the Stoic idea that a conflagration periodically brings the world to an end and is followed by its reconstitution.[41] One expression of this idea is preserved in Eusebius, *Praep. ev.* 15.14, "At certain destined periods of time the whole world is consumed by fire (ἐκπυροῦσθαι); then it is once more constituted an ordered manifold world." The Stoics also spoke of the word as that according to which this occurs. If the author intends to evoke this pic-

---

41. Bauckham, *Jude, 2 Peter,* 300–301; Neyrey, *2 Peter, Jude,* 240–41.

ture, however, it is most likely that he integrates it into the biblical picture of judgment by fire. To mention only one point, the parallel with destruction of the world by water in the time of Noah has no place in Stoic thought.

The elements that, burning, will be dissolved or melted (3:10, 12) are probably earth, air, fire, and water.[42] The author may picture the dissolution of the world that consists of various combinations of these elements as resulting from the complete conversion of earth, air, and water into fire. If so, he is adopting the Stoic description of the conflagration that ends the world.

However, the author of 2 Peter does not envision the destruction of everyone at the end of the world, but only the destruction of the impious. In this the author fundamentally diverges from the Stoic understanding of the conflagration, even though he seems to have adopted the Stoic picture of this conflagration. Just as Noah and his family escaped God's ending of the world by the flood, so the upright will escape God's ending of the world by fire.

As we have noted in discussing 2 Pet 3:4 above, vv. 5–13 are a riposte to the challenge in v. 4. The author invokes the value of purity by referring to holiness and piety (v. 11) on one hand, and impiety (v. 7) on the other. In this way the author calls the addressees to purity and warns them to avoid impurity.

Sacred texture. The passage has much to say about God. There were of old heavens and earth created and then destroyed by the word of God (vv. 5–6). The present heavens and earth have been treasured up by God's word for fire on the day of judgment (v. 7), which is also the day of God (v. 12). Assuming that "Lord" in vv. 8 and 9 refers to God, the passage also tells us that time is different for God than for humans (v. 8) and that God is not slow to keep the promise of Jesus' return and all that will accompany it, but is patient, wanting all to repent (v. 9). In these ways the passage presents God as the creator of all, who sustains all he has created in existence until the time appointed for its dissolution. This presentation implies that God directs the course of world history.

When the author speaks of "our Lord and savior" in 3:2, he probably refers to Jesus. In vv. 8 and 9 the title "Lord" probably refers to God; in v. 10 it might refer either to Jesus or to God. Use of "Lord" as a title for both God and Jesus, and the frequent ambiguity about which is the referent, both in this passage and elsewhere in 2 Peter, is another aspect of 2 Peter's presentation of Jesus as divine.

---

42. See Neyrey, *2 Peter, Jude*, 243; Green, *Jude & 2 Peter*, 330. According to Bauckham most commentators instead see the elements as the sun, moon, and stars (*Jude, 2 Peter*, 315–16); Bauckham himself agrees with this, as do Harrington ("Jude and 2 Peter," 289) and Davids (*2 Peter and Jude*, 284–86).

Rhetorical Force

One striking aspect of 2 Pet 3:5–13 is its thoroughly apologetic use of apocalyptic discourse. The entire letter is an argument against those who doubt the second coming of Jesus. In 1:16—2:10a the author is mainly concerned to show that this expectation is well-founded. In 3:5–13 he responds to more specific concerns, namely the arguments that the second coming of Jesus is unprecedented and that it should have happened already. This requires him to use apocalyptic discourse to show that the second coming of Jesus is not unprecedented and to account for what seems to be a delay in its arrival. The author's concluding exhortation to live virtuously in light of eschatological hope is more typical of apocalyptic discourse.

The persuasive power of this apocalyptic apology derives partly from the author's explanation of the "delay" of the second coming, which pictures God as outside time and as benevolent. But it also derives from the author's vivid portrayal of the end of the world, which is patterned on the deluge, i.e., from his eschatography. Earlier in the letter the author has mentioned aspects of the end, but only now does he describe it fully.

In the letter opening he spoke of the hope that the addressees "become sharers of divine nature, having escaped the corruption in the world by desire" (1:4) and that they enter "the eternal kingdom of our Lord and savior Jesus Christ" (1:11). As he argued in the middle of the letter that the second coming of Jesus is not a myth, he said that false teachers would arise at the end of the world, who would live immoral lives and undergo destruction (2:1–3, 10b–22; cf. 3:3–4). He implied that their destruction, and the salvation of the pious, would be like the previous judgments of God that he described (2:4–8), but he did not describe the final judgment itself. In 3:5–13 the author finally gives a full description of the end that he has so frequently mentioned. In this way his portrayal of the end of the world reaches a crescendo in 3:5–13, elaborating and completing the eschatography of the entire letter.

Like 2:4–10a, 3:5–13 paints a picture of the end of the world that is intended to replace the different picture of world history espoused by the scoffers (see 3:4), as well as other non-apocalyptic views of world history found in the Greco-Roman world. Second Peter's picture has some affinity to the Stoic view of the world as ending in conflagration. However, 2 Peter reconfigures this Stoic picture in apocalyptic terms by understanding the end of the world as eliminating evil, and the new world that follows as one in which justice dwells.

Appendix A: Terms used earlier in 2 Peter and repeated in 3:1-4

ταύτην (this—3:1, 3) was used earlier in 1:4, 5, 8, 9, 10, 12, 13, 15, 17, 18, 20; 2:12, 17, 19, 20.

ἀγαπητοί (beloved—3:1) was used earlier in 1:17 and is cognate to ἀγάπη (love) used in 1:7.

ὑμῖν (you—3:1 [twice], 2) was used earlier in 1:2, 5, 8, 10, 11, 12, 13, 15, 16, 19; 2:1, 3, 13.

γράφω (write—3:1) is cognate to γραφή (Scripture) used in 1:20.

διεγείρω ὑμῶν ἐν ὑπομνήσει (I arouse in your remembrance) in 3:1 is very similar to διεγείρειν ὑμᾶς ἐν ὑπομνήσει (to arouse you by remembrance) in 1:13.

μνησθῆναι (to remember—3:2) is cognate to ὑπομνήσει in 3:1; a verb cognate to the latter ὑπομιμνήσκειν (to remind) was used in 1:12; a noun cognate to the former μνήμην (remembrance) was used in 1:15.

ἁγίων (holy—3:2) was used earlier in 1:18, 21; 2:21.

προφητῶν (prophets—3:2) was used earlier in 2:16; the cognate προφητικόν (prophetic) was used in 1:19; the cognate προφητεία (prophecy) was used in 1:20, 21; the cognate ψευδοπροφῆται (false prophets) was used in 2:1.

ἀποστόλων (apostles—3:2) was used earlier in 1:1.

ἐντολῆς (commandment—3:2) was used earlier in 2:21.

κυρίου (lord—3:2) was used earlier in 1:2, 8, 11, 14, 16; 2:9, 11, 20; the cognate κυριότητος (dominion) was used in 2:10; the synonym δεσπότην (master) was used in 2:1.

σωτῆρος (savior—3:2) was used earlier in 1:1, 11; 2:20.

τοῦτο πρῶτον γινώσκοντες (first knowing this—3:3) was used in 1:20.

πρῶτον (first—3:3) was used earlier in 1:20; 2:20.

γινώσκοντες (knowing—3:3) was used earlier in 1:20; the cognate verb γνωρίζω (to make known) was used in 1:16; the cognate verb ἐπιγινώσκω (to know fully) was used twice in 2:21; the synonym οἶδα (to know) was used in 1:12, 14; 2:9; the antonym ἀγνοοῦσιν (to be ignorant) was used in 2:12; the cognate noun ἐπίγνωσις (full knowledge) was used earlier in 1:2, 3, 8; 2:20; as was the cognate noun γνῶσις (knowledge) in 1:5, 6.

ἐσχάτων (last—3:3) was used earlier in 2:20.

ἡμερῶν (days—3:3) was used earlier in 1:19; 2:8 [twice], 9, 13.

ἰδίας (their own—3:3) was used earler in 1:3, 20; 2:16, 22.

ἐπιθυμίας (desires—3:3) was used earlier in 1:4; 2:10, 18.

αὐτῶν (their—3:3, 4) was used earlier in 1:3, 5, 9, 17, 18; 2:1, 2, 3, 8, 11, 12, 13, 19 (twice), 20, 21 (twice), 22.

πορευόμενοι (going—3:3) was used earlier in 2:10.

ἐπαγγελία (promise—3:4) is cognate to ἐπαγγέλματα (promises) used in 1:4 and ἐπαγγελλόμενοι (promising) used in 2:19.

παρουσίας (coming—3:4) was used earlier in 1:16.

γάρ (for—3:4) was used earlier in 1:8, 9, 10, 11, 16, 17, 21; 2:4, 8, 18, 19, 20, 21.

πατέρες (fathers—3:4) was used earlier in 1:17.

πάντα (all—3:4) was used earlier in 1:3, 5, 20.

οὕτως (thus—3:4) was used earlier in 1:11.

Appendix B: Terms used earlier in 2 Peter and repeated in 3:5–13

γάρ (for—3:5) was used earlier in 1:8, 9, 10, 11, 16, 17, 21; 2:4, 8, 18, 19, 20, 21; 3:4.

αὐτούς (them—3:5, 7, 10, 13) was used earlier in 1:3, 5, 9, 17, 18; 2:1, 2, 3, 8, 11, 12, 13, 19 (twice), 20, 21 (twice), 22; 3:3, 4.

τοῦτο (this—3:5, 8, 11) was used earlier in 1:4, 5, 8, 9, 10, 12, 13, 15, 17, 18, 20; 2:12, 17, 19, 20; 3:1, 3.

οὐρανοί (heavens—3:5, 7, 10, 12, 13) was used earlier in 1:18.

ἔκπαλαι (long ago—3:5) was used earlier in 2:3; the cognate πάλαι (past) was used in 1:9.

δι' with genitive (through—3:5, 6) was used earlier in 1:3, 4 (twice).

θεοῦ (God—3:5, 12) was used earlier in 1:1, 2, 17, 21; 2:4.

λόγῳ (word—3:5, 7) was used earlier in 1:19; 2:3.

κόσμος (world—3:6) was used earlier in 1:4; 2:5, 20.

ἀπώλετο (be destroyed—3:6, 9); its cognate ἀπωλείας (destruction—3:7) was used earlier in 2:1 (twice), 3; the synonym φθορά (corruption) was used earlier in 1:4; 2:12 (twice), 19 as was its cognate φθαρήσονται (to be corrupted) in 2:12.

τηρούμενοι (kept—3:7) was used earlier in 2:4, 9, 17.

ἡμέραν (day—3:7, 8, 10, 12) was used earlier in 1:19; 2:8 (twice), 9, 13; 3:3.

κρίσεως (judgment—3:7) was used earlier in 2:4, 9, 11; the cognate κρίμα (judgment) was used in 2:3; the cognate κατέκρινεν (to condemn) was used in 2:6.

ἀσεβῶν (impious—3:7) was used earlier in 2:5, 6; a noun with an opposite meaning εὐσεβείαις (pieties—3:11) was used earlier in 1:3, 6, 7; the cognate adjective εὐσεβεῖς (pious) was used in 2:9.

ἀνθρώπων (human beings—3:7) was used earlier in 1:21 (twice); 2:16.

ὑμᾶς (you—3:8, 9, 11) was used earlier in 1:2, 5, 8, 10, 11, 12, 13, 15, 16, 19; 2:1, 3, 13; 3:1 (twice), 2.

ἀγαπητοί (beloved—3:8) was used earlier in 1:17; 3:1 and is cognate to ἀγάπη (love) used in 1:7.

κυρίῳ (lord—3:8, 9, 10) was used earlier in 1:2, 8, 11, 14, 16; 2:9, 11, 20; 3:2; the cognate κυριότητος (dominion) was used in 2:10; the synonym δεσπότην (master) was used in 2:1.

ἐπαγγελίας (promise—3:9) was used earlier in 3:4; the cognate ἐπάγγελμα (promise—3:13) was used earlier in 1:4; the cognate verb ἐπαγγελλόμενοι (to promise) was used in 2:19.

ἡγοῦνται (consider—3:9) was used earlier in 1:13; 2:13.

πάντας (all—3:9, 11) was used earlier in 1:3, 5, 20; 3:4.

ἔργα (works—3:10) was used earlier in 2:8.

οὕτως (thus—3:11) was used earlier in 1:11; 3:4.

ὑπάρχειν (to be—3:11) was used earlier in 1:8; 2:19.

ἁγίαις (holy—3:11) was used earlier in 1:18, 21; 2:21; 3:2.

ἀναστροφαῖς (lives—3:11) was used earlier in 2:7; the cognate verb ἀναστρεφομένους (to live) was used in 2:18.

παρουσίαν (coming—3:12) was used earlier in 1:16; 3:4.

δικαιοσύνη (justice—3:13) was used earlier in 1:1; 2:5, 21; the cognate adjective δίκαιος (just) was used earlier in 1:13; 2:7, 8; as was ἄδικος (unjust) in 2:9; the cognate noun ἀδικία (wrongdoing) 2:13, 15; and the cognate verb ἀδικούκμενοι (to be wronged) in 2:13.

Appendix C: Terms Introduced and Repeated in 3:5–13 and in One Case Later in 2 Peter

λανθάνει (escape the notice of) is used in 3:5, 8.

γῆ (earth) is used in 3:5, 7, 10, 13.

ὕδατος (water) is used in 3:5 (twice), 6.

πυρί (fire) is used in 3:7 and the cognate verb πυρούμενοι (to burn) is used in 3:12; the synonym καυσούμενα (set on fire) is used in 3:10, 12.

ἕν (one) is used three times in 3:8.

χίλια (thousand) is used twice in 3:8.

βραδύνει (delay) and its cognate βραδύτητα (delay) are used in 3:9.

στοιχεῖα (elements) is used in 3:10, 12.

λυθήσεται (dissolve) is used in 3:10, 11, 12.

προσδοκῶντες (await) is used in 3:12, 13 and later in 3:14.

καινούς (new) is used twice in 3:13.

Section 5: 2 Peter 3:14–18

Letter Closing

The closing section of 2 Peter is prophetic discourse blended with apocalyptic, priestly, and wisdom discourse. It is prophetic discourse in that it consists of a final warning against the influence of the false teachers. Apocalyptic discourse is blended with this (as it has been throughout the letter) because rejection of the false teachers is rejecting their denial of apocalyptic expectation. The addressees should await the day of judgment described in the preceding verses of the letter (v. 14), regard the patience of the Lord as salvation (v. 15), and grow in grace and knowledge of the Lord and Savior Jesus Christ to the day of eternity (v. 18). The false teachers are headed for destruction (v. 16). Wisdom discourse is also blended into this exhortation in that it is supported by an appeal to the wisdom of Paul (vv. 15–16), and the addressees are urged to avoid error (v. 17) and grow in knowledge (v. 18). Priestly discourse is evoked in the exhortation that the addressees be without spot or blemish (v. 14). The doxology with which the letter ends is also priestly discourse (v. 18b).

14 Διό, ἀγαπητοί, ταῦτα προσδοκῶντες[1] σπουδάσατε ἄσπιλοι καὶ ἀμώμητοι αὐτῷ[2] εὑρεθῆναι ἐν εἰρήνῃ 15 καὶ τὴν τοῦ κυρίου ἡμῶν μακροθυμίαν σωτηρίαν ἡγεῖσθε, καθὼς καὶ ὁ ἀγαπητὸς ἡμῶν ἀδελφὸς Παῦλος κατὰ τὴν δοθεῖσαν αὐτῷ σοφίαν ἔγραψεν ὑμῖν, 16 ὡς καὶ ἐν πάσαις ἐπιστολαῖς λαλῶν ἐν αὐταῖς περὶ

---

1. In 3:12–13 the author used this verb to refer to awaiting τὴν παρουσίαν τῆς τοῦ θεοῦ ἡμέρας and καινοὺς δὲ οὐρανοὺς καὶ γῆν καινήν; they are the antecedents of ταῦτα here.

2. αὐτῷ may be taken with the preceding adjectives, indicating with respect to whom the readers are to be ἄσπιλοι καὶ ἀμώμητοι, or with the following verb, indicating by whom the readers are to be εὑρεθῆναι. In either case the pronoun refers to God (Bigg, *St. Peter and St. Jude*, 299).

τούτων, ἐν αἷς ἐστιν δυσνόητά τινα, ἃ οἱ ἀμαθεῖς καὶ ἀστήρικτοι στρεβλοῦσιν³ ὡς καὶ τὰς λοιπὰς γραφὰς⁴ πρὸς τὴν ἰδίαν αὐτῶν ἀπώλειαν. 17 Ὑμεῖς οὖν, ἀγαπητοί, προγινώσκοντες φυλάσσεσθε, ἵνα μὴ τῇ τῶν ἀθέσμων πλάνῃ συναπαχθέντες ἐκπέσητε τοῦ ἰδίου στηριγμοῦ, 18 αὐξάνετε δὲ ἐν χάριτι καὶ γνώσει τοῦ κυρίου ἡμῶν καὶ σωτῆρος Ἰησοῦ Χριστοῦ. αὐτῷ ἡ δόξα καὶ νῦν καὶ εἰς ἡμέραν αἰῶνος.⁵ [ἀμήν.]⁶

14 Therefore, beloved, awaiting these things, be eager to be discovered by him spotless and unblemished in peace. 15 And consider the patience of our Lord salvation, as also our beloved brother Paul wrote to you according to the wisdom given to him, 16 so also in all his letters speaking in them about these things, in which [letters] there are some things hard to understand which the ignorant and unstable twist, as they also do the rest of the Scriptures, to their own destruction. 17 Therefore you, beloved, knowing these things beforehand, be on guard in order that you may not fall away from your firm footing, having been led astray by the error of the lawless. 18 But grow in favor and knowledge of our Lord and savior Jesus Christ. To him be glory both now and into the day of eternity. Amen.

Rhetography

The letter closing pictures Peter as concluding his letter with some final prophetic exhortations, briefly repeating the main points he has argued earlier in the letter. He supports these exhortations by appealing to Paul as someone who taught the addressees the same things, and ends by praying a doxology. The appeal to Paul that is central to this section pictures Paul as a teacher of wisdom and implies that the author's entire prophetic, apocalyptic message is wisdom teaching.

3. There is some uncertainty whether the original text read στρεβλοῦσιν or στρεβλώσουσιν. The former is found in ℵ, A, and B; the latter in P⁷². The latter may have been a correction intended to help present 2 Peter as Peter's prediction of future events.

4. ὡς καὶ τὰς λοιπὰς γραφὰς (v. 16) is elliptical, presupposing the verb στρεβλοῦσιν which is not repeated.

5. αὐτῷ ἡ δόξα καὶ νῦν καὶ εἰς ἡμέραν αἰῶνος is also elliptical; the verb "to be" is understood. The understood verb could be indicative, implying that glory belongs to Jesus Christ, or optative, implying that glory should be given to him, as in the translation given above (Bauckham, *Jude, 2 Peter*, 119).

6. It is difficult to decide whether the original text included ἀμήν (v. 18) or not, hence the brackets in the Greek text. On the one hand P⁷², ℵ, A, and many other manuscripts include it; on the other hand B and a few others do not include it, and it is easier to understand its addition to the text than its omission (Metzger, *A Textual Commentary*, 637–38).

In v. 14 the author pictures the addressees as awaiting the dissolution of this world and the arrival of new heavens and a new earth, as he has just said in 3:12–13. He urges them to be eager, thus envisioning them in this emotional state. They should be eager to be discovered by Jesus, when he comes again, spotless and unblemished in peace. The addressees will resemble unstained fabric or animals suited to be sacrificial victims; these are metaphors for ethical rectitude. Envisioning the addressees as being discovered in peace may refer to their being exempt from judgment at the second coming of Jesus.

In v. 15a the author urges the addressees to consider the patience of our Lord salvation, envisioning them as having the attitude toward the time of the parousia that he expressed in 3:9, where he rejected the view of some that it was delayed. The author pictures the addressees as thinking that the timing of the parousia derives from divine patience that allows people time to repent so they will not be destroyed at the end of the world. This is a mental image of their thoughts.

In vv. 15b–16 the author appeals to the letters of Paul as support for what he has just said. In v. 15 he refers to Paul as our beloved brother (ἀδελφός), picturing him as having the same intimate relationship with the author and addressees as exists between them, i.e., being beloved. More specifically, Paul is like a family member, a brother. The author had also spoken of the addressees as his brothers in 1:10.

The author speaks of Paul as having had wisdom given to him, probably implying that it was given by God. He pictures Paul as having written the same things to the addressees that the author himself has written. These things are most likely to be what the author has just said in vv. 14–15a. The author pictures Paul as having written these things not only in letters directed to the addressees of 2 Peter, but also in all his letters. Thus the author pictures the existence of a collection of letters written by Paul.

In v. 16b the author acknowledges that there are some things in Paul's letters that are hard to understand and says that the ignorant and unstable twist these complex elements of Paul's letters to their own destruction. The metonymy of referring to these people by mentioning qualities rather than names emphasizes this characterization of them. The author also emphasizes it by using the rare word ἀστήρικτος (unstable) for a second time (it is also found in 2:14).

The author pictures the false teachers and their followers as interpreters of Paul, but ones who twist the meaning of his letters rather than understanding them correctly. The author also says that they do the same with the rest of the Scriptures. The author regards the letters of Paul as comparable to the Jewish Scriptures; cf. the reference to Scripture in 1:20. Together they constitute the beginning of the bible as Christians know it today. The false teachers' misinterpretation of the Jewish Scriptures might mean specifically that they reject the interpretation of the Jewish Scriptures the author proposed in 2:4–10a.

The author urges the addressees to be on guard lest they fall away from their own firm footing, having been led astray by the error of the lawless. He pictures them as being alert to repel enemy attack so that they maintain the firm footing they presently have. The author has used the rare word στηριγμός for "firm footing," another metaphor for a moral state. The alternative is to fall away from this, becoming unstable like those who misinterpret Paul. The author emphasizes this contrast by the paronomasia ἀστήρικτοι (unstable)—στηριγμοῦ. Falling away from this firm footing would result from being led astray by the error of the lawless. The lawless are the false teachers who were earlier said to have gone astray (2:15; cf. 2:18). They resemble the lawless people of Sodom from whom God rescued Lot (2:7).

In v. 18 the author urges the addressees to grow in favor and knowledge of our Lord and savior Jesus Christ. The author envisions the addressees as growing in favor, something for which he prayed on their behalf in 1:2. Growing in knowledge of Jesus summarizes in a very general way, without specifying what exactly is to be known, the main message of the letter. The author pictures the addressees as progressively acquiring more and deeper knowledge of Jesus. The author ends with a doxology praying that Jesus will have glory now and in the day of eternity. This may envision Jesus as radiant (cf. 1:17) or possibly as renowned, famous, both now and in the day of eternity. The latter is the day of the Lord on which the new age begins.

Textural Analysis

Intertexture. Verses 14–15 are a *recitation* that summarizes a span of text, namely the letter(s) written by Paul to the addressees of 2 Peter. If 2 Pet 3:1 implies that 2 Peter, like 1 Peter, is addressed to the diaspora exiled in Pontus, Galatia, Cappadocia, Asia, and Bithynia, the only surviving letters of Paul that might be recited in vv. 14–15 are Galatians, Ephesians, and Colossians. The most likely of these letters to be meant is Ephesians. Second Peter 3:14 and Eph 4:3 both use the verb σπουδάζω (to be eager) and the noun εἰρήνη (peace). Despite the similarity in vocabulary, however, the two passages make rather different points. The Ephesians passage calls for unity among believers, while the verse in 2 Peter urges believers to be found morally upright on the day of the Lord.

Eph 4:3 σπουδάζοντες τηρεῖν τὴν ἑνότητα τοῦ πνεύματος ἐν τῷ συνδέσμῳ τῆς εἰρήνης

2 Pet 3:14 σπουδάσατε ἄσπιλοι καὶ ἀμώμητοι αὐτῷ εὑρεθῆναι ἐν εἰρήνῃ

Notice, however, that 2 Pet 15a most closely resembles Rom 2:4, which was obviously not written to any of the recipients of 1 Peter.[7] Both of these passages use the noun μακροθυμία (patience) and express the idea that God's patience is for the benefit of humans.

Rom 2:4 τῆς ἀνοχῆς καὶ τῆς μακροθυμίας καταφρονεῖς, ἀγνοῶν ὅτι τὸ χρηστὸν τοῦ θεοῦ εἰς μετάνοιάν σε ἄγει;

2 Pet 3:15a τὴν τοῦ κυρίου ἡμῶν μακροθυμίαν σωτηρίαν ἡγεῖσθε

Romans 2:4 is even more closely related to 2 Pet 3:9.

Verse 16a expands the recitation of the letter(s) Paul wrote to the addressees of 2 Peter into a *recitation* that summarizes all of Paul's letters. In addition to the connections with the letters of Paul just mentioned, we previously noted that 2 Pet 3:10 cites 1 Thess 5:2. Gilmour discusses this and other possible uses of Paul's letters by 2 Peter, but concludes that they do not indicate literary dependence.[8] The possible instances of literary dependence mentioned by Gilmour include, in the order he discusses them:

1. 2 Pet 2:19 resembles the thought of Rom 6:16;
2. 2 Pet 3:9 resembles Rom 2:4;
3. 2 Pet 1:13–14 uses the same imagery as 2 Cor 5:1–4; and
4. 2 Pet 3:15 refers to the wisdom given to Paul; Paul refers to himself in similar terms in 1 Cor 3:10.

Moreover, the understanding of the human predicament and its origin in 2 Pet 2:18–20 is similar to that of Rom 8:20–21, understood as a summary of 1:18–32. And we have earlier noted other places where the thought of 2 Peter resembles that of Paul's letters. The understanding of the completion of salvation as becoming incorruptible in 2 Pet 1:4 is similar to that of 1 Cor 15:50–55.[9] And the idea that the earth and the works on it will be discovered at the end of the world (3:10) is similar to what Paul says in 1 Cor 3:12–15.

---

7. According to Gilmour (*Significance of Parallels*, 102n39) some have seen this as reason to think that 2 Peter was written to Christians in Rome. Specifically, Gilmour mentions Mayor, *St. Jude and St. Peter*, 164.

8. Gilmour, *Significance of Parallels*, 100–105.

9. See Callan, "Soteriology of the Second Letter of Peter," especially 552–53, 556–57.

Social-cultural texture. Jeffrey A. D. Weima has identified a number of conventional elements belonging to the conclusions of ancient letters, both Greek and Semitic.[10] The most common convention of both is the farewell wish. Greek letter conclusions also include the health wish, the greeting, the autograph, the illiteracy formula, the dating formula, and the postscript. The health wish, dating formula, and postscript are also sometimes found in Semitic letters; Semitic letter conclusions regularly include a signature. Many Greek letters, however, have no closing formulas; they simply end.[11] The conclusion of 2 Peter does not include any conventional elements of ancient letter conclusions; however, it ends with a doxology. This serves as a closing formula, but is not a convention of ancient letter conclusions.[12]

Inner texture. Several terms mentioned earlier in 2 Peter are *repeated* in 3:14–18 (see Appendix A).

The conclusion of 2 Peter repeats a number of terms used at the beginning of the letter (inclusio). Jesus Christ is called our (ἡμῶν) savior (σωτῆρος) in 1:1 and 3:18; he is called Lord (κυρίου) in 1:2 and 3:18. Favor (χάρις) is also mentioned in 1:2 and 3:18. In addition, knowledge is mentioned in 1:2 and 3:17, 18; glory is mentioned in 1:3 and 3:18; and peace (εἰρήνη) is mentioned in 1:2 and 3:14. All of these repetitions serve to end the letter by returning to topics mentioned at the beginning.

As is appropriate for a concluding exhortation, the author also repeats other terms previously used in the course of the letter, especially in 3:1–13. Verses 12–14 are linked by the repetition of different forms of a verb meaning "await," προσδοκῶντας—προσδοκῶμεν—προσδοκῶντες, which is transplacement. The author urges the addressees to be eager as he had in 3:12. They should be eager to be discovered by Jesus, when he comes again, spotless and unblemished in peace. The author had referred to the discovery that will occur at the second coming of Jesus in 3:10. Being spotless and unblemished will make the addressees the opposite of the false teachers who are spots and blemishes (2:12). The author had prayed that peace would be multiplied for the addressees in 1:2.

In v. 15a the author urges the addressees to consider the patience of our Lord salvation (σωτηρίαν), recommending that they take the attitude toward the time of the parousia that he expressed in 3:9. In 3:9 the author said that the Lord was patient so that people could avoid destruction. This suggests that salvation is rescue from destruction. Jesus is called savior

---

10. Weima, *Endings*, 28–56 (Greek), 63–76 (Semitic).
11. Ibid., 30.
12. Ibid., 141. Jude also ends with a doxology.

(σωτῆρος) in v. 18, repeating the term used in 3:2, because he rescues people from eschatological destruction.

In 3:18 the author distinguishes between now (νῦν) and the day of eternity (ἡμέραν αἰῶνος). This mirrors the references in 3:7 to the present (νῦν) heavens and earth on one hand, and on the other hand to the day (ἡμέραν) of judgment and destruction (ἀπωλείας) of impious human beings on which they will burn up. The author has further described this day in 3:10, 12. The author again refers to eschatological destruction (ἀπώλειαν) in 3:16.

In two cases (in addition to the use of salvation in v. 15 and savior in v. 18) the author repeatedly uses a term from 3:1–13 in 3:14–18. In vv. 14 and 17 the author again calls the addressees beloved (ἀγαπητοί), returning for a third and fourth time to the picture of them as people with whom he has an intimate relationship earlier evoked in 3:1 and 8. Similarly in v. 15 he refers to Paul as our beloved brother (ἀδελφός).

The most significant repetition in 3:14–18 is the use of ἀμαθεῖς (ignorant) in v. 16, προγινώσκοντες (know beforehand) in v. 17, and γνώσει (knowledge) in v. 18; the latter two are cognate to γινώσκοντες (knowing) used in 3:3. This brings to a conclusion one of the main topics of the letter. Those who do not understand the letters of Paul properly are ignorant (v. 16), like the false teachers (see 2:12). The danger of ignorance has been implicit in the author's emphasis on the importance of knowledge throughout the letter, as well as in the references to the danger of forgetting in 1:9 and the importance of remembering in 1:12–15; 3:1–2.

Here the emphasis on the importance of knowledge is first expressed positively in the reference to the addressees as knowing these things beforehand (v. 17). The things they know beforehand are most immediately that the false teachers twist the meaning of the Scriptures. However, their foreknowledge probably includes knowledge of the dissolution of this world and the arrival of new heavens and a new earth that the author has just described. And the author may also be thinking of the other content of the letter as well. In any case, the author presumes that they know these things by way of his letter, though he does not presume that this is the only way they have learned them.

In v. 18 the author concludes the letter by urging the addressees to grow in favor and knowledge of Jesus Christ. In 1:2 the author had prayed that favor and peace would be multiplied for the addressees by full knowledge of God and Jesus their Lord. Taken together with 1:2, v. 18 strongly suggests that the addressees will grow in favor by growing in knowledge; an increase in divine favor will result from an increase in knowledge. In 1:3 the author said that Jesus' divine power has given him and the addressees all things for life and piety through full knowledge of him. Taken together with 1:2 this suggests that divine favor consists of all things for life and piety.

In 1:8 the author said that possessing and exceeding in the virtues listed in 1:5-7 leads to an increase of full knowledge of Jesus. Taken together with 3:18, this suggests that the addressees will grow in knowledge of Jesus through a life of virtue. In 2:20-21 the author said that one escapes the defilements of the world through full knowledge of Jesus, and warns that the last state of one who is again implicated in these defilements after having escaped them, is worse than his initial state. Taken together with 1:8 and 3:18, this suggests that one avoids implication in the defilements of the world by a life of virtue. Taken together with 1:3, 2:20-21 implies that escaping the defilements of the world is a negative equivalent of receiving all things for life and piety.

Another significant repetition within 3:14-18 is the use of ἀστήρικτοι (unstable) in v. 16 and the cognate στηριγμοῦ (firm footing) in v. 17. Those who do not understand the letters of Paul properly are not only ignorant, they are also unstable people (like those enticed by the false teachers according to 2:14, and probably the false teachers themselves). The addressees have a firm footing (as the author also said in 1:12), but need to be on guard so as not to fall away from it. Another significant repetition is the use of ἴδιος (one's own) in vv. 16 and 17. This emphasizes the close connection between twisting the Scriptures and destruction on one hand (v. 16), and between being on guard and maintaining firm footing on the other (v. 17).

Verses 14-15a are a double *enthymeme*,[13] arguing on the basis of vv. 5-13 that the addressees should live well and consider the forebearance of the Lord salvation. This is signaled by the use of διό (therefore) in v. 14. The argument can be restated:

> One who expects new heavens and earth in which justice dwells will strive to be virtuous.
>
> The addressees do expect new heavens and earth in which justice dwells.
>
> Therefore, they should be eager to be found spotless and blameless.
>
> One who expects the destruction of the impious on the day of judgment (v. 7) will consider an opportunity for repentance salvation.

---

13. Watson, *Invention*, 136.

> The patience of the Lord leading to delay of the day of judgment is an opportunity for repentance (v. 9).
>
> Therefore, the addressees should regard the patience of the Lord as salvation.

Verses 16b–17 form another enthymeme signaled by use of οὖν (therefore) at the beginning of v. 17. The argument can be restated:

> One who knows that incorrect interpretation of Scripture is dangerous will guard against it.
>
> The addressees know that the ignorant and unstable twist the meaning of the Scriptures leading to their own destruction.
>
> Therefore, the addressees should be on guard so they do not fall away from their own firm footing.

Sacred texture. On the assumption that "Lord" in v. 15 (as in 3:8–9) refers to God, the passage repeats the message of 3:9 that any delay in Jesus' return should be seen as God's forebearance for the sake of salvation. In v. 18 Jesus is explicitly called Lord and savior. Use of the title "Lord" both for God and for Jesus is probably another indication of Jesus' divine status. Verse 18b is a doxology praising Jesus. In praying this doxology, the author pictures Jesus as having divine status because such a doxology is ordinarily addressed to God. Elsewhere in the New Testament this kind of doxology is reserved for God. For example, the letter of Jude ends with the following doxology (vv. 24–25):

> Now to him who is able to keep you from falling, and to make you stand without blemish in the presence of his glory with rejoicing, to the only God our Savior, through Jesus Christ our Lord, be glory, majesty, power, and authority, before all time and now and forever. Amen.

The doxology in 2 Peter suggests that the author regards Jesus as God. This accords with what we have seen in earlier sections of the letter.

Ideological social-cultural texture. As we have noted earlier, writing in the name of Peter means that the author speaks on behalf of the most eminent leader of the Christian church. The claim that Paul agrees with what he says invokes the authority of another eminent church leader. Both of these imply that the author represents the *dominant* powers in his context. It is clear, however, that others interpret the letters of Paul in a different way than does the author of 2 Peter. This is another reflection of the contest between the author and the false teachers for recognition as the authentic teachers of Christian faith.

Social-cultural texture. The author continues to invoke the value of *purity* by exhorting the addressees to be spotless and blameless (v. 14)[14]—the opposite of the false teachers according to 2:13—and to avoid the error of the lawless (v. 17), whose lawlessness makes them similar to the inhabitants of Sodom and Gomorrah (2:7) and to Balaam (2:16).

The value of *group-oriented personality*[15] is reflected in the reference to the wisdom given to Paul (v. 15). This wisdom comes from another, namely God, and is presumably something God wants others to recognize in Paul. According to Neyrey, "group-oriented persons take their cue from God and honor those whom God honors."[16]

Obviously the value of *honor vs. shame* is also reflected in this description of Paul, as it is in the ascription of glory to Jesus (v. 18), a topic mentioned earlier in 1:3, 16 and 2:11. The patron-client relationship underlies the exhortation that the addressees grow in knowledge of Jesus, i.e., recognition of him as Lord and savior.

Rhetorical Force

As is fitting for the conclusion of the letter, in 3:14–18 the author restates his major theme: the necessity that the addressees behave properly as they await the second coming of Jesus. In this section he appeals, for the first time explicitly, to Paul and his letters as presenting a message in agreement with his own. And he implies that these letters have an authority like that of the Jewish Scriptures. This is a striking portrayal of his message as that of the authoritative teachers of the Christian church.

The author again refers to the divinity of Jesus. As we have noted earlier in commenting on 1:16–18, the author sees the divine status of Jesus as an important support for his belief that Jesus will come again. This may mean that one element of the false teachers' rather different understanding of Christianity was a low Christology.

By making an appeal to the wisdom of Paul the central element of his conclusion, and by urging the addressees to avoid error and grow in knowledge, the author presents his message as the wisdom in which Christians should be educated. This wisdom has intensified prophetic and apocalyptic features and is associated with priestly praise of Jesus as divine.

---

14. Neyrey, *2 Peter, Jude*, 247–49.
15. On this see ibid., 17–19.
16. Ibid., 249.

Appendix A: Terms Mentioned Earlier in 2 Peter and Repeated in 3:14–18

διό (therefore—3:14) was used earlier in 1:10, 12.

ἀγαπητοί (beloved—3:14, 15, 17) was used earlier in 1:17; 3:1 and is cognate to ἀγάπη (love) used in 1:7.

ταῦτα (these—3:14, 16) was used earlier in 1:4, 5, 8, 9, 10, 12, 13, 15, 17, 18, 20; 2:12, 17, 19, 20; 3:1, 3, 5, 8, 11.

προσδοκῶντες (await—3:14) was used earlier in 3:12, 13.

σπουδάσατε (be eager—3:14) was used earlier in 1:10, 15; the cognate noun σπουδή (eagerness) was used in 1:5.

ἄσπιλοι καὶ ἀμώμητοι (spotless and unblemished—3:14) is cognate to the phrase σπίλοι καὶ μῶμοι (blots and blemishes) used in 2:13.

αὐτῷ (him—3:14, 15, 16 [twice], 18) was used earlier in 1:3, 5, 9, 17, 18; 2:1, 2, 3, 8, 11, 12, 13, 19 (twice), 20, 21 (twice), 22; 3:3, 4, 5, 7, 10, 13.

εὑρεθῆναι (find—3:14) was used earlier in 3:10.

εἰρήνη (peace—3:14) was used earlier in 1:2.

κυρίου (lord—3:15, 18) was used earlier in 1:2, 8, 11, 14, 16; 2:9, 11, 20; 3:2, 8, 9, 10; the cognate κυριότητος (dominion) was used in 2:10; the synonym δεσπότην (master) was used in 2:1.

ἡμῶν (our—3:15, 18) was used earlier in 1:1 (twice), 2, 3 (twice), 4, 8, 11, 14, 16, 18; 2:20.

μακροθυμίαν (patience—3:15) is cognate to μακροθυμεῖ (to be patient) used in 3:9.

σωτηρίαν (salvation—3:15) is cognate to σωτῆρος (savior—3:18), which was used earlier in 1:1, 11; 2:20; 3:2.

ἡγεῖσθε (consider—3:15) was used earlier in 1:13; 2:13; 3:9.

καθώς (as—3:15) was used earlier in 1:14.

ἀδελφός (brother—3:15) was used earlier in 1:10; the cognate φιλαδελφία (brotherly love) was used twice in 1:8.

ἔγραψεν (write—3:15) was used earlier in 3:1; the cognate γραφή (Scripture—3:16) was used earlier in 1:20.

ὑμῖν (you—3:15, 17) was used earlier in 1:2, 5, 8, 10, 11, 12, 13, 15, 16, 19; 2:1, 3, 13; 3:1 (twice), 2, 8, 9, 11.

πάσαις (all—3:16) was used earlier in 1:3, 5, 20; 3:4, 9, 11.

letter closing

ἐπιστολαῖς (letters—3:16) was used earlier in 3:1.

λαλῶν (speak—3:16) was used earlier in 1:21.

ἀστήρικτοι (unstable—3:16) was used earlier in 2:14; the cognate στηριγμοῦ (firm footing) is used in 3:17; the cognate ἐστηριγμένους (to establish) was used in 1:12.

ἰδίαν (their own—3:16, 17) was used earlier in 1:3, 20; 2:16, 22; 3:3.

ἀπώλειαν (destruction—3:16) was used earlier in 2:1 (twice), 3; 3:7; the cognate verb ἀπόλλυμι (to destroy) was used in 3:6, 9; the synonym φθορά (corruption) was used earlier in 1:4; 2:12 (twice), 19 as was its cognate φθαρήσονται (to be corrupted) in 2:12

ἀμαθεῖς (ignorant—3:16) is an antonym of προγινώσκοντες (to know beforehand—3:17) that is cognate to γνῶσις (knowledge—3:18), which was used earlier in 1:5, 6, to ἐπίγνωσις (full knowledge) used earlier in 1:2, 3, 8; 2:20, to γινώσκοντες (to know) used earlier in 1:20; 3:3, to γνωρίζω (to make known) used earlier in 1:16, and to ἐπιγινώσκω (to know fully) used twice in 2:21; the synonym οἶδα (to know) was used in 1:12, 14; 2:9; the antonym ἀγνοοῦσιν (to be ignorant) was used in 2:12.

φυλάσσεσθε (be on guard—3:17) was used earlier in 2:5.

ἀθέσμων (lawless—3:17) was used earlier in 2:7.

πλάνη (error—3:17) was used earlier in 2:18; the cognate verb ἐπλανήθησαν (to go astray) was used in 2:15.

χάριτι (favor—3:18) was used earlier in 1:2.

Ἰησοῦ Χριστοῦ (Jesus Christ—3:18) was used earlier in 1:1 (twice), 8, 11, 14, 16; 2:20; Ἰησοῦ (Jesus) was also used in 1:2.

δόξα (glory—3:18) was used earlier in 1:3, 17; 2:10.

νῦν (now—3:18) was used earlier in 3:7.

ἡμέραν (day—3:18) was used earlier in 1:19; 2:8 (twice), 9, 13; 3:3, 7, 8, 10, 12.

αἰῶνος (eternity—3:18) is cognate to αἰώνιον (eternal) used in 1:11.

Bibliography

Abbott, E. A. "On the Second Epistle of St. Peter." *The Expositor* 2:3 (1882) 49–63, 139–53, 204–19.
Aland, Barbara et al., eds. *The Greek New Testament*. Fourth Revised Edition. Stuttgart: Deutsche Bibelgesellschaft, 1993.
———. *Novum Testamentum Graecum. Editio Critica Maior* vol. 4 Catholic Letters. Stuttgart: Deutsche Bibelgesellschaft, 2000.
Bartchy, S. Scott. *Mallon Chresai: First Century Slavery and 1 Corinthians 7:21*. Society of Biblical Literature Dissertation Series 11. Missoula, MT: Scholars, 1973.
Bauckham, Richard J. "2 Peter: An Account of Research." *Aufstieg und Niedergang der Römischen Welt: Geschichte und Kultur Roms im Spiegel der Neuren Forschung*. Teil II: Principat 25:5, 3713–52. Berlin: Walter de Gruyter, 1988.
———. *Jude, 2 Peter*. Word Biblical Commentary 50. Waco, TX: Word, 1983.
Bigg, Charles. *A Critical and Exegetical Commentary on the Epistles of St. Peter and St. Jude*. International Critical Commentary. New York: Scribner, 1901.
Brown, Raymond E. *An Introduction to New Testament Christology*. New York: Paulist, 1994.
———. *Jesus: God and Man*. London: Chapman, 1968.
Callan, Terrance. "The Christology of the Second Letter of Peter." *Biblica* 82 (2001) 253–63.
———. "Comparison of Humans to Animals in 2 Peter 2:10b–22." *Biblica* 90 (2009) 101–13.
———. *Dying and Rising with Christ: The Theology of Paul the Apostle*. New York: Paulist, 2006.
———. "A Note on 2 Peter 1:19–20." *Journal of Biblical Literature* 125 (2006) 143–50.
———. *The Origins of Christian Faith*. New York: Paulist, 1994.
———. "Second Peter." In Duane F. Watson and Terrance Callan, *First and Second Peter*, 129–219. Paideia. Grand Rapids: Baker Academic, 2012.
———. "The Soteriology of the Second Letter of Peter." *Biblica* 82 (2001) 549–59.
———. "The Style of the Second Letter of Peter." *Biblica* 84 (2003) 202–24.
———. "The Syntax of 2 Peter 1:1–7." *Catholic Biblical Quarterly* 67 (2005) 632–40.
———. "Use of the Letter of Jude by the Second Letter of Peter." *Biblica* 85 (2004) 42–64.
Cavallin, H. C. C. "The False Teachers of 2 Pt as Pseudoprophets." *Novum Testamentum* 21 (1979) 263–70.

Chaine, Joseph. *Les Épitres Catholiques: La Seconde Épitre de Saint Pierre, Les Épitres de Saint Jean, L' Épitre de Saint Jude*. Paris: Gabalda, 1939.

Charles, J. Daryl. *Virtue Amidst Vice: The Catalog of Virtues in 2 Peter 1*. Journal for the Study of the New Testament Supplement Series 150. Sheffield, UK: Sheffield Academic, 1997.

Charles, R. H., ed. *The Apocrypha and Pseudepigrapha of the Old Testament in English* vol. 2 *Pseudepigrapha*. Oxford: Clarendon, 1913.

Charlesworth, J. H., ed. *The Old Testament Pseudepigrapha* vol. 2. Garden City, NY: Doubleday, 1985.

Chase, F. H. "Second Epistle of Peter." *Hastings Dictionary of the Bible*, 3:796–818. Edinburgh: T. & T. Clark, 1900.

Collins, Raymond F. *1 & 2 Timothy and Titus: A Commentary*. New Testament Library. Louisville: Westminster John Knox, 2002.

Combes, I. A. H. *The Metaphor of Slavery in the Writings of the Early Church: From the New Testament to the Beginning of the Fifth Century*. Journal for the Study of the New Testament Supplement Series 150. Sheffield, UK: Sheffield Academic, 1998.

Cullmann, Oscar. *The Christology of the New Testament*. Translated by S. C. Guthrie and C. A. M. Hall. Philadelphia: Westminster, 1959.

Danker, Frederick W. "2 Peter 1: A Solemn Decree." *Catholic Biblical Quarterly* 40 (1978) 64–82.

———. *Benefactor: Epigraphic Study of a Graeco-Roman and New Testament Semantic Field*. St. Louis: Clayton, 1982.

Davids, Peter H. *The Letters of 2 Peter and Jude*. Pillar New Testament Commentary. Grand Rapids: Eerdmans, 2006.

Deissmann, Adolf. *Bible Studies*. Translated by A. Grieve. Edinburgh: T. & T. Clark, 1901.

Dittenberger, Wilhelm, ed. *Orientis Graeci Inscriptones Selectae. Supplementum Sylloges Inscriptionum Graecarum* vol. 2. Leipzig: Hirzel, 1905.

Donelson, Lewis R. *I & II Peter and Jude: A Commentary*. New Testament Library. Louisville: Westminster John Knox, 2010.

Dunn, J. D. G. *Christology in the Making: A New Testament Inquiry in the Origins of the Doctrine of the Incarnation*. Philadelphia: Westminster, 1980.

du Toit, Andrie. "Vilification as a Pragmatic Device in Early Christian Epistolography." *Biblica* 75 (1994) 403–12.

Elliott, John H. "II Peter." In R. A. Martin, *James*. John H. Elliott, *I–II Peter/Jude*, 117–58. Augsburg Commentary on the New Testament. Minneapolis: Augsburg, 1982.

Exler, Francis Xavier J. *The Form of the Ancient Greek Letter of the Epistolary Papyri (3rd c. B.C.–3rd c. A.D.): A Study in Greek Epistolography*. Washington, DC: Catholic University of America, 1923.

Fauconnier, Gilles, and Mark Turner. *The Way We Think: Conceptual Blending and the Mind's Hidden Complexities*. New York: Basic, 2002.

Fiore, Benjamin. *The Pastoral Epistles: First Timothy, Second Timothy, Titus*. Sacra Pagina. Collegeville, MN: Liturgical, 2007.

Fitzmyer, Joseph A. "Aramaic Epistolography." In *A Wandering Aramean: Collected Aramaic Essays*, edited by Joseph A. Fitzmyer, 183–204. Chico, CA: Scholars, 1979.

———. *The One Who Is To Come*. Grand Rapids: Eerdmans, 2007.

Fornberg, Tord. *An Early Church in a Pluralistic Society: A Study of 2 Peter*. Coniectanea Biblica New Testament Series 9. Lund: Gleerup, 1977.

Fuller, Reginald H. *The Foundations of New Testament Christology*. New York: Scribner, 1965.
Gerdmar, Anders. *Rethinking the Judaism-Hellenism Dichotomy: A Historiographical Case Study of Second Peter and Jude*. Coniectanea Biblica New Testament series 36. Stockholm: Almqvist & Wiksell, 2001.
Giese, Curtis P. *2 Peter and Jude*. Concordia Commentary: A Theological Exposition of Sacred Scripture. St. Louis: Concordia, 2012.
Gilmour, Michael J. *The Significance of Parallels Between 2 Peter and Other Early Christian Literature*. Academia Biblica 10. Atlanta: Society of Biblical Literature, 2002.
González, Catherine Gunsalus. *1 & 2 Peter and Jude*. Belief. Louisville: Westminster John Knox, 2010.
Gowler, David B. et al., eds. *Fabrics of Discourse: Essays in Honor of Vernon K. Robbins*. New York: Trinity, 2003.
Green, Gene L. *Jude & 2 Peter*. Baker Exegetical Commentary on the New Testament. Grand Rapids: Baker Academic, 2008.
———. "Second Peter's Use of Jude: *Imitatio* and the Sociology of Early Christianity." In *Reading Second Peter with New Eyes: Methodological Reassessments of the Letter of Second Peter*, edited by Robert L. Webb and Duane F. Watson, 1–25. Library of New Testament Studies 382. London: T. & T. Clark, 2010.
Green, Michael. *The Second Epistle General of Peter and the General Epistle of Jude*. Tyndale New Testament Commentaries 18. Grand Rapids: Eerdmans, 1987.
Grundmann, Walter. *Der Brief des Judas und der Zweite Brief des Petrus*. Theologischer Handkommentar zum Neuen Testament 15. Berlin: Evangelische Verlagsanstalt, 1974.
Gunn, David M., and Paula M. McNutt, eds. *"Imagining" Biblical Worlds: Studies in Spatial, Social and Historical Constructs in Honor of James W. Flanagan*. Journal for the Study of the Old Testament Supplement Series 359. Sheffield, UK: Sheffield Academic, 2002.
Hafemann, Scott J. "The (Un)conditionality of Salvation: The Theological Logic of 2 Peter 1:8–10a." In *Getting "Saved": The Whole Story of Salvation in the New Testament*, edited by Charles H. Talbert and Jason A. Whitlark, 240–62. Grand Rapids: Eerdmans, 2011.
Hahn, Ferdinand. *The Titles of Jesus in Christology: Their History in Early Christianity*. Translated by H. Knight and G. Ogg. London: Lutterworth, 1969.
Harrington, Daniel J. "Jude and 2 Peter." In Donald. P. Senior and Daniel. J. Harrington, *1 Peter, Jude and 2 Peter*, 159–299. Sacra Pagina 15. Collegeville, MN: Liturgical, 2003.
Harris, Murray J. *Jesus as God: The New Testament Use of Theos in Reference to Jesus*. Grand Rapids: Baker, 1992.
Harvey, Robert, and Philip H. Towner. *2 Peter & Jude*. The IVP New Testament Commentary Series. Downers Grove, IL: InterVarsity, 2009.
Head, Barclay V. *Catalogue of Greek Coins. Corinth, Colonies of Corinth, Etc.* London: Longmans, 1989.
Hengel, Martin. *The Son of God*. Translated by J. Bowden. Philadelphia: Fortress, 1976.
Hiebert, D. E. "The Prophetic Foundation of Christian Life." *Biblia Sacra* 141 (1984) 158–68.

Hofmann, J. Chr. K. v. *Die heilige Schrift neuen Testaments 7.2 Der zweite Brief Petri und der Brief Judä*. Nördlingen: Beck'schen, 1875.

Holmes, Michael W. *The Greek New Testament SBL Edition*. Society of Biblical Literature and Logos Bible Software, 2010.

Ilan, Tal. *Lexicon of Jewish Names in Late Antiquity. Part I: Palestine 330 BCE 200 CE*. Texts and Studies in Ancient Judaism 91. Tübingen: Mohr Siebeck, 2002.

James, Montague R. *The Second Epistle General of Peter and the General Epistle of Jude*. Cambridge Greek Testament for Schools and Colleges. Cambridge: University Press, 1912.

Johnson, Luke T. *The First and Second Letters to Timothy*. Anchor Bible 35A. New York: Doubleday, 2001.

———. "The New Testament's Anti-Jewish Slander and the Conventions of Ancient Polemic." *Journal of Biblical Literature* 108 (1989) 419–41.

Käsemann, Ernst. "An Apologia for Primitive Christian Eschatology." In *Essays on New Testament Themes*, translated by W. J. Montague, 169–95. Studies in Biblical Theology 41. Naperville, IL: Allenson, 1964.

Keating, Daniel. *First and Second Peter, Jude*. Catholic Commentary on Sacred Scripture. Grand Rapids: Baker Academic, 2011.

Kelly, J. N. D. *The Epistles of Peter and of Jude*. Harper's New Testament Commentaries. New York: Harper and Row, 1969.

Knoch, Otto. *Der Erste und Zweite Petrusbrief. Der Judasbrief*. Regensburger Neues Testament. Regensburg: Verlag Friedrich Pustet, 1990.

Kolenkow, Anitra B. "The Genre Testament and Forecasts of the Future in the Hellenistic Jewish Milieu." *Journal for the Study of Judaism* 6 (1975) 57–71.

Kraus, Thomas J. "Παρὰ κυρίου, παρὰ κυρίῳ oder *omit* in 2Petr 2,11." *Zeitschrift für die Neutestamentliche Wissenschaft* 91 (2000) 265–73.

———. *Sprache, Stil und historischer Ort des zweiten Petrusbriefes*. Wissenschaftliche Untersuchungen zum Neuen Testament 136. Tübingen: Mohr Siebeck, 2001.

Kümmel, Werner Georg. *Introduction to the New Testament*. Translated by H. C. Kee. Nashville: Abingdon, 1973.

Kurz, William S. "Luke 22:14–18 and Greco-Roman and Biblical Farewell Addresses." *Journal of Biblical Literature* 104 (1985) 251–68.

Lapham, F. "The Second Epistle of Peter." In *Peter: The Myth, the Man and the Writings. A Study of Early Petrine Text and Tradition*, 149–71. Journal for the Study of the New Testament Supplement Series 239. New York: Sheffield, 2003.

MacDonald, Dennis R. "Paul's Farewell to the Ephesian Elders and Hector's Farewell to Andromache: A Strategic Imitation of Homer's *Iliad*." In *Contextualizing Acts: Lukan Narrative and Greco-Roman Discourse*, edited by Todd Penner and Caroline Vander Stichele, 189–203. Society of Biblical Literature Symposium Series 20. Atlanta: Society of Biblical Literature, 2003.

Marshall, I. Howard. "The Development of the Concept of Redemption in the New Testament." In *Reconciliation and Hope: New Testament Essays on Atonement and Eschatology*, edited by Robert Banks, 153–69. Grand Rapids: Eerdmans, 1974.

Martin, Dale B. *Slavery as Salvation: The Metaphor of Slavery in Pauline Christianity*. New Haven: Yale University Press, 1990.

Mayor, Joseph B. *The Epistle of St. Jude and the Second Epistle of St. Peter*. New York: Macmillan, 1907.

Metzger, Bruce M. *A Textual Commentary on the Greek New Testament*. Second Edition. Stuttgart: German Bible Society, 1994.

Miller, Robert J. "Is There Independent Attestation for the Transfiguration in 2 Peter?" *New Testament Studies* 42 (1996) 620–25.

Moo, Douglas J. *2 Peter and Jude*. The NIV Application Commentary. Grand Rapids: Zondervan, 1996.

Moore, George F. *Judaism in the First Centuries of the Christian Era, the Age of the Tannaim*. New York: Schocken, 1971. [original publication 1927, 1930].

Mounce, Robert H. *A Living Hope: A Commentary on 1 and 2 Peter*. Grand Rapids: Eerdmans, 1982.

Murphy-O'Connor, Jerome. *Paul the Letter-Writer: His World, His Options, His Skills*. Good News Studies 41. Collegeville, MN: Liturgical, 1995.

Neyrey, Jerome H. "The Apologetic Use of the Transfiguration in 2 Peter 1:16–21." *Catholic Biblical Quarterly* 42 (1980) 504–19.

———. *2 Peter, Jude*. Anchor Bible 37C. New York: Doubleday, 1993.

Norden, Eduard. *Die antike Kunstprosa vom VI. Jahrhundert v. Chr. Bis in die Zeit der Renaissance*. Leipzig: Teubner, 1898.

Paulsen, Henning. *Der Zweite Petrusbrief und der Judasbrief*. Meyer Kommentar. Göttingen: Vandenhoeck & Ruprecht, 1992.

Perkins, Pheme. *First and Second Peter, James and Jude*. Louisville: Westminster John Knox, 1995.

Reese, Ruth Anne. *2 Peter and Jude*. Two Horizons New Testament Commentary. Grand Rapids: Eerdmans, 2007.

———. "Narrative Method and the Second Epistle of Peter." In *Reading Second Peter with New Eyes: Methodological Reassessments of the Letter of Second Peter*, edited by Robert L. Webb and Duane F. Watson, 119–46. Library of New Testament Studies 382. London: Continuum, 2010.

Reicke, Bo. *The Epistles of James, Peter and Jude*. Anchor Bible 37. Garden City, NY: Doubleday, 1964.

Rengstorf, Karl H. "διδάσκω κτλ." *TDNT* 2:135–65.

Riesner, Rainer. "Der zweite Petrus-Brief und die Eschatologie." In *Zukunftserwartung in biblischer Sicht: Beiträge zur Eschatologie*, edited by Gerhard Maier, 124–43. Wuppertal: Brockhaus, 1984.

Robbins, Vernon K. "Conceptual Blending and Early Christian Imagination." In *Explaining Christian Origins and Early Judaism: Contributions from Cognitive and Social Science*, edited by Petri Luomanen et al., 161–95. Biblical Interpretation Series 89. Leiden: Brill, 2007.

———. "The Dialectical Nature of Early Christian Discourse." *Scriptura* 59 (1996) 353–62.

———. *Exploring the Texture of Texts: A Guide to Socio-Rhetorical Interpretation*. Valley Forge, PA: Trinity Press International, 1996.

———. *The Invention of Christian Discourse* vol. 1. Blandford Forum: Deo, 2009.

———. "Rhetography: A New Way of Seeing the Familiar Text." *Words Well Spoken: George Kennedy's Rhetoric of the New Testament*, edited by Duane F. Watson and Clifton C. Black, 81–106. Waco, TX: Baylor University Press, 2008.

———. "Socio-Rhetorical Interpretation." In *The Blackwell Companion to the New Testament*, edited by David Aune, 192–219. Malden, MA: Wiley-Blackwell, 2010.

———. *The Tapestry of Early Christian Discourse: Rhetoric, Society and Ideology.* London: Routledge, 1996.
Robinson, John A. T. *Redating the New Testament.* Philadelphia: Westminster, 1976.
Rose, H. J. *Outlines of Classical Literature.* New York: World, 1959.
Schelkle, Karl H. *Die Petrusbriefe. Der Judasbrief.* Herders theologischer Kommentar 13/2. Freiburg: Herder, 1961.
Schmidt, Karl M. *Mahnung und Erinnerung im Maskenspiel: Epistolographie, Rhetorik und Narrative der Pseudepigraphen Petrusbriefe.* Freiburg: Herder, 2003.
Schrenk, G., and G. Quell. "πατηρ κτλ." *TDNT* 5:945–1022.
Senior, Donald. *1 and 2 Peter.* New Testament Message 20. Wilmington, DE: Glazier, 1980.
Sidebottom, E. M. *James, Jude, and 2 Peter.* New Century Bible. London and Edinburgh: Nelson, 1967.
Smallwood, E. Mary. *Documents Illustrating the Principates of Gaius, Claudius and Nero.* Cambridge: Cambridge University Press, 1967.
Smith, Terence V. *Petrine Controversies in Early Christianity: Attitudes towards Peter in Christian Writings of the First Two Centuries.* Wissenschaftliche Untersuchungen zum Neuen Testament 2. Reihe 15. Tübingen: Mohr Siebeck, 1985.
Spicq, Ceslas. *Les Épitres de Saint Pierre.* Sources Biblique. Paris: Gabalda, 1966.
Spitta, Friedrich. *Der zweite Brief des Petrus und der Brief des Judas.* Halle: Waisenhaus, 1885.
Stauffer, Ethelbert. "Abschiedsreden." *Reallexikon für Antike und Christentum,* 1:29–35. Edited by T. Klauser et al. Stuttgart: Hiersemann, 1950.
Starr, James M. *Sharers in Divine Nature: 2 Peter 1:4 in its Hellenistic Context.* Coniectanea Biblica New Testament Series 33. Stockholm: Almqvist and Wiksell, 2000.
Sylva, Dennis, D. "A Unified Field Picture of Second Peter 1:3–15: Making Rhetorical Sense Out of Individual Images." In *Reading Second Peter with New Eyes: Methodological Reassessments of the Letter of Second Peter,* edited by Robert L. Webb and Duane F. Watson, 91–118. Library of New Testament Studies 382. London: T. & T. Clark, 2010.
Targum Neofiti 1: Numbers translated, with Apparatus and Notes by M. McNamara; *Targum Pseudo-Jonathan: Numbers* translated, with Notes by E. G. Clarke. Collegeville, MN: Liturgical Press, 1995.
Thurén, Lauri. "The General New Testament Writings." In *Handbook of Classical Rhetoric in the Hellenistic Period: 330 BC–400 AD,* edited by S. E. Porter, 587–608. Leiden: Brill, 1997.
———. "Hey Jude! Asking for the Original Situation and Message of a Catholic Epistle." *New Testament Studies* 43 (1997) 451–65.
———. "Style Never Goes out of Fashion: 2 Peter Re-Evaluated." In *Rhetoric, Scripture and Theology: Essays from the 1994 Pretoria Conference,* edited by S. E. Porter and T. H. Olbricht, 329–47. Journal for the Study of the New Testament Supplement Series 131. Sheffield, UK: Sheffield Academic, 1996.
Trobisch, David. *Paul's Letter Collection: Tracing the Origins.* Minneapolis: Fortress, 1994.
Vögtle, Anton. *Der Judasbrief/Der 2. Petrusbrief.* Evangelisch-Katholischer Kommentar zum Neuen Testament 22. Solothurn, Düsseldorf: Neukirchener, 1994.

———. *Die Tugend- und Lasterkataloge im Neuen Testament: Exegetisch, Religions- und Formgeschichtlich Untersucht.* Münster: Aschendorfschen Verlagbuchhandlung, 1936.

Wand, J. W. C. *The General Epistles of St. Peter and St. Jude.* London: Methuen, 1934.

Watson, Duane F. *Invention, Arrangement, and Style: Rhetorical Criticism of Jude and 2 Peter.* Society of Biblical Literature Dissertation Series 104. Atlanta: Scholars, 1988.

———. "The Oral-Scribal and Cultural Intertexture of Apocalyptic Discourse in Jude and 2 Peter." In *The Intertexture of Apocalyptic Discourse in the New Testament*, edited by Duane F. Watson, 187–213. Society of Biblical Literature Symposium Series 14. Atlanta: Society of Biblical Literature, 2002.

Weima, Jeffrey A. D. *Neglected Endings: The Significance of the Pauline Letter Closings.* Journal for the Study of the New Testament Supplement Series 101. Sheffield, UK: Sheffield Academic, 1994.

Wendland, P. "Σωτηρ. Eine religionsgeschichtliche Untersuchung." *Zeitschrift für die Neutestamentliche Wissenschaft* 5 (1904) 335–53.

Wilson, W. E. "Εὑρεθήσεται in 2 Pet. Iii.10." *Expository Times* 32 (1920–21) 44–45.

Windisch, Hans. *Die Katholische Briefe.* Handbuch zum Neuen Testament 15. Tübingen: Mohr Siebeck, 1951.

Witherington III, Ben. *Letters and Homilies for Hellenized Christians, Volume 2: A Socio-Rhetorical Commentary on 1–2 Peter.* Downers Grove, IL: InterVarsity Academic, 2007.

Wohlenberg, G. *Der erste und zweite Petrusbrief und der Judasbrief.* Leipzig: A. Deichert, 1915.

Young, F. "Two Roots or a Tangled Mass." In *The Myth of God Incarnate*, edited by John Hick, 87–121. London: SCM, 1977.

Author Index

Bartchy, S. Scott, 111n56
Bauckham, Richard J., 11, 12n10, 14, 16, 17, 20, 24, 27n42, 29n44, 33n45, 33n47, 34, 36, 37, 38n61, 45n20, 48n29, 54n50, 55n51, 59n63, 62nn67-68, 64n70, 65n72, 66n75, 67nn76-77, 69n80, 72n83, 72n85, 74nn87-88, 76n90, 77, 78, 79n102, 81, 82n108, 90nn10-11, 91, 94, 95, 96n26, 101n38, 104n43, 106n44, 108nn47-48, 109n49, 110n52, 112n59, 118n74, 120n79, 123n84, 130n3, 130n6, 132n11, 137n22, 139n29, 145n37, 147n40, 151n46, 157n55, 164nn5-6, 165n7, 166, 168n14, 170n18, 170n20, 170n22, 171n26, 173n27, 175n31, 175n34, 178n37, 180n40, 181n41, 182n42, 189n5
Bigg, Charles, 17n19, 23n33, 27n42, 29n43, 33, 36, 37nn58-60, 38, 40n4, 45n20, 48n29, 51n34, 54n50, 59n63, 67n76, 76n90, 101n38, 106nn44-46, 118n74, 130nn2-3, 139n26, 164n5, 165n7, 166n11, 168, 170nn18-20, 180n40, 188n2
Braun, Willi, 20n29
Brown Raymond E., 48nn29-30
Callan, Terrance, 14n13, 15n17, 16n19, 42n11, 47n25, 51n38, 57n57, 58n58, 97n30, 98n34, 102n39, 136n18, 143n32, 148n42, 192n9
Chaine, Joseph, 16n19, 34n50, 36, 37

Charles, J. Daryl, 11n5, 20n28, 56n53, 69n80, 72n84
Charles, R. H., 42n12, 78n98, 148n44
Charlesworth, J. H., 42n12
Collins, Raymond F., 11n9
Combes, I. A. H., 47n22
Cullmann, Oscar, 42n11, 43n13, 44n15, 96n30
Danker, Frederick W., 55, 57, 66n74
Davids, Peter H., 11n5, 17n19, 36, 48n29, 55n51, 59n63, 62n67, 67n76, 68n78, 69n80, 94nn17-18, 95n21, 101n38, 104n43, 108n47, 112n59, 118n74, 123n84, 130n3, 130n6, 139n28, 146n37, 147n40, 164n5, 168n13, 171n26, 175n31, 175n34, 178n37, 180n40, 182n42
Deissmann, Adolf, 24n36, 56n53, 97n31
Dittenberger, Wilhelm, 72n84
Dunn, J. D. G., 20, 97n30
du Toit, , Andrie, 113n65, 114, 144n34, 154n52
Exler, Francis Xavier J., 44n17, 44n19
Fauconnier, Gilles and Mark Turner, 3n4
Fiore, Benjamin, 11n9
Fitzmyer, Joseph A., 42n11, 44n18
Fornberg, Tord, 24n34, 29n44, 35n51, 48n29, 62n67, 74n88, 83, 90n10, 112n59, 115n69, 132n11, 175n31, 178n37
Fuller, Reginald H., 42n11, 96n30
Gerdmar, Anders, 118n74, 166n11
Giese, Curtis P., 33, 36

author index

Gilmour, Michael J., 17n19, 46n21, 95n23, 147n41, 165, 166, 175n31, 192
Gowler, David B., L. Gregory Bloomquist and Duane F. Watson, 20n29
Green, Gene L., 11n5, 17, 33, 48n29, 54n50, 55n51, 59n63, 62nn67–68, 66n75, 67n76, 74nn87–88, 90n10, 94n17, 95n25, 96n27, 101n38, 104n43, 108n47, 114n67, 118n74, 123n84, 130n3, 130n6, 137n20, 139n28, 146n37, 151n46, 164nn5–6, 165n7, 166n11, 168n16, 175n31, 175n34, 178n37, 180n40, 182n42
Green, Michael, 11n5, 33, 36
Grundmann, Walter, 11n5, 17n19, 34n50, 36, 59n63, 62nn67–68, 67n76, 69n80, 132n11, 135n16, 136n19, 140n29, 154n49, 178n37
Gunn, David M. and Paula M. McNutt, 3n4
Hahn, Ferdinand, 42n11, 44n15, 96n30
Harrington, Daniel J., 11n5, 17n19, 36, 37, 101n38, 130n3, 139n28, 145n37, 178n37, 182n42
Harris, Murray J., 24n38, 48n26, 48nn29–30
Harvey, Robert and Philip H. Towner, 11n5, 33, 36
Head, Barclay V., 96n28
Hengel, Martin, 96nn29–30
Ilan, Tal, 41n9
James, Montague R., 36
Johnson, Luke T., 11n9, 113n65
Käsemann, Ernst, 19, 20n25, 29n43, 178n37
Kelly, J. N. D., 11n5, 14n13, 17n19, 27n42, 29n43, 36, 37, 45n20, 48n29, 54n50, 59n63, 62n67, 90n10, 98n33, 101n38, 104n43, 112n59, 132n11, 139n29, 145n37, 147n40, 164nn5–6, 168, 170nn18–20, 171n26, 178n37, 180n40
Kline, A. S., 137n21

Kloppenborg, John S., 20n29
Knoch, Otto, 11n5, 17n19, 20n26, 34n50, 36, 37, 48n29, 59n63, 67n76, 94, 112n58, 139n29, 145n37, 151n46, 178n37
Kolenkow, Anitra B., 83n110
Kraus, Thomas J., 130n4, 166n11
Kümmel, Werner Georg, 35n53
Kurz, William S., 82, 83
Lapham, F., 17n19, 164n5
MacDonald, Dennis R., 82n109
Marshall, I. Howard, 111n57
Martin, Dale B., 24n36
Mayor, Joseph B., 16n19, 34n50, 36n54, 166n11, 192n7
Metzger, Bruce M., 40n2, 51n33, 51n35, 51n37, 52n45, 100n36, 115nn69–70, 130n4, 130nn7–8, 145n35, 170n22, 170n25, 189n6
Michel, C., 55n52
Miller, Robert J., 95n24
Moo, Douglas J., 17n19, 33, 36
Moore, George F., 96n29
Mounce, Robert H., 33, 36
Murphy-O'Connor, Jerome, 35n52
Neyrey, Jerome H., 11n5, 17n19, 18, 24nn36–37, 29n44, 34, 47nn23–24, 55n51, 66n74, 67n76, 72n82, 73n86, 74n88, 79nn104–105, 83, 94n17, 97n32, 100n37, 101n38, 104, 108n48, 112n59, 113nn60–64, 122n82, 123nn83–85, 139n28, 143n33, 154nn50–51, 165n7, 169n17, 175n31, 178n37, 181n41, 182n42, 197
Norden, Eduard, 14, 15n15
Paulsen, Henning, 11n5, 17n19, 36, 59n63, 67n76, 69n80, 90n8, 94n16, 95n21, 101n38, 112n58, 140n29, 168n14, 171n26, 178n37
Perkins, Pheme, 17n19, 36, 37
Reese, Ruth Anne, 22n31
Reicke, Bo, 11n5, 14, 15, 22n30, 36, 37, 48n29, 64n70, 139n27
Rengstorf, Karl H., 109nn50–51
Robbins, Vernon K., ix, 1, 2, 3, 18, 23n32, 39n1, 89n1
Robinson, John A. T., 33n46

Schelkle, Karl H., 11n5, 16n19, 20n26, 36, 37, 59n63, 69n80, 96n27, 101n38, 130n3, 132n11, 139n29, 145n37, 147n40, 152n47, 168n15, 178n37, 180n40
Schrenk, G. and G. Quell, 96n29
Senior, Donald, 17n19, 36n54
Sidebottom, E. M., 16n19, 17n20, 36
Sisson, Russell B., 20n29
Smallwood, E. Mary, 43n14, 44n16, 48n28, 96n28
Spicq, Ceslas, 11n5, 36, 37, 48n29, 59n63, 62n67, 67n76, 90n8, 95n25, 96n27, 101n38, 106n45, 140n29, 178n37
Starr, James M., 51n34, 58n62, 60n64, 62n67, 72n85, 74n88
Stauffer, Ethelbert, 82n109
Sylva, Dennis D., 53n47
Thurén, Lauri, 108n48

Trobisch, David, 35n52
Vögtle, Anton, 11n5, 17n19, 36, 69n80, 94n18, 96n26, 140n29
Wachob, Wesley H., 20n29
Wanamaker, Charles A., 20n29
Watson, Duane F., 13, 14n13, 17n19, 20n29, 61n66, 63n69, 64n70, 77n96, 94n18, 95, 96n26, 104, 108n48, 109n49, 110n52, 112n59, 129n1, 135n17, 139n25, 162n1, 164n6, 166, 173n29, 174, 175, 178n38, 195n13
Weima, Jeffrey A. D., 193
Wendland, P., 43n13
Wilson, Bryan, 18
Windisch, Hans, 11, 16n19, 59n63, 69n80, 95n25, 139n29, 178n37
Wohlenberg, G., 17n19, 33, 36
Young, F., 96–97nn30

Ancient Document Index

OLD TESTAMENT

Old Testament/Hebrew/
Jewish Scriptures/Jewish bible
    17, 21, 25, 26, 35, 43, 47, 95, 97,
    100, 104–5, 106, 107, 109, 111,
    114, 116, 121, 123, 124, 144, 166,
    190, 191, 197

Septuagint (LXX)
    14

Genesis

	17, 104, 172
1–7	16, 174
1:2, 6–9	171
3	31, 74
6:1–19:29	16
6:1–4	116, 121
6:5–9:29	117, 122, 171
6:5	122
7:11	171
18–19	117, 122
19:4–11	118

Numbers

	17, 143
22–24	134, 137
22	16
22:22–35	135
22:28–30	138
24:17	17, 104
25	138
31:8	138
31:16	138

Leviticus

1:3	133n13
25:47–55	111

Deuteronomy

14:1	97
32:6	96
32:22	172, 174

1 Samuel

10:5–6, 10–13	105

2 Samuel

7:14	97

1 Kings

2:1–9	77n97
22:5–28	109

2 Kings

6:8–23	96

Judith

10:18	90n7

2 Maccabees

8:12; 15:21	90n7

Job

7:21 (LXX)	53n49
24:13	16, 148

Psalms

	17, 104
2	94
2:7	17, 91, 95
24:5 (LXX 23:5)	43
33, 34	38
49:12, 20 (LXX 48:13, 21)	136
90:4 (LXX 89:4)	16, 38, 174, 177

Proverbs

	17, 154
21:16, 21	148
26:11	16, 148

Ecclesiastes

2:7	111
10:16–17	136–37

Wisdom

2:23	72
14:12–31	158
14:22–28	144

Isaiah

	17, 104
5:11	136
6	105
32:16	174, 175
34:4	17, 175
42:1	17, 95
65:17	16, 175
66:15–16	174
66:22	16, 175

Jeremiah

1	105
2:13	135n17
25:11–12	106
28	109
29:10	106

Daniel

9:2, 3, 21–27	106

Amos

1:3–2:3	144
2:4–16	144
7:14–15	105

Habbakuk

2:3	17, 174, 175
3:10, 12	17

Zephaniah

1:18	174

Malachi

2:17	166
3:19	17, 174, 175

TARGUMS

Neofiti

138

Pseudo-Jonathan

138n24

PSEUDEPIGRAPHA

1 Enoch

	17
6.2	122
10.7	122
12.4–6	122
86–88	116n72
89.1–8	116n72
93.4	116n72

2 Baruch

56.10–14	116n72
56.15–16	116n72
78–86	11, 12, 77–78, 79

Assumption of Moses

18

Testaments of the Twelve Patriarchs   11, 12

The Story of Ahikar
8:15/18   16, 148

Psalms of Solomon
17.21–39   42

3 Maccabees
    90n7

NEW TESTAMENT (EXCLUDING 2 PETER)

New Testament
    2, 3, 11, 14, 17, 24n36, 33, 34, 37, 43n13, 44, 49n31, 66nn73–74, 71, 72, 73, 75, 109, 110, 196

Synoptic gospels
    31, 71, 91, 92, 93, 94

Matthew
    17, 66n73, 91
4:18–19	41
5:27	137
5:44, 45–48	69
7:6	148
10:2–4	41
10:15	116n72
12:45	16, 147, 153
16:18	41
17:1–8	16, 90, 95
17:5	16, 89n5, 95
21:32	148
22:1–14	54
23	145
24:3	90n9
24:6	76n90, 81
24:27, 37, 39	90n9
24:37–39	116n72
24:43–44	175n32

Mark
1:16–18	41
3:13–19	41
9:2–8	33, 90, 93, 95
9:47–48	71
12:31	69n79

Luke
1:33	71
2:11	43n13
5:1–11	41
6:13–16	41
10:12	116n72
11:26	16, 147, 153
12:39–40	175n32
13:6–9	44
17:26–27	116n72
17:28–30, 32	116n72
22:29–30	71
24:34	41

John
	17, 25
1:1	49n31
1:1–2	24, 49
1:41–42	41
4:42	43n13
13:34–35	69n79
15:1–17	53n48
18:36	71
20:28	48, 49n31
21	41
21:18–19	16, 33, 77, 82

Acts
1:15–26	41
2:37	41
4:21	121n80
5:1–6, 12–16	41
5:31	43n13
12:22	48
13:1	109
13:23	43n13
15:14	40n2
20:17–38	77n97, 82n109
20:29–30	114

Letters of Paul

16, 17, 28, 35, 36, 46, 50, 66n73, 67, 104, 164, 190, 191, 192, 194, 195, 196, 197

Romans

	35, 41n10, 47
1:18–32	192
1:29–31	144
2:4	192
5:3–5	61
5:12–21	31
6:15–23	152
6:16–23	111
6:16	192
7:7–12	75
8:20–21	192

1 Corinthians

	41n10
1:9	74
3:10	192
3:12–15	173, 192
3:12	72
3:13–15	174
6:12–20	151
6:19–20	111
7:22–23	111
10:16	74
11:17–22	136
12:28–29	109
13	68
15:5	41
15:23	90n9
15:24	71
15:50–55	29, 192
16:17	89n7

2 Corinthians

	41n10
5:1–4	192
7:6, 7	90n7
10:10	89n7

Galatians

	41n10, 157, 191
3:13	111
4:5	111

5:6	67

Ephesians

	35, 41n10, 191
4:3	34, 191, 192
4:11	109
5:5	71
5:23	43n13

Philippians

	47
1:26	90n7
2:12	89n7
3:10	74
3:20	43n13
4:8	66n74

Colossians

	41n10, 191
1:13	71
4:16	34

1 Thessalonians

	17, 179
2:19	90n9
3:13	90n9
4:15–17	90
4:15	90n9
5:2	16, 175, 192
5:3–11	180
5:23	90n9

2 Thessalonians

1:12	48
2:1, 8	90n9

1 Timothy

	41n10, 46, 50
1:4	95
4:7–8	64n71
4:7	95

2 Timothy

	11, 41n10, 46, 50
1:10	43n13
3:1–5	114
4:1	71

4:3–4	114
4:4	95

Titus
	41n10, 46, 47, 50
1:1–2	64n71
1:4	43n13
1:14	95
2:13	43n13
3:6	43n13

Hebrews
1:8	49n31
6:4–6	147n40
10:26	147n40

James
	44, 47, 50
1:1	44
2:14–26	67
3:1	109
5:7, 9	90n9

1 Peter
	16, 17, 33, 34, 35, 38, 41n10, 47, 50, 164, 165, 168, 191, 192
1:1	34
1:2	46, 165
1:2a	15
1:18–19	111
1:19	166
2:9	66n74, 165
2:12	166
3:2	166
3:18–20	166
4:11	166

1 John
2:28	90n9
4:14	43n13

2–3 John
	50

Jude
17, 33, 34, 38, 47, 50, 121, 139, 140, 143, 154, 168, 193n12

1	34, 46
4–18	16, 108, 165
4	109
4(–5)	109
5–8a	121
5	109
6	116n72, 122
7	116n72, 122
8	136
8b–13	135
9	18, 136
10	136
11	136, 137, 143
12–13	139
12	130n8, 136
13b	16, 136
14–15	17
16	147
17	16
17–18	165
24–25	196

Revelation
3:3	175n32
4	22
5:9	26, 111
11:15	71
14:4	111
16:15	175n32
17:4	72
17:14	54
18:12	72

GRECO-ROMAN WRITINGS

Aristotle, *Rhetoric*
119n75

Cicero
14

Coins
Corinth
96

Ephesus
97

Demetrius, *On Style*
16	58n59
18	58
22–24	119n75
106–11	173n29

Diodorus Siculus, *Bibliotheca historica*
15.7.1; 36.2.2	111

Hesiod, *Theogony*
729–31	123

Homer, *Iliad*
1.9	97
1.544	96
4.68	96
4.235	96
5.33	96
6	82n109

Horace, *Epistles*
1.2.26	149

Inscriptions
24n36

Asia Minor
72

Boeotia
44, 48

Caria
43

Iasos
55

Nemrud Dagh
15, 57

Tarsus
97

Stratonicea
56–57

Josephus, *Jewish Antiquities*
1.22	95
1.73–75	122
4.109–10	139
4.309–19	77, 79
9.51–59	96
19.345, 347	48n27

Ovid, *Amores*
1.4	137

Philo
66n74

De Abrahamo
139	122

De aeternitate mundi
5	155
37	155n53

De confusione linguarum
11	117n73
141, 159	156

De vita contemplativa
77	117n73

De Iosepho
220	121n80

De vita Mosis
1.146	155n53
1.263–99	137
1.269	139

De opificio mundi
2	95

De praemiis et poenis
22	155n53

Quaestiones et solutiones in Genesin
2.22   155n53

De sacrificiis Abelis et Caini
28   108n47

De specialibus legibus
3.8   117n73

De virtutibus
40   117n73

Plato
Gorgias
491E   121n80

Phaedo
115–18   82–83

Republic
614B-21D   83

Pliny, *Epistulae*
10.96.7   49n31

Plutarch
Alcibiades
22.3   90

De Pythiae Oraculis
397 B-C   105

De sera numinis vindicta
563B-68   83

Moralia
89C   121n80
91D   121
452C   121n80
1008B   121n80

Suetonius, *Life of Domitian*
13.2   48

Quintilian, *Institutio Oratoria*
9.4.125   58n59
9.4.128   58

EARLY CHRISTIAN WRITINGS

1 Clement
    46, 47, 50
23.3–4, 5; 27.4   166

2 Clement
11.2–4; 16.3   166

Acts of John
90   90n11, 92n13

Acts of Peter
20   90n11, 91n11, 92n13
36–41   33

Acts of Thomas 1
43   90n11, 92n13

Apocalypse of Peter
    90n11, 92n13
22, 28   37

Apostolic Fathers
    14

Epistle of Barnabas
15.4   38

Eusebius
Ecclesiastical History
3.3.1   37
3.25.3   37
6.25.8   37

Praeparatio evangelica
15.14   181

Gospel of Philip
58, 5–10   90n11, 92n13

Shepherd of Hermas
Similitude
9.17.5–18.2   147n40

Vision
3.8.7   61

Irenaeus, *Against Heresies*
5.32.2   38

Justin, *Dialogue with Trypho*
35.3   106n44
81   38
82.1   38

Letters of Ignatius of Antioch
    50

To the Ephesians
1.1   49n31
7.2   49n31
12.2   35
15.3   49n31
19.3   49n31

To the Romans
4.3   35

To the Smyrnaeans
1.1   49n31

Letter of Polycarp
    46, 50

Melito, *Homily on Passover*
    38

Origen, *Commentarii in evangelium Johannis*
5:3   37

Venerable Bede, Commentary on 2 Peter
    69n80, 178n37

www.ingramcontent.com/pod-product-compliance
Lightning Source LLC
Chambersburg PA
CBHW062021220426
43662CB00010B/1425